The Bamboo Gulag

The Bamboo Gulag

Political Imprisonment in Communist Vietnam

NGHIA M. VO

McFarland & Company, Inc., Publishers
Jefferson, North Carolina, and London

LIBRARY OF CONGRESS CATALOGUING-IN-PUBLICATION DATA

Vo, Nghia M., 1947–
    The bamboo gulag : political imprisonment in communist Vietnam / Nghia M. Vo.
        p.   cm.
    Includes bibliographical references and index.

    ISBN 0-7864-1714-5 (softcover : 50# alkaline paper)

    1. Political Prisoners — Vietnam.   2. Concentration Camps — Vietnam.   3. Torture — Vietnam.   I. Title.
HV9800.5.V6   2004
365'.45'09597 — dc22   2003025324

British Library cataloguing data are available

©2004 Nghia M. Vo. All rights reserved

No part of this book may be reproduced or transmitted in any form or by any means, electronic or mechanical, including photocopying or recording, or by any information storage and retrieval system, without permission in writing from the publisher.

Manufactured in the United States of America

McFarland & Company, Inc., Publishers
  Box 611, Jefferson, North Carolina 28640
   www.mcfarlandpub.com

To the Vietnamese who suffered or died
in communist jails, and
to the Vietnam War veterans who
fought for freedom

Table of Contents

Preface   1

I. North and South   5
II. The Last Heroes   10
III. Prelude to a Tragedy   23
IV. Bamboo Fences   31
V. A Police State   46
VI. Incarceration   53
VII. Southern Gulags   68
VIII. Northern Gulags   93
IX. Starvation   117
X. Executions, Tortures, and Confinements   133
XI. Thought Reform   143
XII. Hard Labor and Poor Medical Care   151
XIII. Defense Mechanisms   159
XIV. Well-Known Prisoners   167
XV. Post-Reeducation Ordeal   173
XVI. New Economic Zones   188
XVII. Disillusion   198

XVIII.	Of Cemeteries	207
XIX.	Epilogue	215
	Glossary	223
	Notes	225
	Bibliography	235
	Index	241

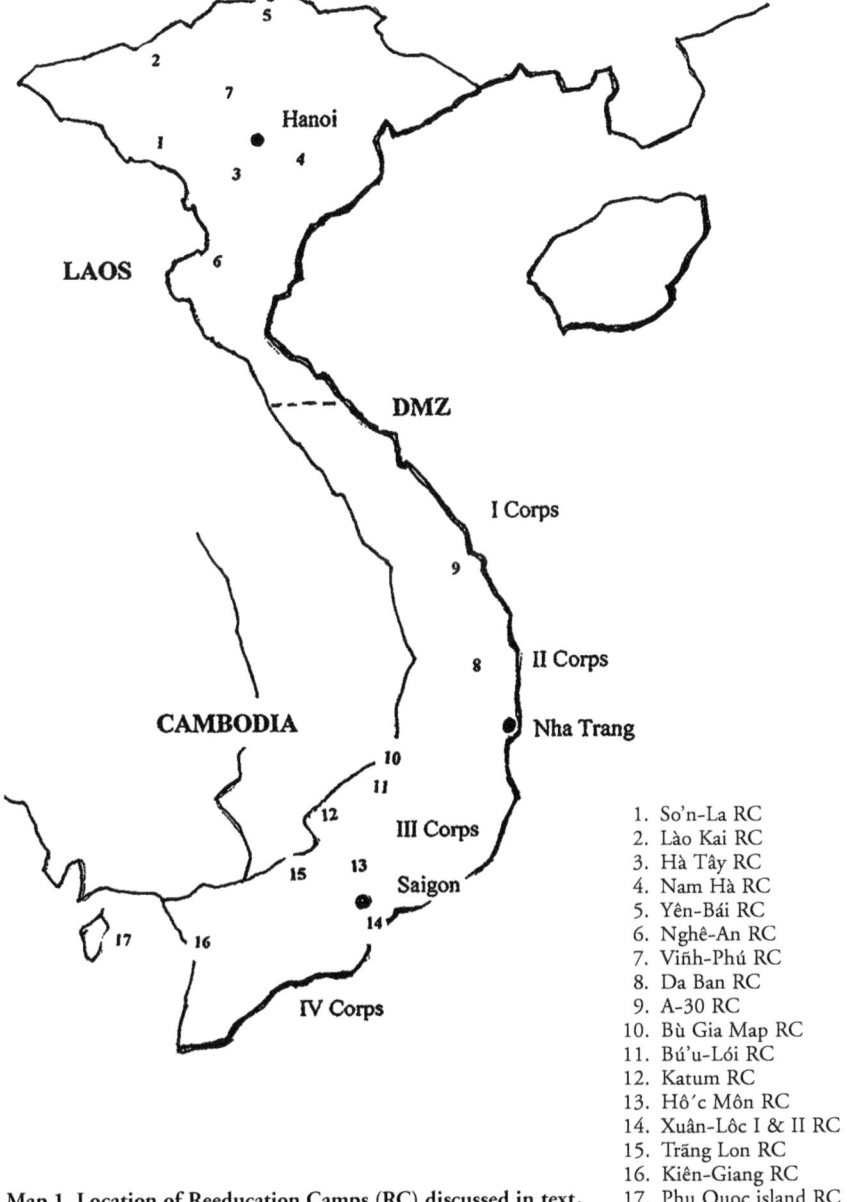

Map 1. Location of Reeducation Camps (RC) discussed in text.

1. So'n-La RC
2. Lào Kai RC
3. Hà Tây RC
4. Nam Hà RC
5. Yên-Bái RC
6. Nghê-An RC
7. Viñh-Phú RC
8. Da Ban RC
9. A-30 RC
10. Bù Gia Map RC
11. Bú'u-Lói RC
12. Katum RC
13. Hô'c Môn RC
14. Xuân-Lôc I & II RC
15. Trăng Lon RC
16. Kiên-Giang RC
17. Phu Quoc island RC

Preface

The bamboo curtain fell on South Vietnam after the communist takeover of Saigon on April 30, 1975. What happened behind this curtain was not known for some time until the first news about the reeducation camps leaked out of the country with the escape of the boat people. The boat people had either witnessed the horrors of the camps from which they had escaped or been released, or they simply relayed stories from relatives or friends who were not fortunate enough to escape.

These were stories of execution, torture, starvation, forced labor, inhumane treatment, and poor medical care. As more news came out with each new load of boat people, the picture of the bamboo gulags began to take form. The stories about these Stalinist or Maoist-type camps were strikingly similar except for differences in time, location, and individuals involved. They therefore could not be dismissed as coming from opponents of the new regime. Alerted by these reports, international organizations started probing the Hanoi government, which first denied any such camps existed. It later let a few communist countries visit an exemplary site to deflect the accusations. The friendly nations of course did not see anything wrong with the incarceration system. As organizations and governments continued to raise questions about the camps, they were finally allowed to visit a few "ideal camps" in 1979. Ginetta Sagan from Amnesty published her report titled "Violations of Human Rights in the Socialist Republic of Vietnam" in 1983.

The overall picture of the camps to this day is far from complete. For almost three decades, the Hanoi regime has not released any information about them, probably fearing it would confirm Hanoi's violations of human rights. We thus have to rely on reports from boat people supplemented by occasional official reports from the Hanoi regime as well as statements from former communist officials who escaped from Vietnam. Although some of these reports were published in the form of memoirs, confusion remains about these camps among the general public. Were the camps no worse than any "regular" prisoner-camp some people wonder, or were they the *Enfer Rouge* (Red Hell) described by one refugee who landed in France?

One way to assess the severity of the punishment system is to evaluate the number of fatalities occurring during the process. It has been estimated that 100,000 to 250,000 prisoners died during this forced incarceration,[1] mostly from starvation, malnutrition, illnesses, and executions. This disturbing ten percent attrition or mortality rate was certainly higher than that seen in any regular jail. It raised many interesting questions: Why was the attrition rate so high? What were the causes of this mortality? Were the deaths intentional?

This book answers some of these questions. But as one former detainee suggested, "There is no difference in the end with the two routes: killing people quickly in gas chambers, or killing them slowly by forcing them to work to death, denying them food and water, and making them succumb to disease."[2]

Two other factors — lack of due process and length of detention without trial — also deserve to be evaluated. Although all detainees were listed as "political prisoners," none of them had ever been prosecuted or convicted by a court of law. They should have been convicted or set free from the beginning. The Socialist Republic of Vietnam (SRV) should acknowledge its errors and reimburse the prisoners for the damages, financial as well as moral, they incurred during these long years of incarceration. This is a vital moral obligation for any nation that desires to clean up its act in order to join the free world.

The fact that the SRV had jailed at one time more than two million "dissidents" out of the 30 million southerners also raises serious questions about the legality of the regime and about the war itself. Although the majority had been released a long time ago, a few detainees remained jailed twenty-two years later and reported they were working in communes or being "reeducated." Were their errors serious enough to deserve such a long incarceration? This length of their incarceration not only suggests the vindictiveness of the regime but also the threat some inmates might pose to the regime by exposing its ruthlessness and disregard of laws. Even Sheehan, who believed that the communists "behaved with comparative restraint,"[3] had to acknowledge "what started as a wartime measure then acquired a bureaucratic inertia, years drifted by, and the experiment at changing minds degenerated into simple punishment."[4]

The *raison d'être* of this book is not only to describe the devastating and degrading treatment inflicted on the South Vietnamese as a whole, but also to highlight the greatness of human spirit in the face of adversity. In writing this book, I have tried to retrace the path they took from the last months of the war to their escape from Vietnam as well as the emotions that gripped them throughout their stay in the camps. Although the prisoners all went through similar misfortunes, the feelings they experienced varied depending on their philosophical, emotional, or moral constitutions and beliefs. What seemed to be trivial for some took on exponential meaning for others.

This book tries to reflect the voices and feelings of these internees. The emotions they experienced were so complex and profound that no inmate could or dared remember in detail what he or she (there were a few female inmates) had felt during this long banishment. Such a reconstruction serves as a "memoir" for all those who were at one time incarcerated in the camps.

Communists should not have used their power to treat their countrymen inhumanly through isolation, incarceration, hard labor, starvation, torture, and summary execution. There was no reason for a government to degrade, break down, and render a whole nation destitute because many people simply did not share the communist view. Though there were many ways to build up a country anew, this certainly was not one of them.

One could look at the difference in behavior between American and Vietnamese victors after their respective civil wars to predict the future these politicians were leading their nations to. Lincoln reunified and rebuilt the country by incorporating the defeated southerners into his government; Ho's followers took the opposite path. Ho decided to eradicate the South Vietnamese society and exclude the southerners by sending them to the gulags. In the latter situation, the resentment and bad feelings toward the Hanoi government were bound to occur and linger for decades. The economic effect of the exclusion of half of the population was enormous and is difficult to evaluate.

It was no wonder Senator John McCain, while visiting Saigon at the 25th anniversary of its fall, uttered his now famous comments: "The wrong guys won. [Vietnam] lost millions of their best people who left by boat, thousands by execution and hundreds of thousands who went to reeducation camps."[5]

The 1954–1975 Vietnam war claimed at least two million lives, one each from the North and South, while twelve million additional people were displaced,[6] not including those who were summarily executed by the communist regime. These numbers are staggering. One would like to ask why Ho Chi Minh and his communists started a revolution that was based on an unproven theory only to lead the Vietnamese and Southeast Asians to poverty, destitution and death. Was the revolution worth the human cost? What was the revolution trying to prove? And the biggest question remains: Why did Ho, who was present in the Soviet Union in 1930 and witnessed the Great Russian Terror and its effect on the population, impose the same treatment on his people? Was he so blinded by his ego or his hate of colonialists that he lost all his morals?

I would like to express my sincere thanks to A. J. Dommen, a knowledgeable Vietnamologist and remarkable historian, for his invaluable comments and for taking the time to review the manuscript. My thanks to Jeff Wallace for his suggestions and Tung Tri Thien for allowing me to use her thoughtful poems.

Grateful acknowledgment is made for permission to reprint excerpts from Huynh Sanh Thong, *An Anthology of Vietnamese Poems* (1996), by Yale University Press. Sincere thanks to Nguyen Chi Thien for allowing me to reprint his poems from *Flowers from Hell*, a bilingual collection of poems, selected and translated from the Vietnamese by Huynh Sanh Thong and published by the Council on Southeast Asia Studies *Lac Viet* series, Yale University (1984).

Last, but not least, I would like to thank the survivors of the camps who told me their stories and opened my eyes to the world of the bamboo gulags. Without their recollections, the writing of this book would not have been possible. I hope this work will serve as a testament to the Gulag's tragic victims and fortunate survivors. This is their story.

I

North and South

To understand the Vietnam War, one needs to focus on the basic differences and the long-standing antagonism between North and South Vietnam. At its birth, a few millennia ago, Vietnam was circumscribed to a small area in the Red River Delta in present-day North Vietnam. South Vietnam, on the other hand, had its beginning in the early 17th century.

In the first millennium, the Indo-Chinese peninsula was occupied by, besides Vietnam, two Indianized civilizations, the Chams and the Khmers, who flourished respectively in present-day central and South Vietnam. Through the process of *nam tien* (southern expansion), the Vietnamese moved out of the Red River Delta and pushed south as early as the 13th century A.D. In the process, they displaced the Chams and the Khmers out of their lands and completed the conquest of central and South Vietnam in 1780. The *nam tien* was similar to the American westward expansion in the 19th century. This population shift resulted in two groups of Vietnamese people with different social, political, and religious backgrounds: those who stayed put in the north and the pioneers who migrated south.

In 1558, tired of the political maneuverings at the Le king's court in Thang Long (present day Hanoi), Duke Nguyen Hoang, one of the northern pretenders to the throne, decided to move to Thuan Hoa in today's central Vietnam and found his own "empire." In 1600, he completely broke away from the north, refusing to pay taxes to Thang Long.[1] That date marked the official division of Vietnam into two separate states: the north (Dang Ngoai) then controlled by the Trinh-Le kings and the lands south of the Gianh River (roughly at the 17th parallel) known as Dang Trong, which fell under the leadership of the Nguyen. A fifty-year war broke out between the northern Trinh and the southern Nguyen in 1627 and ended in a stalemate in 1677 (first Vietnamese civil war).

Profiting from the stalemate, the southerners slowly moved farther south at the expense of the Chams and the Khmers. The Chams, who flourished in present-day central Vietnam between the 7th and 15th centuries, survived on trade and pillages of surrounding countries. The Khmers, whose civilization peaked between the 9th and 14th centuries, lived in what is presently known as South Vietnam. They were the builders of the magnificent Angkor temples and the forefathers of the Cambodians. The Vietnamese displaced both Chams and Khmers during their southern expansion.

The southern Nguyen government developed the newly conquered land and engaged in trade with other southeastern countries.[2] In 1698, they conquered Prey Nor from the Khmers and renamed it Saigon. By 1780, they acquired the province of Ha Tien at the southernmost part of Vietnam through the death of Mac Thien Tu.[3] Present day South Vietnam became a unified state. The conquest and establishment of South Vietnam took 180 years during which the south remained a completely separate entity from the north. Thus, for more than 180 years, South and North Vietnam were two separate and different political and economic entities, although they shared the same language and Chinese influence.

In the late 18th century, Nguyen Hue, a southern lord, was able to reunify the whole country under his command after defeating the northern warlords and the Chinese who came to the rescue of the northerners. Asian history in general and Vietnamese history in particular would have been completely different had Nguyen Hue, who was crowned King Quang Trung in 1788,[4] been able to establish and secure his own dynasty. He unfortunately died in 1792, at the age of 40,[5] after a short but brilliant reign. Ten years later in 1802, Nguyen Anh, another southern prince conquered the northern land and for the second time reunified Vietnam.[6] He established his capital at Hue in central Vietnam and founded the Nguyen dynasty that lasted until 1945 when King Bao Dai abdicated.

The French colonialists took over the country in 1867 and kept it divided into three regions: North (Tonkin), Central (Annam), and South (Cochinchina) Vietnam for almost a century. The south became a colony while Annam and Tonkin formed a French protectorate under the Nguyen rule. The Geneva Accords in 1954 formally divided the country into North and South at the 17th parallel.

During the period of southward expansion (1600–1780), the South Vietnamese "adopted and adapted whatever aspects of indigenous cultures and traditions they believed useful" to assimilate the local population.[7] They became liberal and flexible. They "borrowed, blended, and absorbed extensively from the cultures of the Chams and other people in the region."⁸ From the Chams, they borrowed their deity Po Nagar, the cult of the whale and the trade with other southeastern nations. From the Khmers, they learned wet rice culture. The conquest of new lands and the assimilation of the Cham and Khmer nationalities generated a new breed of people: the South Vietnamese. The South Vietnamese transformed by time, space, as well as assimilation of new ideas and cultures, became different from the northerners in social, political, and cultural ways. They became not only richer by the acquisition of new lands and new freedom, but also more versatile and tolerant by having to deal with different cultures, such as the Chams and Khmers. They also became more moderate and respectful of other minorities.⁹

They adopted Buddhism as their main religion¹⁰ at the expense of Confucianism, which was still prevalent in the north. As a frontier country, rules became more relaxed and less enforced and enforceable by central authorities. The southern country was lush and fertile as a result of the Mekong River; land was plentiful and rice abundant. The southerners also took over the foreign trade business, which was previously the domain of the Chams. Bathed in this new prosperity, they became more progressive and tolerant of the diversity that surrounded them. They were in general trustful, easy-going, gullible, pragmatic, and individualist. Like all pioneers, they liked their freedom and did not care much about a strong central authority.

The northerners, who did not have to interact with different cultures, remained constrained by their rigid Confucian rules, regulations, and formalities. The Red River Delta soon became crowded, and people had to fight hard against each other for a place to live, farm, and grow. One could look at the Vietnamese countryside to see major differences between north and south. Northern farmers were allocated small parcels of land delineated by hedges around an enclosed community while southern farmers lived scattered and free among their vast lands. The arid and mountainous regions of the north surrounding the small Red River Delta contrasted sharply with the vast and lush southern rice fields bathed by the Mekong River. The weather was harsh in the north with heavy monsoon rains during summer (the classic fight between the spirit of the Mountains and the spirit of the Sea) and drizzly, damp, and cold during the winter months.¹¹ On the other hand, the weather was generally warm year round in the south.

Life in general was rough and difficult in the north and the fight for survival became the focal point of people's lives. Northerners had to fight so much for a living that fighting became part of their nature. They bonded themselves to communities and villages in order to improve their chances for survival. They were respectful towards the authorities and believed in a centralized government. They were persevering, hard working, and conservative to the point of being almost puritanical. At their worst they could be deceptive, manipulative, ruthless, and greedy. All these traits made them susceptible to communist teachings. The communists liked the northerners' simplicity and obedience and vowed to turn them into well-regimented soldiers, the "Prussians of the East."

Just as history and geography shaped the minds of the northern and southern Vietnamese, politics also played a major role. North Vietnam became a fertile ground for nationalists who were looking for ways to regain independence from France. On one end were Phan Boi Chau and Phan Chu Trinh. The former, founder of the Viet Nam Quoc Dan Dang, favored an arm struggle against the French. Phan Chu Trinh, a more moderate nationalist, chose cooperation as a way to gain independence. On the other end of the spectrum was Ho Chi Minh who circled the world between 1910 and 1940 and became an unabashed communist while studying in Moscow. Despite witnessing the Great Russian Terror of the '30s, Ho plowed ahead believing that communism was the way to go. Over the years, Ho and his followers ruthlessly eliminated Chau and nationalists from other parties.[12] He even temporarily cooperated with the French to eliminate opposition members to his party.[13] The Communist Party officially took control of North Vietnam in 1946. South Vietnam remained under French control another eight years. After the Dien Bien Phu battle, the 1954 Geneva Agreement effectively divided Vietnam at the 17th parallel into a communist north under Ho Chi Minh and a free democratic south under Ngo Dinh Diem.

After being a French colony for more than eighty years, South Vietnam catapulted itself onto the world scene in 1954 as a free democratic country that espoused western ideals of democracy. With freedom came a cacophony of political voices, including the Catholics, Buddhists, Hoa Hao, Cao Dai, and other groups vying for a piece of the action. President Diem ruled over a tumultuous time. He tried to introduce democracy to a previous colony, investment from the free world, and especially education and health care. He helped to resettle a million northerners, who willingly left everything behind to escape the ruthless communist rulers.[14] The majority were Catholics. The resettlement was a gigantic task; South Vietnam at that time had a population of roughly 15 million people. At the same time, Diem fought against the National Liberation Front, a creation of the communist party.

In a way, President Diem was successful in reviving South Vietnam from its deathbed, for everyone was pessimistic about its chances of survival after 1954. The French had not built any political or economic infrastructure for the locals to thrive on before they left. Diem reorganized the military system, gave land to the peasants, stabilized the country, and established the roots for democracy. Nevertheless, he could not rely on anyone else except his family, especially his brother Ngo Dinh Nhu and his sister-in-law. He surrounded himself with northern Catholics and in the process antagonized the southerners, Buddhists, and generals. His image as an incorruptible Mandarin, his authoritarian stance, and his political strength was too much for these people who did not like to be ordered around. Diem became a victim of his style and time. He would have been successful in the north. A military coup took place in November 1963 during which Diem and Nhu were both murdered.

In the North, Ho ruthlessly launched a Marxist revolution crushing all freedoms as well as all political opponents, nationalizing industries, spreading a reign of terror, and impoverishing the whole population. In 1959, Ho decided to conquer the south with the help of China and the Soviet Union. The tragedy was Ho did not believe in history and in the complexity and duality of the Vietnamese mind. The fact that he was outside Vietnam for thirty years might account for this error. Blinded by Marxism, he wrongly assumed that only socialism was the cure for all problems. Convinced that all the Vietnamese would submit to his will, he refused to acknowledge the existence of basic human rights and freedoms; those concepts only sounded good on paper.

Historically, the north and south had been divided between two states and two states of mind as early as 1600. Without the nam tien, Vietnam would not have been as it is today. But with it, the chasm between northerners and southerners grew wider. Geographically, economically, and politically, Vietnam is a land of imbalances, which were further accentuated by Ho's introduction of communism to the north. "The North was a Maoist, badly planned economy; here (the South) we have a strictly private-enterprise economy.... This is a two-country nation. The tail wags the dog."[15]

II

The Last Heroes

On April 30, 1975, Saigon fell under the advance of twenty-two northern communist divisions. What Hanoi could not achieve politically, by persuasion, intimidation, or by free elections for twenty-one years, it did outright by force. South Vietnam fell not because the people liked the communist theory and revolted against the Saigon government, but as a result of aggressive attacks by a ruthless army of an authoritarian regime. It fell under the guns and the artillery of a well trained and well supplied army. "As a people's war, the Vietnamese revolution was a fraud."[1]

The communists had insisted all along they would not invade South Vietnam. This turned out to be the biggest lie they had ever told besides pretending to talk peace in Paris between 1969 and 1973 while continuing to invade South Vietnam. After two decades of war, all eyes turned to Paris hoping that peace would finally settle in the land of the Ascending Dragon. Alas, this was only a reprieve in this long war, which would be broken a few months after the accords were signed.

The Aftermath of the Paris Accords

The 1973 accords not only allowed the Americans to withdraw all their troops out of ravaged, war-torn Vietnam, but also permitted the 150,000 North Vietnamese troops (some people put the number as high as 300,000) to remain in South Vietnam. This condoned de-facto occupation of the free democratic South Vietnam sealed its fate. South Vietnamese president Thieu "wept" when he was presented with a copy of the accords drafted by the United States and North Vietnam. He remarked that the bargain was "tantamount to a surrender."[2] He would not sign the accords, but was finally convinced by the Nixon government that the Americans would help him defend his country in case of any outright invasion by the North Vietnamese.[3] Many South Vietnamese, from the left to the right were angered that Thieu had agreed to sign on the accords. They talked about Thieu being bought out by the Americans. But he could not do anything else; this was a take it or leave it proposition. Had he not signed on the dotted lines, the U.S. government would most likely have cut funding to the country; and without funding, the war was lost anyway.

The Watergate fallout forced Nixon to resign and effectively sealed the fate of South Vietnam. The new Ford administration was considered "weak," and not as committed to the war in South Vietnam as the Nixon government. Military aid amounted to 2.2 and 1.5 billion dollars respectively for the fiscal years 1973 and 1974. With no one to help defend South Vietnam's cause, the U.S. Congress unilaterally cut all funding to Saigon, and from there on it was a rapid downhill slide towards oblivion. While the Soviet Union continued to provide North Vietnam with state-of-the-art artillery, tanks, guns, and ample amounts of ammunitions, of the 1.5 billion fiscal year 1975 aid request for South Vietnam from the Defense Attaché Office in Saigon, only $700 million was appropriated. An additional $300 million worth of equipment was charged against the 1975 budget instead of the '74 fiscal year and another $200 million was also subtracted as transportation costs.[3] As a result Saigon was left with $200 million for the entire 1975 year. Even Van Tien Dung, a North Vietnamese general, wrote in his diary in the fall of 1974, "Nguyen Van Thieu [was] forced to fight a poor man's war."[4]

With ammunition and supplies running short, the ARVN restricted its engagements with the enemy by half and could not effectively defend against communist attacks. The rising fuel costs following the Arab oil boycott in 1974 forced half of the air force to be grounded.[5] South Vietnam, with a population of roughly 20 million people, maintained an armed force of over one million soldiers. The bulk of this force, however, was used to protect roads, rivers, and bridges and to provide security for the population and the cities. It was a huge, largely immobile and defensive force. The remainder of the fighting forces comprised "nine Infantry divisions, one airborne division, fourteen Ranger groups, six Air divisions, one Marines division and a Navy fleet." Only 150,000 of the million-man army were assault troops. Colonel Edward Lansdale back in 1960 had suggested that the ARVN should be small and mobile.[6] But his advices went unheeded and the ARVN became large, immobile, and inefficient thanks to Pentagon leaders. The North Vietnamese on the other hand had 500,000 combatants out of a force of 1.2 million men.

Theirs was a mobile army geared towards attack. During the last months of the war, they sent all their divisions south except one to protect Hanoi.[7]

The North Vietnamese by 1974 massed their divisions close to the demilitarized zone, which divided Vietnam into two states: North and South. In full violation of the Paris Accords, they had stockpiled ammunitions and brought into South Vietnam "antiaircraft weaponry, heavy artillery, and tanks ... built hundred of miles of pipelines for moving fuels ... and constructed hundreds of miles of highways in order to reduce transportation times in South Vietnam." They had "nineteen divisions throughout South Vietnam, artillery, antiaircraft and sapper battalions ... along with seven reserve divisions in North Vietnam and one in Laos."[8] From September 1974 to April 1975, the North Vietnamese sent 178,000 fresh troops, including six reserve divisions stationed in the North into South Vietnam again in violation of the Paris Accords. Confident in their strength, they embarked on a third spring offensive. The first two, in 1968 the Tet Offensive and in 1972 the Easter Tide Offensive were repulsed with the help the Americans. Now that the Americans were gone, the North blatantly invaded the South expecting no response from the Ford government.

President Thieu was a shrewd politician. In the middle of internecine political maneuverings and plots, he had always been able to get the upper hand and keep his adversaries at bay. Between 1963 and 1965, many governments came and went, but Thieu remained in power from 1965 to 1975. The fact that he was able to remain afloat during all these years belies his ingenuity and shrewdness. On one end, he had to deal with the American government and its ambassador who pressed for reforms while keeping his constituency, the army and the generals, happy. He also had to fend off the flashy Marshall Ky who was circling close by and was always willing to take over his job. A more and more vocal civilian opposition had to be deflected. On the other end, he had to fight against an unending and devastating war and an enemy who was bound to no international laws or democratic rules.

Even though his generals gave him "high marks as a military commander, others stated he was inept as a political and military leader." Like Diem before him, Thieu was from central South Vietnam, a poor and arid region. "His character and moral values were strongly influenced by the hard life in his native village where the lands are poor and rocky."[9] He knew he had to fight hard to keep what he had earned. His upbringing and the murky political situation made him suspicious of others; he could not confide to any one and was afraid of plots. He was aware that out there a few generals were ready to topple him. He did not want the Corps generals to meet together for he was afraid they would be plotting against him. He was not afraid of a "soft" plot during which he would be simply removed from power, but of a "hard" one like the one that killed Diem and his brother Nhu.

Convoy of Tears

Unable to secure extra funding from the Americans, Thieu gambled and decided to pull his troops out of the sparsely populated highlands (military Corps II). Although he had thought lengthily about this option, he had not discussed it with anyone in his government until then. Pressed by the losses of Phuoc Long and Ban Me Thuot in February and March 1975, with his forces spread too thin, he decided to gather the remnant of his army in order to strengthen the coastal areas.[10] He did not have too many options: either pull his forces out of the highlands or face immediate assaults from the communists, against which he could not defend. He could not discuss the option with U.S. Ambassador Martin who was at that time on vacation at his home in North Carolina.[11] Thieu met with general Phu, the II Corps Commander at the Cam Ranh airport on March 15 and ordered him to withdraw from the highlands. Phu argued that the "morale of every Vietnamese soldier would plummet if retreat were ordered." After ninety minutes of heated discussion, Thieu gave Phu two choices: "carry out the order, or be replaced and jailed. Phu accepted the order"[12]

General Phu left the evacuation process to general Tat.[13] Although the idea sounded good on paper, pulling the troops out without any concrete planning and right on the heels of the losses of Phuoc Long and Ban Me Thuot proved to be devastating for the morale of the soldiers. The withdrawal was poorly executed, without the protection of the U.S. B-52 bombers. The soldiers felt that the Americans had already given up on South Vietnam, and, as a result, the withdrawal turned into a debacle. South Vietnamese soldiers became confused and lost their will to fight. The confusion stemmed not only from the American policy in Vietnam, but also from the feeling of loss of Vietnamese sovereignty, the lack of direction of the war, the continuous bickering among politicians and generals, and the length of the war: "In no time was it the policy of the American side to win the war.... Total victory was banned."[14]

When local people overheard the news of the pullout, they immediately decided to follow the retreating column. They understood that communism could not bring anything but devastation, despair, repression, and poverty. They chose freedom over enslavement by the communists. As soon as they heard the communists were coming, they uprooted their families, children and extended families, although this meant leaving everything behind including ancestral lands and facing a bleak future. They piled up their prized belongings and ran away from the enemy. They did not know where they were going; they only knew to follow the military convoy. Since fuel was scarce in times of war, and since the decision of leaving the town was made on the spur of the moment, the only means of transportation were bikes, oxcarts or their feet. The Montagnards were particularly upset: they lived in these regions and had been loyal to the Saigon government throughout these years. But since they could not abandon their ancestral lands, they decided to stay put and refused to fight any longer.

Civilians were overpowered by fear and uncertainty and started shedding tears. They escaped through overcrowded and mined roads, steep hills and valleys. Since many bridges had been blown apart, the 20th Engineer Group had to repair roads and bridges on the spot.[15] Since food and water were not available on short notice, every ounce of water was savagely protected. In their rush to get out of the fighting zones, they pushed, shoved and trampled on each other. The fight to escape became a fight for life. Decency and respect were ignored. Children and elderly people, unable to fight against this unruly crowd were the first to suffer from the long and dangerous march: they were dropped by the sides of the roads while the stronger ones kept going until they too fell of hunger, thirst, or fatigue. Many people died during this trip from the highlands to the coastal area. This was the biggest inland exodus since the one generated by the formation of the states of India and Pakistan.

For the first few days, the trip was uneventful except for snipers' shots, road difficulties and the usual hardships of a jungle trip. Then the unexpected thing happened: mortars and shells suddenly exploded on and around the convoy and tore it apart. Yells and screams of horror filled the air. The escapees realized the enemy had caught up with them and was pounding them right and left. The communists had no qualms about killing them: they aimed straight at the flow of fleeing people and army. And the pounding of the enemy's artillery went on for hours followed by the firing of AK 47 automatic machine guns.

Blood splattered everywhere while body parts and pieces of flesh flew in all directions. The sight was gruesome and the stench unbearable. The smell of powder from detonated shells and charred bodies caused people to become sick while heavy black smokes slowly drifted upward. People either died instantaneously or were covered with bloody wounds. When silence finally came, the survivors saw the grisly scenery that lay bare in front of their eyes. A Martian landscape had replaced the greenery they had seen a few hours ago. The thick forests covered with hundred-year-old trees had given way to a vast clearing. Trees were denuded of their branches or had their trunks cut down by the unrelenting shelling. Torn branches, wood splinters and burned tree trunks lay disorganized among the charred remains of destroyed military trucks, armored vehicles, and canons. Bomb craters filled with bodies of soldiers and civilians, young and old, had replaced the asphalted road. The laughter of the children was replaced by the mourning cries of the relatives.

One Saigon reporter wrote in *Chinh Luan*, a Saigon newspaper: "Refugees moving on foot were hit by communist machine guns, falling down on the road. The blood flowed on the road like a tiny stream. The sound of roaring artillery and small arms, the screams of seriously wounded people at death's door, and children, created a voice out of hell."[16]

Civilians and soldiers did not have time to count their losses. Horrified, they took a long time to gather themselves but had to keep going because of the insecurity of the area. They traveled on dirt roads, up mountains and along rivers; they went through jungles and bushes. And the shells kept following them and soon reduced the long convoy to scattered groups of ragged, tired and injured people. Besieged by thirst, hunger, and fear, they kept walking until they were worn out by fatigue and hunger. They fell on the ground only to be awoken by hordes of hungry mosquitoes and bugs. No one could tell the misery each of them had gone through trying to escape the communists. Others just stopped in the middle of their run and cried. The rest of the convoy forged ahead.

What was uplifting during this tragic period was that the communists had never won the hearts and minds of these people. Despite their hopelessness and fear, they just kept on hanging behind the nearly destroyed military convoy. The same thing had happened during the 1968 Tet Offensive. The communists then attacked more than a hundred cities hoping to cause people to rebel against their government. Alas, they waited in vain for a spontaneous insurrection that never came.

By the time the convoy arrived in the coastal areas, the II Corps army was reduced to a few wandering souls and had ceased to exist. Only 20,000 of the 60,000 troops made it through, and of the 400,000 civilians, only 100,000 reached the coastline.[17] The convoy was remembered as the Convoy of Tears. But no one in the free world had condemned the ruthlessness of the communists who had shelled indiscriminately at civilians and soldiers, mothers and children.

The war went on and the discouraged soldiers, sensing the end had arrived, did not want to fight any longer. Full divisions were destroyed or surrendered and after twenty-one years of war, the North Vietnamese took over South Vietnam in a few months.

The Last Battles

Xuan Loc was a town of 38,000 people situated on Highway 1, about thirty-eight miles northeast of Saigon. It represented the last outpost facing the incoming communist forces that had been traveling along Highway 1, which linked North and South Vietnam. The 2,500-man regiment of the 18th ARVN division defended the town. The 18th division, formerly baptized as the 10th division, had been the laughingstock of the army because of its poor fighting capabilities. After 1973, it received a new commander, one star general Le Minh Dao, a no nonsense general who climbed the army ranks from lieutenant to general as a result of his ability not by politics. General Dao rapidly reenergized the soldiers by rebuilding troop morale as well as its fighting capability. The division soon became the most reliable and important defense forces of Saigon.

On April 9, 1975, it was hit with 2,000 enemy shells. This was followed by an all out assault by two communist divisions. The communists overran the South Vietnamese troops, but the 18th division fought back and recaptured the town by nightfall.

The communists threw in two more divisions, but were still held back. The communists decided to cut off Highway 1, preventing reinforcement forces to arrive to Xuan Loc. Dao's 2,500-man regiment was at one time separated from his forces inside the town, which were led by colonel Le Xuan Hieu. The 18th division soldiers, however, were holding on and were fighting better every day. They repulsed one attack after another. The town was almost completely devastated by the shelling and all the town dwellers caught boats to escape by sea. The only things left standing were brick walls. Two more communist divisions were sent to the combat zone. Dao brought in another regiment to counterattack and to free Highway 1 but to no avail. Another reinforcement brigade sent in by Saigon was ambushed by a North Vietnamese division and pushed back.

For almost two weeks, they held on by fighting attack after attack, hiding from long-range artillery shelling and direct attacks by tanks. On the 21st of April 1975, the communists threw in two divisions for a final assault. A ferocious shelling never experienced before by the defenders fell on the devastated town and blew up the remaining defenses. The outposts around Xuan Loc fell one after another. The fight became hopeless. General Dao finally gave the order to retreat. He was left with 600 men who had to fight against "a combined tank, artillery and infantry force of about 10,000 North Vietnamese."[18] A total of 20,000 rockets and artillery shells fell on the defending forces, which, however, destroyed thirty-seven communist T-54 tanks and killed more than 5,000 attackers.[19] This was the South Vietnamese Alamo.

II. THE LAST HEROES

General Dao received a coded message from the Americans advising him about the evacuation in Saigon and asking him to go along. The general said he wouldn't go. He stayed with his troops and later had to surrender to the North Vietnamese. The latter were especially angry with Dao, who they thought had ordered the Cluster Bomb Unit (CBU55) to be dropped on them on April 21st. In reality, Major General Homer Smith gave the official go-ahead to Saigon to use the bomb.[20] This super napalm bomb had never been used before anywhere and was designed to kill by robbing those on the ground of oxygen. Two hundred and fifty enemy soldiers were killed instantaneously. A few other CBU55 bombs along with multiple cluster bombs had been dropped on the enemy line.

General Dao was later sent to the re-education camps in the North only to be released seventeen years later. He became almost blind during his incarceration; the cause of the illness was unknown although it was thought to be due to malnutrition. Under the Orderly Departure Program, he was offered another chance to be flown to America but refused. He thought he could have left Vietnam in 1975 while he was still strong and healthy; but now that he was disabled, he thought there was no need to go anywhere. He lived quietly in South Vietnam for a while declining interviews, and later changed his mind and came to the U.S.

General Ly Tong Ba was born in South Vietnam in 1931. He attended the Dalat Military Academy and was commissioned in 1952 as officer. In 1975, he became brigadier general and commander of the 25th ARVN division, which was deployed in Tay Ninh, fifty-five miles northwest of Saigon. His division along with other ones formed a defensive belt around the capital of the free and democratic South Vietnam. General Ba was the hero who in May 1972 had repulsed the North Vietnamese attacks on Kontum in the central highlands.[21] He too had the chance to fly out of the country in late April 1975 at the urge of the Americans who saw him as a prized prisoner in case of a communist takeover. But he decided to remain behind to defend his country against the invading North Vietnamese communist forces. He had asked his American friend to take his wife and children to safety to America. As long as his family remained in a safe place abroad, he could fully dedicate his heart and mind to fight the incoming enemy.

This brave and heroic decision to hold still and fight the communists gave the Americans crucial time to initiate a seemingly orderly, although highly chaotic, evacuation of the last American forces and Vietnamese civilians out of Saigon. Without the resistance of these forces around Saigon, the enemy would have trapped and caught many more Americans and Saigonese. Had this happened, the front pages of worldwide newspapers bearing the news of thousands of Americans held prisoner by the communists would have dealt the Ford government a devastating blow.

General Ba's forces were pounded continuously by the enemy's long-range artillery, hit directly by the guns of huge T-54 tanks and even bombarded from above by captured South Vietnamese A-37 jets. His division fought a force of three North Vietnamese divisions. Unable to sustain this massive and concentrated attack from air and ground, he surrendered to the invading North Vietnamese forces on the 29th of April 1975. The general, wounded in the leg and dressed as a farmer, escaped with an aide by "lying on his back under the water of a flooded rice paddy, trying to poke his nose above the surface in order to breathe without being seen."[22] He was finally captured while trying to get back to Saigon on foot and spent one year of reeducation in Hoc Mon, South Vietnam, along with twenty-seven other generals.

To add salt to his wound, not only was he caught, but his wife and children were also not picked up by the departing Americans; they were still holed up in Saigon. He was then transferred to North Vietnam to do hard labor in a camp in Yen Bai, then Ha Dong, in "a compound of small brick buildings with barred windows" and finally in another camp in Phu Ly for a total of twelve years and eight months. He was finally freed in December 1987. By that time, he had lost forty-five pounds. After his release, he mentioned to a reporter, "I fought for my country. I did my duty. I did the best I could. And I lost. Yet, I am proud still."[23] He never thought about committing suicide because this was very "egoistical." He thought he was not a Mandarin who was going to die for the emperor.

The Last Heroes

Nguyen Khoa Nam enrolled in 1953 at the Thu Duc Military Academy. He later became commander of the ARVN 7th division, and his last post was that of a three-star general and commander of the IV Corps in South Vietnam. He was well liked by his soldiers and used to drop by in the middle of a military operation to enquire about their well being. He was a Buddhist and ate vegetarian food two weeks each month. He had a girlfriend but vowed not to get married until the war was over. He, therefore, was not linked to any bribe, which was usually channeled through the officer's wife. With the fall of An Loc and Xuan Loc in late April 1975, there was talk about pulling all the troops down to the IV Corps and holding there. General Nam and his assistant, two-star general Le Van Hung, looked at all the options and planned to receive the troops within the new capital in Can Tho. They were two of the few generals who remained at their post until the end.

II. The Last Heroes

General Nam had ordered his field commanders to stay put and fight. As a fighter, he did not understand and was particularly offended by the retreats and lack of resistance of the army in the highlands. He even shot a province chief at Sa Dec as the man insisted on leaving with the American evacuation. When the Kien Giang province chief left his post by boat, he had "three helicopters pursue the boat and sink it with rocket and machine-gun fire."[24] The IV Corps area was quiet and the communists did not stage any fight during the last days of April 1975.

When "Big Minh," who had been unanimously voted as president by the South Vietnamese Congress three days earlier, went on radio at 10:30 A.M. on April 30, 1975, to issue an unconditional surrender to the invading North Vietnamese army, General Nam was flabbergasted. He and General Hung stood under the flag of the command post and bid farewell to each other. Then General Nam went to the Phan Thanh Gian Military Hospital in downtown Can Tho to bid farewell to hospitalized soldiers. He did not know what to do except empathize with them. He told them he did not know what the future had in store for them once the Viet Cong took over the city. When he returned to his command post, he heard that his second-in-command had killed himself.

General Le Van Hung was respected while he was a young officer for his bravery in military combat. He was known as one of the "Tiger officers" of the ARVN. He rapidly moved up the ladder and became general commander of the 5th ARVN division a few days before the Eastertide campaign in 1972. At that time, the Vietcong under the command of General Vo Nguyen Giap threw an ambitious three-pronged attack on Quang Tri, near the DMZ zone (I Corps) on Kontum in the highlands (II Corps) and on An Loc (III Corps). The four North Vietnamese divisions, 5th, 7th, 9th and Binh Long, attacked the South Vietnamese 5th, 18th, and 21st divisions. General Le Van Hung and his 5th division held on at An Loc for ninety-five days defeating overwhelming enemy forces. All these attacks were repulsed with the help of the American firepower and B52 bombers. The North Vietnamese, having suffered massive casualties, decided to change the military command with general Van Tien Dung replacing general Vo Nguyen Giap as commander-in-chief. As for general Hung, he was promoted as deputy to General Nam.

In late April 1975, the United States had offered thrice to evacuate the two generals and their families,[25] but they refused. As of 4 P.M., April 30, 1975, General Hung was still proclaiming that he "would not surrender to communists." He met with his wife and advised her to be brave and to raise their son as a man. He told her, "I would rather die than have my hands tied and watch the invasion of the Viet Cong." He gathered his soldiers and told them, "I will not abandon you in order to evacuate my family. I cannot surrender in this shameful situation. If I have yelled at you on occasions when mistakes are made, please forgive me."

He shook hands with his men, ordered them to leave, and locked himself in his office. A gunshot was later heard. Mrs. Hung and the staff who were hanging around found the general still convulsing with blood all over his shirt, his arms outstretched, his body halfway out of his chair. He had shot himself in his heart. It was 8.45 P.M. on April 30, 1975.[26]

At 11 P.M., General Nam called Mrs. Hung to offer his condolences. She heard a long sigh at the end of the line. As a man of war, he did not believe in surrendering to people he did not like and felt he could defeat. He put on his official white military uniform along with all his medals, sat on his desk and shot himself through his right temple. His body was taken to the morgue and he was buried at the Can Tho Military Cemetery.

General Pham van Phu, the man who issued the order of withdrawal from the II Corps in March 1975 under President Thieu's request, committed suicide on April 30, 1975, rather than surrender to the enemy. Back in 1954 then captain Phu parachuted with his company in Dien Bien Phu to reinforce the French and South Vietnamese troops. He was taken prisoner and was released back to South Vietnam in July 1954. Since that time, he had sworn never to fall again into enemy's hands.

General Le Nguyen Vy was colonel under the command of General Hung at the famous 1972 An Loc battle. He single handedly took an M-72 antitank gun to blast a North Vietnamese T-54. He became deputy commander of the 21st ARVN division and in 1974 went to the United States for military training. He returned as commander of the 5th ARVN division. When Big Minh surrendered, General Vy bid farewell to his soldiers, went into his office and killed himself with a Beretta 6.35. When the North Vietnamese officer came to the camp to take the surrender, he calmly saluted the body and said, "This is how a general should behave."[27]

General Tran Van Hai, then a colonel, had parachuted himself at the famous battle of Khe Sanh in 1968. He became commander of the 7th ARVN division in 1974 and was known not only as a brave and clean officer but also as one who cared for his soldiers. President Thieu had offered to evacuate one week before the fall of Saigon, but he refused. He remained at his post and had reports of a growing concentration of enemy troops along the Cambodian side of the border. He himself called his CIA contact for help: "Where are your bombers? We have them in the open. Now it is the time to get them. They are marshaling in front of my men. I need help. Help me, CIA man." As no help was coming, the enemy forces crossed the border and overran his compound. On April 30, 1975, he committed suicide instead of surrendering.[28]

II. THE LAST HEROES

In the middle of Saigon in front of the Assembly House, Police Lieutenant Colonel Long, dressed in full military regalia, stood in front of the military statue honoring war soldiers, made a final salute then shot himself in the head.[29] He died shortly after arriving at the hospital.

The following poem written by Tung Tri Thien was dedicated to these heroes who remained behind and fought the invading communists so that millions of other people could fly or sail out of Vietnam safely in late April 1975. Without them, not too many South Vietnamese could have escaped from the enemy.

A River Runs Through It

Against a clear blue sky of a Spring Day,
Pink-laden cherry blossoms, its branches sway.
Harvard, Yale, Berkeley sprawling green grass,
Contemplating peaceful crowds moving en mass.
I wonder why, such a feeling of Sadness?
Yet multi-million dollars Success
Of twenty-five years and no less,
Overcome not that gnawing ball of Emptiness.

A dream of last night seized upon me,
Dream or Real Life? Brought down to my knees.
Twenty-one years ago, my country's battlefield,
Under enemy's pressure, my father held still.
Protecting our country, he knew the end was near,
Trained as a soldier, he had no fear.
Weighing the loss of lives, Surrender he would not hear.
His life to save one life and his peers.
"Go, take your wives to safety,
We shall hold it, a few brave men 'til Victory!
Remember these men in your hearts,
Unknown soldiers of Quang-Tri, Hue, Xuan-Loc, DarLac."

Reaching the banks of the River,
Its waters, a color of red blood, simmer.
Carrying boatloads of people to safer shores,
Mixed with the soldiers' blood, Tears of Sadness tore
A gray, stormy sky of Death and Fear,
A River runs through Sweat, Blood, and Tears.

My cheeks wet with warm, salty tears,
Laying down his life, the unknown soldier is near.

Peaceful in death, he looked downstream,
The rice paddies, again lush and green.
From the soldier's River of Sacrifice,
A cupful, so I may have a full Life.
Certainly, you did not die in vain,
My life worthy of your gift, whatever pains.

Future generations, the Source of the River
Engraved in young hearts forever.

—Tung Tri Thien

III

Prelude to a Tragedy

Ho Chi Minh was born Nguyen Tat Thanh in 1890 in the province of Nghe An, North Vietnam. His father was a personal friend of Phan Boi Chau, a prominent Vietnamese Nationalist. In 1911, he took a job in the kitchen of a French ship and left his country only to return to Vietnam thirty years later. He traveled widely, returned to France in 1917, and was active in left-wing political circles. In 1920, he became one of the founding members of the French Socialist Party and the first Vietnamese communist. Since he had a great admiration for Lenin, he rapidly converted to Leninism and became an international communist.[1] He trained in Moscow in 1923 and wrote fervently about Lenin at the time of his funeral on January 1924: "He was our father, teacher, comrade, and adviser. Now he is our guiding star that leads to social revolution. Lenin lives on in our deeds. He is immortal."[2]

One could surmise he was a hardcore communist from then on. He was sent to Canton, China, at the end of 1924 to represent the Comintern (Communist International founded by Lenin). From 1924 onward, he traveled frequently between Shanghai, Thailand and Moscow.

He returned to Pac Bo, Vietnam, in 1941 and founded the Viet Minh (League for the Independence of Vietnam), following which he launched an armed resistance against the French. Numerous other Vietnamese Nationalist parties, especially the VNQDD (Vietnamese Nationalist Party) and the Dai Viet (Greater Vietnam) competed for the same goal. The French had eliminated many of these nationalist leaders (Phan Boi Chau, Phan Chu Trinh … among others) in the '20s and '30s with the secret help of Ho. During World War II, Japanese troops pushed the French aside and took over

Vietnam using it as a base for the conquest of Asia. Profiting from the political vacuum left by the Japanese surrender in 1945, Ho took over Hanoi in 1945 and proceeded to eliminate all other parties during the bloody August Revolution.

The Geneva Agreement in 1954 stipulated that the Vietnamese nationalists and the French move to the South, the communist forces to the North, and Vietnam be officially divided into North and South at the 17th parallel. About a million northerners moved from the North to the South while a smaller number of people moved the other way. However, many of the southern communists stayed put and formed the nucleus of the National Liberation Front or Viet Cong. In 1960, Ho Chi Minh called for the "liberation" of the South, an all-out war to take over the South. And in 1961, Ho officially started sending regular armed forces to the South.

Throughout its history, the revolution proved to be ruthless and unforgiving. Its credo had always been to eliminate the opposition in any way and in complete secrecy. Therefore, there was little tangible evidence to its work.

The 1945 August Revolution

To consolidate his power, Ho targeted members of other parties, including the Trotskyites, the VNQDD, the Dai Viet and so on. Overall 10,000 "enemies" had been ruthlessly eliminated.[3] The Hanoi Central Prison was at that time filled with alleged "enemies of the people," "traitors," and "anti-revolutionary elements": "Tens of thousands remained under detention ... during which time local committees often confiscated or requisitioned their properties."[4]

Two prominent opponents of the communists, the conservative Pham Quynh and the court official Ngo Dinh Khoi, brother of the future South Vietnamese President Ngo Dinh Diem, were arrested in Hue and executed in early September 1945.[5] In the South, communist Tran Van Giau used the scorched earth policy to terrorize and assassinate local people, sect leaders, and rivals.[6] Later, the communists continued to eliminate the remaining opposition elements.[7]

Truong Chinh, General Secretary of the communist party, not only acknowledged the purge but also regretted he had not been aggressive enough in his role. He wrote in 1946, "Immediately after the establishment of revolutionary power, we did not firmly eliminate the various categories of traitors.... We regret only that the repression of the reactionaries during the August Revolution was not carried out fully within the framework of its possibilities."[8]

Since September 1945 as head of the provisionary government, Ho personally had secretly negotiated with the French colonialists without the knowledge of the Nationalists.[9] He then allowed the French to return to Hanoi after June 1946, causing the Nationalists to cry foul. The communists, in close cooperation with the French, proceeded to eliminate the remaining nationalist parties (mostly VNQDD and Dong Minh Hoi) that had refused to welcome the return of the French. Hundreds of Nationalists were rounded up and executed and territories held by the Nationalists were turned over to the communists.[10] Toward the end of 1946, Ho and his communists had almost complete control of North Vietnam.

The 1953–56 Northern Land Reform

The communist leaders let loose a horror of their own in the North in 1954 (1953 in certain areas): a Chinese style "land reform" campaign orchestrated by Truong Chinh, then general secretary and ideologue of the ICP (Indo-Chinese Communist Party). The main goal was the total control of the population, which had not been overwhelmingly receptive to the communist takeover.

First, a team of land reform descended to an area and each cadre moved in with a family. As the cadre encouraged family members to talk, he collected all information related to local landowners, members of "reactionary" parties, or people critical of the communist regime. In the next stage, he tried to "instill hatred for the landlords" and to coach people to speak up against them.

Once the peasants were adequately prepared, a "people's tribunal" was scheduled with the presence of the accused landlord. The "defendant" not only was not allowed to respond but was also forced to kneel before the court with his or her head bent as a sign of submission. A pseudo victim came forward and accused the landlord of such and such crime. On other occasions, charges were outright "manufactured" by the peasants because failure to participate in the denunciation of the landlord could be interpreted as harboring "pro-landlord" thoughts.[11] The "tribunal" then asked the people whether or not the defendant was guilty. A few cadres mixed in the crowd would scream "Guilty! Guilty!" and the crowd would soon follow suit. The "judge" would ask for the sentence and the crowd had no choice but shout "Death to the landlord!" at the urge of the same cadres.

Thus, thousands of real or purported landlords were tried before such kangaroo courts. They were beaten and shot, and their families were isolated and left to starve. Nguyen Ngan's grandfather was executed in 1956 because he had "two acres of land and had hired one peasant to work it for him."[12] The fact that a person owned ten square meters of land could land him in jail because he was "cruel, bad, and greedy...."[13] If there were not enough landlords, rich peasants were targeted next because the land reform team had to reach a minimum quota. The quota was gradually "increased during the various phases of the land reform campaign."[14]

Then started a wild chase for all owners. Once caught, they were paraded around town, smeared, jailed, and killed. Landlords who had supported the revolution in the past were also branded as fake and subjected to the same treatment. Such was the case of Nguyen Thi Nam who became the first female landlord to be executed on the advice of a Chinese adviser. He thought she was a "cruel landlord." Ho Chi Minh was notified about the case but would not intervene because he did not dare contradict the Chinese adviser.[15]

The cruelties of the land reform worsened as the process moved forward. Like the French revolution of 1789, Ho's revolution started to feed on itself. Spilling more and more blood, it started to uncover "new enemies" every day. Ho Chi Minh had even addressed the land reform cadres like a general sending his troops to war:

> Land reform is a revolutionary task.... It is a glorious and heavy task. The fighter is not only the man who kills the enemy at the front. You are fighters, too: fighters to the anti-feudal front....
> Heroes are not only to be found among the soldiers at the battlefront. They can be found among you, fighting on the anti-feudal front together with the peasants....
> In the coming ... land reform, those among you who perform outstanding deeds will be awarded medals, just like soldiers fighting the enemy.[16]

The most brutal aspect of the land reform campaign was the policy of "isolation" applied towards family members of the convicted landlords. As wives and children of the victims of the campaign were unlikely to support the regime, they were "boycotted and shunned by their fellow human beings.... They became creatures at whom children were encouraged to throw stones. Nobody was permitted to talk to them ... they were not allowed to work for a year. In consequence, the majority of them died of starvation."[17]

The human cost of the land reform remained unknown. It was estimated that 50,000 people were executed. The collateral damage (landlords who committed suicide to avoid execution and family members who died of starvation), however, was higher and ranged from three to five hundred thousand people.[18]

The main goal of the reform for Ho and his communists was the ruthless elimination of all opposition factions in order to get complete control for their party. The Hanoi intellectuals reacted strongly against the land reform by publishing poems and articles criticizing the government. The government, in turn, rounded them up and sent them to reeducation camps, a forbearer of the future gulags.

Vo Nguyen Giap, the general commander of the NVA, later acknowledged in the party newspaper *Nhan Dan* (The People) on October 31, 1956, "we ... executed too many honest people ... and, seeing enemies everywhere, resorted to terrorism which became too far widespread.... Worse still torture came to be regarded as a normal practice."

Despite this admission, the reform process went ahead and although Truong Chinh, the architect of the land reform, lost his job he remained a power in the party.

The Quynh Luu Uprising

In November 1956, upset by the land reform and the lack of religious freedom, peasants in the province of Nghe An surrounded Canadian members of the International Commission for Supervision and Control and requested to be allowed to move to South Vietnam. Fights broke out between the mob and the police. Demonstrations spread to other provinces but were suppressed by the army. Six thousand peasants were reported executed or deported.[19]

Viet Cong Atrocities and Repression

In South Vietnam, the Viet Cong, besides fighting a conventional war, targeted government officials and even local population in cities as well as in the countryside. They came to the villages at night to levy taxes, kill officials, or incite hatred against the government. In some areas, village officials were killed so frequently that no one would volunteer to serve in these positions.

Rural terror was intended to gain and maintain control of the populace while urban terror was designed to undermine and discredit the government. One way to control the populace was to undermine the government by killing its officials or disrupting whatever the government did.

Mr Ba Lat became the first casualty in Hung Dien of the Ben Tre province. He fought with the Viet Cong against the French for ten years. After 1954, he retired to his village to become a farmer. When he refused to cooperate with the Viet Cong, he was knifed to death 300 meters from his house. Three youths, aged fifteen or sixteen, were branded as informers for the South Vietnamese government in the Ba Lat's case and killed in front of the peasants.[20] If villagers opposed the communists, the latter usually retaliated by killing the villagers' relatives. On many occasions the communists attacked and burnt down the hamlets killing people, civilians as well as the militia. Villagers moved out and the village became deserted and reverted to a jungle.[21]

At the provincial level, Nguyen Ngan witnessed the indiscriminate shelling by the Viet Cong of a primary school in the Cai Be district causing the death of twenty-one small school children. They even attacked passenger buses in the Dinh Tuong province causing many civilian casualties. They caught private Cao who returned home from duty to visit his parents and decapitated him. His torso was thrown on his father's doorstep while "his head was displayed on a bamboo pike at their front gate."[22]

From January 1st to November 24th 1965, 450 province, district, and hamlet officials were killed and another 709 kidnapped.[23] In the Binh Dinh province, the Viet Cong beheaded a village chief and cut off the arm of his twelve-year-old daughter. These acts of barbarism were designed to intimidate the citizenry, to facilitate collection of taxes and recruitment of men, and to frighten citizens into not revealing Viet Cong's hiding places. There were more than 19,000 communist acts of terrorism in South Vietnam during 1964: attacks on churches, villages, and buses, burning of houses, shelling of markets, gathering areas, and kidnappings.[24]

Urban terror was based on the same hit and run tactic. On March 3, 1965, a bomb exploded in front of the Mayflower Bar killing five people and injuring four others. On March 30, a bomb exploded in front of the U.S. Embassy in Saigon killing twenty-two people, including two Americans and injuring 188 people. On June 25, 1965, the Viet Cong bombed the My Canh floating restaurant on the Saigon River. One hundred, twenty-four casualties were reported including twenty-eight Americans. Soon afterwards, Radio Hanoi approved the terrorist act and commented: "Let us acclaim this great victory by the Saigon revolutionary armed forces.... The South Vietnamese people and our compatriots are overjoyed at this feat of arms...."[25]

On October 3, a blast at the Cong Hoa stadium killed nine people. The killing went on and on, no day passing by without the report of a new terrorist attack.

The record of communist terrorism in Saigon was long and murderous. It consisted of firing automatic weapons at individuals, throwing grenades and setting off bombs in markets, restaurants, and theaters. No one was immune from the attacks and even South Vietnamese Prime Minister Tran

Van Huong was shot at on his way to work. But the main targets were police stations, military installations, the American Embassy, and bars and restaurants frequented by Americans.

The spectrum of Viet Cong repression ranged from assassination, execution, imprisonment, confinement or thought reform. The instrument of repression was the Viet Cong Security Service (An Ninh), which had more than 25,000 agents in 1970. The security cadres usually fomented "hatred and vindictiveness" against the GVN[26] to justify assassination and to destabilize the Saigon government. They were also in charge of executing or abducting people.

A total of 44,000 persons were assassinated (18,000) or abducted (26,000) between January 1966 and December 1969.[27] These numbers, however, might underestimate the true figures because of underreporting and exclusion of large numbers of GVN officials killed as a result of military attacks and other actions not considered to be assassinations.

Overall the Viet Cong had carried out "systematic assassinations of southern leaders" and caused widespread terror among the civilian population throughout the country since 1959.[28] To condone Ho's reign of terror was morally wrong.

The 1968 Tet Offensive

In 1968, the Viet Cong thought the time was ripe for an uprising. On the nights of January 30 and 31, they launched a series of coordinated attacks against South Vietnam's major cities. The Viet Cong were told this was their last battle and the people were ready to support them. The Viet Cong came well prepared and had lists and addresses of everyone who strongly opposed them in the old imperial city of Hue in central Vietnam. They knew exactly where to go to meet their unsuspecting victims thanks to their informers. They rounded up Catholic priests, government officials, military officers, and their families, and either executed them right in front of their doorsteps or marched them to the jungles and got rid of them. They then dumped the bodies into the Huong River, which gently crossed through the city. "The dead floated to the sea for many days after Tet"[29] and the stench was unbearable. In other quarters, "bodies were [placed] in layers like stacks of artillery ammunition." One reporter wrote:

> Gradually, the battling turned the once beautiful city into a nightmare. Hue's streets were littered with dead. A black-shirted communist soldier sprawled dead in the middle of the road, still holding a hand grenade. A

woman knelt in death by a wall in the corner of her garden. A child lay on the stairs, crushed by a fallen roof. Many of he bodies have turned black and begun to decompose, and rats gnawed at the exposed flesh.

Time, February 16, 1968

A few weeks after Hue was retaken, ARVN soldiers found, "hundreds and hundreds of skulls, arms, and legs — everything white because the river washed them for so long" fifteen kilometers Southwest of Hue.[30] The Viet Cong had marched these people to the jungle and had executed them. Many victims had been "beaten to death, shot, beheaded, or buried alive. Many bodies were found bound together in groups of 10 or 15, eyes open, with dirt of cloth stuffed in their mouth."[31]

In one instance in Hue, the Viet Cong exhorted the parishioners to denounce Father Urbain, a French priest. But "when none did, ten of them were shot, and the priest was bound and thrown on top of the bodies." His parishioners were forced to bury him alive.[32] Overall there were between 3,000 and 5,000 South Vietnamese citizens executed in cold blood during this attack.[33]

In the province of Soc Trang,

> every detail and plan had been laid out in case of success.... The execution of all policemen, administrative personnel, secret agents, hamlet chiefs, district chiefs, and so forth would be carried out on the spot without the necessity for consulting with higher authority.[34]

The Viet Cong had similar plans for other cities in the South; luckily the Tet Offensive was crushed and the human cost was held to the minimum. Although that minimum was already high, there was no doubt the toll could have been much worse had the offensive succeeded.

The events of Hue "instilled a fear and horror of the communists, which caused mass flight before them in subsequent offensives."[35] These were the warning signs of what was about to come after the war.

IV

Bamboo Fences

The award of the Nobel Peace Prize to communist Le Duc Tho and U.S. Secretary of State Kissinger for negotiating peace in Vietnam represented an awkward choice that led two members of the Peace Committee to resign in protest. It was certainly ironic given that neither of the two laureates represented the South Vietnamese people; instead they negotiated for the military conquest and the de-facto occupation of South Vietnam in exchange for the pull-out of the American troops. Both of them behaved like modern colonialists who tried to squeeze the most out of the agonizing South Vietnam. The natural consequence was the fall of Saigon in 1975. By negotiating this settlement, the U.S. had "repudiated the sovereignty of their ally, and without an ally the only possible reason for the presence of American armed forces in that country was aggression."[1] By the stroke of a pen, Kissinger had bartered away the freedom of the twenty-five million South Vietnamese he was supposed to protect.

April 30, 1975, marked the end of the free South Vietnamese government as well as freedom in South Vietnam. Not only was it a day of ignominy, but it also marked the beginning of the dark ages for all the South Vietnamese. It marked the enslavement of South Vietnam. Since 1954, the South Vietnamese had been living under the fairly democratic, although at times authoritarian, regimes of Diem and Thieu. People at least could elect their own representatives and choose them from among a long list of candidates; there were a minimum of twenty candidates per open seat. They could at least voice their opinions by demonstrating. In contrast, the communist regime was totalitarian in nature. In retrospect, the Diem and Thieu regimes appeared benevolent and easily tolerable compared to the totalitarian, communist system. Even Lomperis admitted, "However repressive the Saigon regime may have appeared, there was more freedom in the South than in the North."[2]

Peace was equivalent to brutal repression and deportation of 2.5 million southern military personnel and government civilians[3] to concentration camps from which many never reemerged. Peace saw millions of civilians deported to the new economic zones (NEZ) where they were forced to work in agrarian communes. Peace was also equivalent to a complete suppression of freedom of speech, religion, civil liberty, and movement, and the brutal execution of 100,000 to 250,000 South Vietnamese.[4]

Peace saw the dispossession of belongings, homes, lands, and businesses of civilian people by the communists. It sent wave after wave of South Vietnamese to the seas in an attempt to escape the ruthless communist regime, only to fall prey to ruthless barbarians, the sea pirates. Peace meant twenty-five million South Vietnamese would live forever in an "oppressed silence"[5] under a ruthless, totalitarian regime where one misplaced word was equivalent to banishment from the face of the earth.

Since South Vietnam was more progressive and economically rich than the northern socialist regime, the initial plan was to let South Vietnam become a neutralist state, to recognize private ownership and slowly integrate it into the northern system to allow time to resolve certain "realities and specific characteristics of the two zones."[6] But the northern government realized that the south had a higher standard of living than the north. Despite strict regulations the liberal culture of Saigon, in the form of art, books, poetry, music, and movies, was smuggled to the north and reached the northern people.

After two decades of self-sacrifice and self-immolation for the war efforts, the northerners were suddenly confronted with new ideas of freedom, peace, a high standard of living, and material riches. They envied the southerners who seemed to have all the modern conveniences, such as refrigerators, air conditioners, motorcycles, cars, televisions, automatic watches and so on. The northerners, on the other hand, could only aspire for three things: "a bicycle, a radio and a manual watch which had to be rewound twice a day." They started having second thoughts about their government, about its policies, and about whether their sacrifice was worth it. They wondered why they had to sacrifice so much and still come out poorer than the southerners.

Faced with many potentially troubling questions from their own people, the communist leadership immediately decided to unify the country. Otherwise, the government would have difficulty subduing the South Vietnamese and at the same time controlling the north. General elections began in April 1976, one year after the fall of Saigon, and Vietnam became reunified as of that date. It should be noted that this is the third time the country was reunified since 1600: the first was under southern Nguyen Hue (King Quang Trung) from 1788–1792 and the second time in 1802 under southern Nguyen Anh (King Gia Long).

Revenge

Right after the fall of Saigon, the communists began taking revenge first on soldiers, policemen, informers, and intelligence officers. The action was swift and irrevocable. Many officials were taken out of their houses or offices and shot or beaten to death. These incidents were widespread throughout South Vietnam. The war had gone on for such a long time that hard feelings were hard to avoid.

A "bloody and dismembered man was thrown on a communal route near Hoc Mon district" to die. On route 13, soldiers of the 25th ARVN division fought against the Viet Cong. Many South Vietnamese tanks were destroyed and the soldiers were left dying in the torrid sun. The wounded cried in pain but were neglected by the enemy. They "groaned for water but no one dared to take care of them." One Viet Cong designed his own method of torture: he tied a "military security agent behind a coach and dragged him on the road until he died."[7]

In the Vinh Binh province in the Mekong Delta, a teenager, probably a son of a military officer of the Saigon regime, was brought to a soccer field for trial. He was charged with being "a traitor and against the party and the people." Although no proof was given, the youngster was nonetheless condemned to death. Nine other civilians received the same sentence that day and all ten were shot to death by the firing squad. The crowd was then led to a cemetery to watch a bulldozer raze all the southern soldiers' graves. "These people are against us. They are traitors and we have no place for them," yelled a Viet Cong.[8] As for Huynh, he was jailed by the police just for being a student and sent to reeducation camp in June 1975.

Executions

The victims of these summary executions were usually government officials of the former regime: district chiefs, mayors, high-ranking members of the police and the army. Desbarats wrote:

> Most of the executions took place within 18 months of the fall of Saigon. Almost two thirds of all reported executions, and most of those reported

immediately after liberation, occurred in Saigon and the Mekong delta, reflecting the priority placed on the elimination of former regime associates.[9]

In the first week after the fall of Saigon, people were encouraged to witness many trials by the so called "people's court." They were similar to the ones used during the 1954 land reform in North Vietnam. Nguyen Ngan witnessed three teenagers being tried in Saigon for minor charges (stealing a bracelet, a watch and a bicycle respectively) in front of Notre Dame Cathedral. The Viet Cong leader charged that the youngsters were "criminals and children of antirevolutionary families." Antirevolutionary for them simply meant not sharing the communist views. Without further discussion he, a self-appointed prosecutor and judge, determined that they were guilty of "crime against the Revolution." He then asked the onlookers to determine the punishment. One or two voices within the crowd shouted, "Kill them. Kill them." The crowd slowly began to chant these words. There were no arguments or protests because no one wanted to be the fourth one to be tried. The youngsters were tied to a nearby tree and shot to death on the spot by the firing squad. The bodies were then brought to the Saigon market for exhibition for two days. For many days, Nguyen Ngan's wife did not want to leave her house after witnessing these executions.

Throughout the city, these executions were repeated on a regular basis in an attempt to terrorize the Saigonese into a "quick and uncomplaining acceptance of the new regime.[10] No defense was available to the "accused" who were found guilty whether proofs of conviction were present or not.

Captain Trinh, chief of the Kien An district of the Kien Giang province, was a competent and fearless South Vietnamese officer who, before 1975, helped recapture the Hieu Le District in the U Minh Forest from the communists. After the fall of Saigon, the communists immediately captured and executed him.[11]

The Chuong Thien province chief was taken to the heliport in the city, tried before a "people's court," then executed, his body thrown into the jungle. Major Bui Van Ba, the district chief of Vung Liem, Vinh Long province was beaten to death by the communists.[12]

Dr Vu Duc Giang, flight surgeon of the 7th Marine Battalion ARVN was caught on March 25, 1975, by the enemy at the Thuan An bay in central Vietnam along with a Marine brigade. To protect the honor of another physician, he demanded that the jailers respect the physician's human rights. But they beat him up and ordered him to kneel down. He refused and was thrown into jail where he later committed suicide. He was 28 years old that fall of 1976.[13]

After the fall of Saigon, although no major bloodbath took place in the major cities, widespread eliminations and killings were noted in the provinces where no outside observers were encountered. "Over five hundred people in the villages of Hoa Thang, Hoa Tri, Hoa Quang, and Hoa Kien [all in the Tuy Hoa district] were murdered during the first days of [the communist] occupation."[14] Venerable Thich Dieu Bon of the United Buddhist Church in Tuy Hoa was killed because he was suspected of being a CIA agent. He had previously received a citation from the Americans for having helped search for an American MIA. Mr. Tran Pho, a teacher, was stabbed to death at Le Uyen. Mr. Nguyen Huu Tri, a Dai Viet member, was buried alive. Mr. Truong Tu Thien, a Dai Viet Party leader, underwent "extremely atrocious tortures."[15]

In front of the temple of Phuoc Hung before a people's court, eighteen of twenty-five men were condemned to death:

> The communists "took the 18 down into the grave, one by one, and knifed them in the neck, cut the windpipe and jerked the head of the victim in a very professional way. One girl of 18 was executed as an informer to the South Vietnamese side.... Two Viet Cong knifed her at the edge of her grave, and threw her into it, but she was not dead. Another leapt in and knifed her again, but she yelled out, "I'm not dead yet, knife me a few more times."[16]

Nguyen Van Canh had reported many more executions and liquidations in his book.[17]

Nguyen Tuong Lai, a Viet Cong, was put in charge of the Long Tan reeducation camp after 1975. He revealed that the majority of the Hoi Chanh (200,000 former Viet Cong who had rallied to the GVN during the war) and GVN intelligence and security forces were sentenced to death:

> These unfortunate people were killed and nobody knows where. Because Party policy was very clear: Every death sentence should be public to enhance the hatred of the people for the Party's enemies ... but the execution must be done in secret, so the people would not have pity for the victims.[18]

Of all the executions, which took place after 1975, the communist government officially volunteered to report only forty-one:

> The 41 executions reported in detail in the official press the last eight months of 1975, although representing only a small fraction of the total, provide an insight into the vengeful motivations underlying the treatment of the "so called common criminals." Of these 41 death sentences, 36 just happened to involve soldiers of the former "puppet" army.... It is difficult to believe that this group, which made up 7 percent of the adult population of South Vietnam, could justifiably account for 90 percent of all announced

executions for rape, robbery, and murder. Furthermore, in capital cases that involved both former "puppet" soldiers and civilians, former army personnel were much more likely to receive the death penalty.[19]

Eradication of Private Ownership

After 1975, the government took over any house or building it saw fit and it usually did so by force or at gunpoint: the police would show up at a certain house or building and simply "requisition" it for the state. The unlucky owners had no choice but to obey the police, or be sent to reeducation camps. Without warning, they became homeless. In the same vein as the eradication of private commerce, state ownership was promoted: all southerners had to report all their belongings. Those who had two or three houses were allowed to keep only one for shelter; the others had to be handed to the state.

Frequently whole sections of the city were surrounded right after midnight and houses and belongings were confiscated while its citizens were rounded up and driven to a new economic zone (NEZ). They were usually dropped off in the middle of a virgin forested area surrounded by wild animals and infested with malaria-carrying mosquitoes. They were ordered to build new homes, cut down trees and shrubs, till the land, and become farmers (chapter 16).

On September 9th 1975, a businessman in Bac Lieu was jailed and his entire fortune was confiscated. He was said to have "collaborated with the Americans and enriched himself by selling rice" in the three southernmost provinces of South Vietnam. He was released two years later only after the police chief (communist) of the province who sent him to jail had escaped to join the flood of refugees. As the former inmate was trying to get back his house and belongings, he explained that many southerners back in 1975 "were simply arrested so that the cadres could strip them of their fortunes, and divide the booty among themselves. For the majority of arrested people, no records at all were kept."[20]

A middle class family in Saigon was sent to a NEZ so that their house could be converted into a clothing-cooperative.[21] Two weeks after the fall of Saigon in the Vinh Binh province, Huynh's family was driven out of their farm without warning. They were each allowed to take only a shirt and one pair of pants while the police went through their belongings looking for valuables. All his brothers were then sent to reeducation camps and his father almost got executed.[22]

The campaign of confiscation of private property continued in full swing in 1978 with many tragic results. "A lady burned herself to death when security guards broke in to take over her property."[23] She knew she would never have survived by herself in an NEZ, so she decided to take her own life right then rather than die in the NEZ. While the same process of immolation of a Buddhist monk in 1963 brought worldwide coverage, under the communist regime no press coverage was available and the lady burned alone, ignored by the world.

More than one million northern communist officials along with their families moved south to administer Saigon. Buildings requisitioned or vacated by the southerners became state properties and redistributed to northerners. This represented a de-facto civilian occupation of Saigon and the South, which completed the military takeover.

Confiscation of Private Businesses

The North Vietnamese rapidly converted the southern capitalist economy into a socialist regime. Private commerce was abolished in a stroke of the pen. They used taxation as a means to control the economy by levying excessively high taxes on all private businesses and backdating these taxes for ten years. It did not matter that they did not control South Vietnam during these years: the goal was to strip all citizens of their belongings. Since business people were unable to pay all these taxes, they decided to "give their businesses away" to the state.[24] Soon the state owned all the stores, and the people became plain workers. This confiscation process affected every business including bookstores, movie theaters, furniture stores, gas stations, and car and motorcycle dealerships. All of the sudden, merchants were dispossessed of their belongings and means of survival. Not only were they out of a job, but they also had lost all their investments. Commerce went into a standstill. Local people now had to line up at state stores to buy their basic needs *a la Soviet* system.

All heavy as well as light industries, the banking system, foreign trade, transportation, communication, and construction companies became state properties and workers were forced to unionize. The government ended private commerce and centralized all trades under a plan called "two-way commerce."[25] This meant fishermen and farmers, for example, could not sell any product directly to the public: they were forced to sell it cheaply to the government. And in return the government would sell them gas, clothes, seed, and medicines. The public, too, could only buy goods from the government.

The state now owned everything, but many of these riches fell into the hands of the northern communists who made the laws and applied them to their advantages. A northern soldier, who had never owned anything valuable in his life, could become the manager of the state grocery store. He then could allocate ten kilos of rice to a person per month. If he did not have enough rice in reserve, he would cut the ration down to eight kilos per month. If he had an excess of rice, he could hoard the excess, sell it on the black market, and pocket the extra cash. The communist soldier or party member became an owner and capitalist at the expense of the southerners. After 1975, the communists used their military power to shift the balance of economic power to their side.

In a socialist regime, the government did not have to cater to the needs of the consumers; the latter were the ones who had to follow strict government's rules. Since there was no competition, the state could do whatever it wanted. If it had spoiled rice, it could sell it as is, and the consumer had to buy it; otherwise he or she would starve to death or pay a higher price on the black market. Slowly using his position, the northern manager enriched himself at the expense of the southerner who had to sell off his belongings little by little in order to survive.

Things got worse. The so-called "dishonest merchants," the big businessmen who controlled a major share of the market and were thought to be useless in the communist system, were sent to the NEZ. Having lost their businesses as well as investments, they soon faced the loss of their homes and private belongings. They were victimized a second time around and finally ended up broke. Many could not endure all these losses and committed suicide.

A Socialist State

In the new society, almost everyone became a salaried employee. Not having enough cash reserve to pay its employees, the state lowered the wages according to the following scale: factory workers earned 30 dong a month; clerks, 40 dong; engineers, 60 dong; doctors and pharmacists, 80 dong; government minister, 215 dong. The exchange rate was 2.75 dong for one U.S. dollar. The official price of a kilo of rice was 0.45 dong, while it was 6 dong on the black market.

Since officials and their families could not live on such a low income; they had to look elsewhere to fill their pockets. They used their positions of power to extract money from the civilians. Everything could be obtained for a bribe; power bred corruption in a communist state. A permit to visit a husband or relative in a concentration camp cost 300 dong. The price for a commuter's permit valid for one or two months was 50 dong. A civilian had to pay bribes each time he had to deal with a government official. Graft and corruption blossomed and became part of the socialist society. "Cadres vie with each other in stealing, taking bribes, and smuggling prohibited goods."[26] Officials mismanaged state property, treating as private property. Although higher officials were aware of all the mismanagement, they just looked the other way because exposing these grafts would give a bad name to the socialist state. Government property, which included smuggled goods found its way to the black market, as described in the following poem:[27]

> If you come to Thai Nguyen City
> You will see an awful sight,
> For the market, morning till night,
>   Bustles with venality.
> Anything you want to buy
> On the sidewalk is displayed-
> Even what the state forbade,
> God may know how, but not I.
>   Nhu Van Lo

Cassava is a root with so little nutritional value that it was not used for consumption in the south before 1975. When food became scarce after the communist takeover, people had to mix cassava with a small amount of rice to increase the bulk of their meals. Poorer people used cassava as a full substitute for rice as the latter was becoming more expensive. The scarcity of rice was due to many factors, including loss of manpower, agricultural reform leading to decreased production, as well as to the fact that most of the rice was bought at a cheap price and shipped to the north.[28]

People became impoverished as a result of the communist policy and resorted to stealing to survive. Many electric wires were cut down to make counterfeit coins. Sewer grills were stolen and bikers got injured when they fell into the sewer.[29] Hungry people stole cassava from the fields.[30]

In September 1975, all the South Vietnamese banknotes were exchanged for communist notes. All bank accounts were frozen and people were only allowed to exchange a certain amount of money. As a result, the Saigonese lost all their savings during this exchange period.

In May 1978, all the banknotes issued in the north and south became invalid as part of the second currency reform. And each household was allowed to withdraw up to a maximum of 500 dong: 100 each for the first two members, and fifty each for subsequent members. Whatever excess money a household had was kept in reserve in the bank and could be withdrawn in small amounts only if the owner could prove that he or she had earned the money "honestly."³¹ And everything hinged on the definition of honesty. If a businessman made a killing in selling cars, he could be deemed as dishonest, and his bank account could be frozen. But if businessmen knew how to deal with the northern bank manager or gave him a share of the money, he could end up saving a large chunk of the money and his own life. And the manager slowly became richer every time he made a deal.

For the rest of the population who did not have large bank accounts, bribery was out of question. But all these reforms rendered everyone poorer because they were simply dispossessed of their bank and saving accounts. This turned out to be the most dramatic economic change in Vietnamese history, causing the whole southern populace to be impoverished. Had the Thieu regime done it, it would have been taken down and there would have been riots, self-immolation, front-page news, and so on. The fact that Hanoi did it with impunity could only be explained by its ruthlessness.

1975 Land Reform

After 1975, landowners were forced to turn over their lands to the state to be redistributed in parcels to local people who worked for the state without owning the land. However, farmers "destroyed equipment and killed animals rather than hand them over to collective farms.... Only 7 percent of households joined co-operatives, compared to about 90 percent in the north." Harvested rice would be sold to the state at a cheap rate, while the cost of the product on the black market would be three times higher. As the process made the farmers unhappy, they simply refused to work harder causing a rapid decline in rice production.³²

Other factors compounded the problem: state interference, loss of manpower (workers as well as technicians) from the massive exodus of refugees, lack of fertilizers, bad weather, and unsafe fields, which were still loaded with war mines. Vietnam, a major rice exporter in the sixties, had to import rice to satisfy local demands. To offset the decline in rice production, at one time, the state cut the rice quota allowed to each household, and even substituted cassava or cattle feeds for rice.

The irony lies in the fact that land reform had been instituted in 1954 when the communists took over North Vietnam. Landowners were dispossessed, tried as capitalists before kangaroo courts and murdered. The reform, however, failed and was terminated in 1956. The communists, refusing to learn from their mistakes, re-instituted the same policy in the south in 1975, which again failed and led to a shortage of rice. It caused another revolt in the south and was terminated in 1978. Private ownership was re-instituted and farmers were allowed to keep a larger portion of their harvest. Stimulated by these changes, productivity instantly surged and in the late '90s, Vietnam became the third largest rice exporter in the world.

The effects of the revolution were felt everywhere. In the countryside, lands were confiscated and reorganized as agricultural cooperatives with farmers toiling as its employees. Old Man Thuoc, a hard-working farmer, took on any task assigned to him by the cooperative. Because of their hard and dedicated work, both he and his wife earned the respect of all the villagers. Thuoc was enjoying his work and thought about a nice retirement. One day, he advised his fellow workers to go easy on an old buffalo; otherwise it might die on them. The secretary of the party branch, however, misunderstood his remarks and branded him as a "reactionary."

A year later, his son enrolled into the army, but soon went AWOL. The party secretary decided to target Old Man Thuoc, searching his house and stripping him of his job as a foreman and cutting off the ration-coupon system. All of the sudden, he and his wife were ostracized and avoided like pariahs. He had to look for work in another village while his wife was scrounging for snails, crabs and anything edible in the flooded fields to supply their meager food portion. Meanwhile the old buffalo, exhausted by the work, fell sick and slowly died. Disaster had struck as Thuoc had predicted. One meeting was convened after another, but no one in the coop was willing to play the role of the buffalo. Thuoc saw it an opportunity to "atone for his son's sins and earn his way back into the party's favor. He begged for mercy and a second chance." His wife saw him coming out of the meeting with a "toothless grin from ear to ear." He then told her they would take the place of the buffalo. A few days later, everyone saw Old Man Thuoc pulling the plough while his wife followed him silently behind, trying to keep the plough in a straight line.[33]

Because of the revolution, Old Man Seven, a southern blacksmith, let his youngest son move to the north after the Geneva Accords while a million northerners were heading the other way around. One of the northerners told him about the "secret police snooping on people, private properties confiscated, hard work and not enough food to eat in the North." But Old Man Seven did not believe in any of these statements, calling them "false propagandas." For him the revolution was bright and it was "winning independence, peace, freedom and happiness."

Twenty-one years later, the revolution triumphed in the south. Old Man Seven's oldest son was "sent to reeducation camp. His second son's bus was taken away from him — they politely called it a 'requisition.' The Land Transportation Service borrowed his house to use it as an office.... His grandchildren had to do labor for the state and rummage through garbage dumps for scrap paper and tattered nylon bags.... He had to raise a pig and ten chicken to help the village implement its plan for self-sufficiency in food supply." His younger son, now a high official in the revolutionary administration, kept his distance for fear of guilt by kinship. All around him, Old Man Seven "witnessed nothing but hunger and misery, suspicion and hatred."

Old Man Seven's life imitated "the game of the Forty Beasts as he played it once and lost. He betted on a roasted pig: the Revolution laid an egg and hatched a canard."[34]

Suppression of Religious Freedom

In the political arena, religious and political freedoms were harshly suppressed. In the city of Danang, over 1,500 temples, pagodas, and other places of worship were destroyed in early 1985 on the grounds that they helped foster superstition.[35] Seminaries were closed and many priests were sent to reeducation camps.

Many political and religious leaders, who had been free to revolt against the Diem and Thieu regimes were jailed under the communist regime and completely silenced. Tran Van Tuyen, a lawyer who fought against the Thieu regime, was locked up by the new regime and was later reported to have died in reeducation camp, some said of suicide. Monk Thich Thien Minh died in jail in 1978. Other monks like Thich Huyen Quang, Thich Thuyen An and Thich Quan Do were jailed and their fate went unknown.

Thich Tri Quang, the Buddhist monk who toppled the Diem government and caused a lot of trouble for the Thieu regime was jailed in the Chi Hoa prison for sixteen months. He was "kept in a poorly ventilated underground dungeon where he could not even sit without assuming a fetal position. He was let out only fifteen minutes a day. He was reduced to a skeleton and his legs atrophied." He remained confined to a wheelchair for some time.[36] In 1994, he was reported to be "swabbing the latrine floor at the Xa loi pagoda, reduced, like everyone else outside party circles, to a subsistence standard of living."[37] Leaders of the Hoa Hao and Cao Dai sects were also known to have died in concentration camps.

For many years after the fall of Saigon, all churches, pagodas, and other religious institutions were closed. Many monks were defrocked and sent to the NEZs. The leading Buddhist monks were jailed and replaced by northern monks who offered a sympathetic voice more in line with the government.

Social Changes

The first significant change was the burning of four million works previously stored in the Khai Tri publishing house on Saigon's LeLoi Street. Books from the many universities in Saigon were taken out and burned in the streets. Revolutionary youths went from house to house to hunt for "decadent" literature from private libraries and to confiscate it. University professors, doctors, judges, poets, writers, journalists, publishers, actors, and producers were either sent to reeducation camps or thrown into jails.[38]

Children were taught to sing communist songs and to report whatever their parents said at home. "A good citizen is someone who turns you in, kills your relatives, or makes you do exactly what they want you to do."[39]

After 1975, women were also invited to join revolutionary organizations. They first enrolled as a "Patriotic Woman" (Phu nu Yeu Nuoc) to learn the way of the revolution. After a while, if qualified, they proceeded to be a "United Woman" (Phu nu Doan Ket); and with tenure they finally graduated to a "Liberated Woman" (Phu nu Giai Phong). Participation in these organizations exacted tremendous amounts of time, energy, and money.[40] They became so busy attending meetings that they were unable to take care of their homes, families or do their chores. They also had to make time to participate in these organizations at the level of the cell, the precinct, the ward and the district at the expense of their children.

There were similar meetings at their offices. And when workers came home tired from a long day of work at the office, they were "encouraged" to attend the precinct or ward meeting that dragged on endlessly, from 6:00 P.M. to as late as 10:00 or 11:00 P.M. By then, they had not had time to talk to their husband or children or gulp down the evening meal. But they had to show "joy and zeal" to participate in all the discussions that ensued. They continuously studied one new directive after another and brought back a wealth of homework. Once they had mastered the basic concepts, they had to go out and teach them to other organizations. If they were not office workers in the morning, they had to talk people "into going back to their native villages or leaving for the economic zones, [drive] away peddlers, [and hunt] enemies of the state."[41]

Women also had to contribute money to these organizations to defray the costs of running the meetings. In between, they had to make time to go to the market or stand in long lines to buy the meager rations allowed at the government store. And if the stores ran out of items to sell, they had to come back another day to buy them; otherwise there would be nothing to eat. Southern women had to participate in these activities unless they wanted be labeled as "un-revolutionary" and shipped to the NEZ.

Women also had to learn words and phrases of the new official jargon with the purpose of stunning people with the force and ardor of their revolutionary convictions. Words like "struggle," "dialectics," "historical materialism," "militant," and especially "joy and zeal" were frequently used to highlight the report. Women could not simply state, "The work began at 5 A.M. and ended at 8 P.M." They had to elaborate. For example, they might say, "Although the weather suddenly turned cool that morning, all our sisters made a tremendous effort and succeeded in being there at 5 A.M. They vied with one another in having the street swept cleaned by 8 P.M.; thus making our organization worthy of the name that it proudly bears."

Language became more flowery and poetic. The revolution would have been idyllic had it not been for the fact that the workers were forced to "volunteer" for the job unless they were willing to be shipped to the zones to work in unreasonable and unhealthy conditions at less than minimum wage and fifteen hours a day. The following sentence was found in one of the reports: "Most of our sisters studied hard and made a genuine effort to speak up in class" had been reformulated as, "All of our sisters applied themselves with determination to the course of study and enthusiastically vied with one another in expressing their opinions on the subject."[42] The reality was the tired women who attended the meeting had only one wish: to go home and get some rest in order to be able to function the following morning.

Amerasians are children born of unions between American men and Vietnamese women. They lived as "outcasts on the fringes of society,"[43] shunned by other children and the communists. Already abandoned by their fathers, they sometimes were rejected by their mothers. They survived as street children or were sent to new economic zones. They were targeted after the takeover because they were the "enemy's children." They were called the "dust of life" and were denied education as well as opportunities.

After finishing high school, Trang applied to college but was turned down because he was Amerasian. He enlisted in the People's Army and fought the Khmer Rouge in Cambodia. Because he was a good and intelligent soldier, he was selected to attend "an officer candidate school."[44] As soon as it was discovered he was Amerasian and his stepfather was a Saigon policeman, he was sent back to fight in the Cambodian jungle.

Nguyen Kien recounted that, after 1975, his mother had to turn over her house and belongings to her gardener who turned out to be an underground Viet Cong. His application for college was turned down because he was a member of the "reactionary class."[45]

The Looting of South Vietnam

While native southerners were either sent to the NEZ or reeducation camps, the northerners descended on southern cities and took over the administration, industries, businesses, houses and so on:

> They fought each other over houses, cars, prostitutes and bribes. Soldiers and officials brought up in the bleak poverty of North Vietnam and subjected for years to the rigors of military life were suddenly confronted with what seemed to them an almost fairy-tale richness, theirs for the taking. It was as if the city had been invaded by a swarm of locusts.[46]

South Vietnam's gold reserves, which amounted to sixteen tons, were sent to the North on Truong Chinh's order. The Saigon bank deputy suggested that if the gold were invested wisely, it would help finance the reconstruction of Vietnam, but his idea was rejected as capitalist. Two years later, Truong Chinh admitted that most of the gold was "used up in coping with various emergencies."[47]

After the fall of Saigon "much of the equipment (taken from the Long Binh storage base) — mosquito nets, tents, water flasks etc. — was then sold on the market with the profits going into the pockets of corrupt individuals. A lot also disappeared to the North." In 1978, a major campaign was launched against capitalist traders in Saigon without leadership control. "A vast quantity of money, gold, and jewels was simply disappearing, much of it going into the pockets of those conducting the campaign."[48]

The Viet Cong stole gas from tanks or military trucks and sold it on the market. Others took whatever items (barbed wire, tools, wood, steel, iron and aluminum sheets, chemical products, cement, bricks and so on) from South Vietnamese bases and military posts they could get their hands on and sold them. Communist heads stole chemicals and cigarette paper and sold them to the Chinese to make soap and cigarettes.

A sawmill owner in Binh Duong got richer after transferring the ownership to the local government. The communist in charge did not know how to run it. When the saw broke, he called the former owner and asked him to get a new blade or fix it. The owner had the old blade welded, billed the government for a new blade and shared the profit with the communist head. Communist cadres in charge of collective and state farms stole "fertilizers, plants, seeds, gas and oil. Tractor parts were stolen and sold at the junkyards in Cholon. Sweet potatoes, cassava and barley donated by the European Economic Community were sold by cadres on the market."[49]

V

A Police State

In a repressive country, the police force was powerful and could do anything it wanted. It could confiscate a person's car and scooter at will even though the owner had shown the proper titles.¹ It could harass people by subjecting them to interviews for no valid reason. One interview would lead to another, followed by vague threats of being anti-revolutionary or risking the loss of a food-coupon, and people would have to bribe the police in an attempt to avoid jail or being sent to a reeducation camp.

> They never let you go scot-free. If they can't pin you down as a reactionary, then you're a pseudo-pacifist. If you're not a pseudo-pacifist, you're a bourgeois-nationalist. If not a bourgeois-nationalist, you're a decadent. If not a decadent, you're a hooligan. And hooliganism, decadence, bourgeois-nationalism, and pseudo-pacifism are all subtle forms of reaction.²

If military personnel and government officials were sent to reeducation camps located deep in the jungles, lay people, when suspected of "subversion," were thrown into jails and left there to rot until the government could find enough charges to justify the keeping them incarcerated longer.

There were so many arrests—"more kidnappings than legal arrests"—that prisons were overloaded: a cell designed for twenty prisoners under the Thieu regime became home to seventy to eighty inmates under the new regime. In the first year after liberation, some "three hundred thousand people [civilians] were arrested," for there was "no code of laws governing what was to be taken, no authority to which any of these organs were responsible for their decisions, and no protection for those who were seized."³

Truong Nhu Tang, the PRG minister of justice, was so appalled by the lawlessness that he appealed directly to Prime Minister Pham Van Dong in Hanoi for help. Criteria were set and the code became law in March 1976 (almost a year after the fall of Saigon).

But the 3/76 Law was not widely applied after that date either. In the countryside, party cadres continued to take orders directly from the Politburo, and simply disregarded the law. Arrests continued unabated. In Saigon, where before "they did things arbitrarily without a warrant, now they did them arbitrarily with a warrant."[4]

The most renowned civilian prisons were the Ham Tan, Le Van Duyet, and Tran Hung Dao jails. No survivor of the Chi Hoa jail had yet come forward to tell his story.

Ham Tan Camp

This was a police camp, a part of the Thu Duc Detention Center, except that Thu Duc was a Saigon suburb while Ham Tan was ninety miles away. The camp was known as Z30-D; Z30 indicated a prison in Binh Tuy province (central Vietnam) and D meant that it was located in Ham Tan area. It comprised four sub-camps — A, B, C, and D — and was designed as a step down center from all the reeducation camps: for reeducation detainees (political prisoners), it was the last step before freedom. This police camp also housed common law criminals as well as women prisoners.

The camp was run by cadres supported by *trat tu vien* who were detainees appointed to maintain discipline. The latter were mostly criminals serving long sentences. They had been indoctrinated with "class struggle" attitudes and enjoyed every opportunity to get even with "intellectuals." The political prisoners feared the *trat tu vien* as if they were their fathers and the cadres as if they were their grandfathers. They were locked up all the time, more than one hundred in each barrack, and released only during meal times or work hours. There were a couple of latrines for each barrack and prisoners had to line up before 6 A.M. to go to the bathroom.

The overall atmosphere, however, was more relaxed and the work less physical than at the regular reeducation camps. The *trat tu vien*, however, continued to maintain strict discipline by beating inmates whenever they felt like it, and the presence of "antennas" was always feared. Inmates were allowed two meals a day: the average inmate worker got thirteen kilos of rice or its equivalent (*bo bo* sorghum or sweet potato) monthly while those who could not work got only ten and a half kilos.

Prisoners who had committed serious offenses were sent to "disciplinary cells" where they were shackled to the wall. The minimum stay in these cells was one month and no one was released early. One sculptor was locked in the cell for five months for making fun of the Revolution.[5] Inmates were subject to frequent and unexpected searches that could go on for a long time until something was found: cash, letters, textbooks, combs, and chess pieces. At the end of the search, inmates were reshuffled among the various barracks, and a few ended up in the "discipline cell" simply because the study monitor did not like the way they looked or a perhaps "wicked mole" had singled them out.[6]

A few former Viet Cong were also imprisoned at the camp. They were people who had previously "betrayed" the party by surrendering to and by becoming informants for the Saigon government before 1975. After the revolution, they had all been tracked down and sent to the local jail or to the reeducation camps. Others had either committed some petty crimes after 1975 or were politically purged for refusing to submit to the Hanoi government. In the camps, they formed a group apart and rarely interacted with the other inmates. They felt they neither belonged to the new government that had jailed them nor to the other inmates whom they had fought against in the past. Of communists, one of them said, "A communist has limited vocabulary.... The Revolution does not want its followers to use too many words since this might extend the scope of their thinking. The communists want to ensure that everyone speaks and behaves exactly as the revolutionaries do."[7]

Inmates had more free time in the Ham Tan camp than in other camps since political lectures were over. Although they were inching closer to their eventual release, they knew nothing about their future and could always be sent back to the reeducation camps. At night or on weekends, a few inmates, despite years of incarceration, still wondered why they had lost the war. They argued lengthily about the causes of the downfall of the nationalist cause and felt they were not determined enough to stamp out communism when it was still weak. While the North was conducting a full-scale war effort, "leading the whole nation into war," and children as young as six or seven of age were given tasks to perform in the service of the war, the South had only a loose attitude about the war. It was not totally committed to the war effort: only a minority did all the fighting while the majority went on with their daily lives, trying to block out the horrors of the war.[8]

Bien Hoa Jail

A former ARVN colonel, after spending six years in a reeducation camp, attempted to escape by boat, but was caught and sent to the Bien Hoa jail.

He was using a false identity at that time and, therefore, avoided being returned to a reeducation camp where his sentence would have been much harsher. The same 7 × 21 meter ward, which used to house thirty inmates before 1975, was stuffed with 100 inmates in 1981. The overcrowding and the heat from the low ceilings made the cell a suffocating horror. Rice or corn was served twice daily with a little salted vegetable soup. The meager regimen barely kept inmates alive.

In this jail, the colonel met brother Dung, a Catholic priest, who had been jailed from 1975 to 1981 and kept in solitary confinement five of these six years. He was always shackled and was unable to stand up; he could only sit or lie down on a wooden board. He defecated and urinated in a container, which another inmate would clean out every day. His ration was cut in half and family visits were forbidden.[9] This treatment was reserved for inmates condemned for high treason, which usually meant Catholic priests who were thought to be the anti-communist leaders.

Tran Hung Dao Jail

Doan Toai was kidnapped by the communist secret police right in the middle of downtown Saigon after 1975. Although they were looking for another Toai, they simply jailed him for precautionary reasons and would decide on his fate later on. His first cellmate was none other than the dean of the Saigon Law School who had decided to remain in Saigon after 1975 because he thought the communists would not bother a non-politician. The former dean was, however, accused of being a CIA spy. He was jailed and tortured but had nothing to confess because he had not done anything wrong.[10] He was thrown in Toai's cell after a torture session and was taken away a few days later. No one ever heard from him again. For talking to the professor after the torture session, Toai had his right wrist handcuffed to his left ankle behind his back, and his left wrist to his right ankle for two weeks in the "airplane" position.

He was later moved to collective cell A, which was a 50 × 15 foot room designed for twenty but now filled with sixty inmates. At the far end was a tiny room with a hole in the floor and a faucet to serve the inmates' needs. The conditions were terrible because of the overcrowding, the stench, the torture, the awful food, and lack of water. When a prisoner was thrown into a cell, he usually started screaming about his innocence and demanded to be released. After a "few weeks of isolation with only sandy pig rice to eat," he became tamed and "would be happy to just get a bite of meat or sugar."[11] Inmates were shuffled off to other cells every three weeks to prevent the formation of support groups.

Many were further victimized by false denunciations by their neighbors or co-workers who hoped to receive a lighter sentence as a result.

The cell was run by a *hoi chanh*, a former Viet Cong who quit the party in 1972 to rally to the Thieu government. That made him an arch traitor, one who owed a "blood debt" to the revolution. After 1975, he was caught and remained alive only due to the revolution's mercy. He was made head prisoner and enforced an iron regime to keep earning his forgiveness. He imposed a strict silence in the cell: "sixty souls sharing a 100 square yards, and you can hear a pin drop."[12] Conditions in the cell, which were bad to begin with, worsened under the *hoi chanh* discipline. Toai was lucky to be transferred to another jail in September 1975.

Le Van Duyet Jail

The Le Van Duyet jail on September 1975 housed 2,000 inmates, ten times its normal capacity, while the Chi Hoa jail took on 40,000 prisoners, five times its previous high. Everyone had a foot and a half of concrete to sleep on. There was no place for prisoners to walk or exercise. Life was a permanent lockup, unless one was assigned a task outside the cell on rare occasions.

Under these brutal conditions, inmates became irritable, tense, and ready to fight about anything, especially sleeping privileges, food, or water. They segregated themselves into smaller groups based on their social standings: former Viet Cong, *hoi chanh*, students, war profiteers, political prisoners, escapees and so on.

Communists used the "divide and conquer" approach to control inmates. A few of them were used as informers to gather information and sow distrust within the group. No one could trust anyone and no one felt safe for any misstatement would be reported and result in punishment.

Toai began to notice the difference in the treatment of prisoners in the pre- and post–1975 years. Under the new regime, inmates had no rights. They did not have access to lawyers, the press, the Red Cross, or world opinion. They became defenseless.[13] Once they were jailed for whatever reason, they remained jailed until the revolution let them go or got rid of them. On the other hand, under the Thieu regime inmates were at least protected by the rules of law, public, and world opinion. And lawyers or judges could be bought and evidence lost.

With the communist takeover, the *hoi chanh* (former Viet Cong) were hunted down and sent to the Le Van Duyet jail for having turned their back to the revolution.[14] There was also a torture cell in zone B of the jail, where a barber accused of "armed conspiracy" for having a gun in his house was tortured for days.

Toai was dumped into a six feet long, three feet wide and six feet high isolation cell for two weeks with his right wrist cuffed to his left ankle and his left wrist to his right ankle for having bribed a *bo doi* into communicating with his family. He was unlocked twice at meal times during which he could relieve himself in a helmet that served as a toilet. At the end of the sentence, he was taken back to the cell where the other inmates had to nurse him back to health for two weeks.[15]

Water was distributed only fifteen minutes a day by means of a rubber hose poked through a peephole into a water tub that sat next to the door. Inmates had to take turns to sweet talk or bribe the guard in order to get fifteen more minutes of running water.

"At every level, fear was the motivator. It was fear that separates the *bo doi* and the cadres from their essential humanity. And it was the same fear that during the war had given the revolution its internal steel. The revolution had never changed. To achieve its goals it had molded a machine of unearthly strength. And in the course of time it had simply become what it was doing."[16]

Food acted as a drug. "Cut down sufficiently, and people often react like addicts in withdrawal." Starvation led one inmate to steal food and fight with another inmate. For punishment, he was subjected to flogging. He was stripped of his underpants and ordered to lie down. After receiving thirty whips, he was found dead. The administration coldly attributed the death to the inmate having "committed suicide by swallowing his tongue."[17]

After being jailed by the new regime, Nhu Phong, a poet and political commentator decided to start a hunger strike. The *bo doi* threw him into solitary confinement and told him "with us iron became pliant." The strike became a pure battle of wills with the wardens and it was fierce. Nhu Phong did not eat for twenty, then thirty days. The prison commander came by and told him not to commit suicide. They force fed him, but he threw up. He took no food for fifty-five days. At the end, he agreed to eat. He was one of the rare few who were brave enough to challenge the communists.[18]

Through a peephole of his cell, Toai saw a few inmates who were allowed to go into the courtyard: they all looked terrible. Many had swollen feet from malnutrition and their bodies were covered with scaly skin infections. They were allowed to let the healing warmth of the sun play over the skin lesions, as no medication was available for this condition in the infirmary.

Tired of having to endure the terrible jail conditions without reason, Toai challenged the administration to either release him if he were innocent or sentence him if he were found guilty. He was finally let go 863 days after incarceration without any charges being levied against him.¹⁹ He found it ironic to be asked to attest to the communists' humanitarian policies if he ever went abroad. Having enough of the communists' justice system, he bought his way out of the country with sixty taels of gold,²⁰ half of which had to be paid at the time of departure.

VI

Incarceration

While civilians were imprisoned in city or county jails, military personnel were sequestered either in old buildings or newly built camps and guarded by the *bo doi*. The camps were located both in North as well as South Vietnam. They will be reviewed as to their design, location, and goals.

Types of Reeducation

Three types of reeducation were initially planned for South Vietnamese military personnel at the end of the war: the three-day and the ten-day reform classes and the thirty-day intensive classes.[1] But in the end, there were only two types: the three-day classes and the open-ended, labor-intensive concentration camps strewn all over Vietnam from North to South (euphemistically known as re-education camps). There were also thought reform classes reserved for civilian school teachers.

On May 3, 1975, three days after the fall of Saigon, an announcement was made on the radio mandating all former South Vietnamese officials and military personnel to report to the authorities to register their whereabouts. Subsequent directives to this Order Number One specified the dates and locations of the procedure. Generals were to report from May 8th to 9th, colonels from May 8th to 11th, and the remaining officers from May 8th to 14th with their badges, uniforms, and guns. The registration process would be completed by the end of May.

They walked, biked, or were dropped at the registration centers by their friends or family members. They were all sent home after filling out a questionnaire detailing their personal history and past activities from 1945 to

1975. It took them half an hour to an hour to complete the process. The completed questionnaires gave the new government an idea of the number, location, and composition of all southern military personnel living in South Vietnam at that time. The data was later compared to the vital information and files left by the Saigon government and the CIA employees, which in their haste to get out of town they had failed to destroy. This was a treasure trove the Hanoi government did not fail to exploit: they knew exactly who worked for the CIA, the Saigon government and the rank and file of military personnel.

On June 10th, unlisted soldiers and low-ranking civil servants were ordered to report to designated locations. They were advised to bring enough food and clothing for a three-day reeducation course. They were sequestered at local high schools, gymnasiums, or theaters and underwent thought reform classes. After three days, most were sent home.

High-ranking officials, majors and above, were mandated to present themselves on June 15, 1975, with a thirty-day food supply, while officers from captains and below had to do the same on June 23–24 with only a ten-day food supply. The announcement was presented as a clemency act to allow the vanquished to "clear their thoughts" before being reaccepted into the new society. At that time, the South Vietnamese debated vigorously among themselves whether the secret intent of the communists stemmed from a true clemency strategy or whether it was simply a ploy to lock them up for good. No one knew for sure what the communists were thinking, but with the war going for so long, animosity and distrust had a tendency to linger for a long time. Many northerners who had escaped to the South in 1954 remembered that back in the fifties when the communists took over the North, they did send a lot of people to reeducation camps; therefore, they were not to be trusted. But since most of the unlisted soldiers had been released home on schedule, the majority felt comfortable with the government's explanation. On the other hand, they did not have a lot of choices: they could either surrender or escape. And the political and social conditions were still too murky to plan for an escape: curfews were still enforced and since there were no elected officials no one knew who was actually in charge.

Despite all their personal concerns and worries, the majority gave the new government the benefit of the doubt: they were willing to believe the process would last only two to four weeks. Once they were reeducated, they thought it would not be long before they would reunite again with their families. They reluctantly reported to the authorities. Even Truong Nhu Tang, the founding father of the NLF and minister of justice of the new southern communist government (PRG) did not know the exact duration of the reeducation process.

He even convinced two of his brothers who had previously worked for the Saigon government (one was a hospital director and the other head of the foreign exchange division of the National Bank) to surrender and brought them to the camps himself.[2]

On May 15, 1975, Le Duc Tho stated: "We must quickly stabilize the people's lives, maintain public order and security, and resolutely punish counter-revolutionary elements."[3]

The official newspaper of Saigon echoed Le Duc Tho and wrote in June of 1975:

> Let us put the old regime on record. We cannot erase the blood debt owed to us by the U.S. imperialists and their henchmen. Our people must expose and pinpoint all crimes of the old regime, for the clearer we see its ugliness, the more determined ... we are to wipe out its remnants and build a new and better life. We must continue to fight all our enemies in the city, and at the same time, urgently build a better life [Saigon Giai Phong, June 2, 1975].

The setup of the reeducation system required a great deal of planning as well as logistical work. And there was no way the internment of 2.5 million people (according to Hanoi's numbers) could be done on a whim. First, the inmates had to be gathered and transported to the camps, some a few hundred miles away from their homes while hundreds of thousands of others had to be shipped a thousand miles away to the north. Later, they had to be shuffled from one camp to another every three to six months to allay the fear and paranoia of the communists. All these transfers required a lot of bureaucratic work, coordination, and logistical support. The fuel cost alone was astronomical in view of the fact that it had to be imported from the Soviet Union. Second, inmates had to be fed daily: even at a minimum of 0.25 dong per diem, the daily cost would amount to 600,000 dong, which was a lot of money for a poor country coming out of a long and disabling war. Third, they had to be housed somewhere. Even if labor were free and the camps were to be self-sufficient, the state had to provide raw materials like barbed wire, concrete, lumber, tools, and even seeds to start the cultivation process. Fourth, inmates had to be screened, guarded and taught communists' rules, which required extra manpower.

The planning and execution of the program appeared to be political in intent and had to be centralized in Hanoi. The implementation of the reeducation system as conceived would cost a lot of money, time, as well as manpower. And it is regrettable that the Hanoi government would pursue a policy of revenge by establishing and funding such a system of reeducation instead of using the money to rebuild the country and to foster a policy of reconciliation.

Incarceration

Most males went to the designated areas, which usually were local schools. They were triaged, fed, and told to remain in one of the classrooms. Although a few had to wait for a few days in these locations for others to show up, the majority was shipped away the same night. They were told to settle down on the floor and a few made themselves comfortable by hanging up their mosquito nets, spreading out their straw mats, and pulling out their pillows. They did not know what was awaiting them and soon fell asleep. Around midnight, loudspeakers blared and broke the silence, catching the prisoners by surprise. They noticed the *bo doi* running everywhere around the schoolyard and heard them yelling out orders: "Pack up and get ready for departure."

The half-asleep inmates stuffed their belongings in their bags and gathered in the schoolyard. A roll call was initiated, then they were divided into groups forty to fifty and ordered to climb on board of Russian Molotova trucks, which were parked on the nearby streets. Two *bo doi* armed with AK-47 machine-guns guarded each vehicle, one sitting in front and the second in the back of the truck. The tarpaulin was pulled down to prevent prisoners from guessing the direction of their trip. The trucks were crowded and the atmosphere inside the truck suffocating. All these transfers happened in the middle of the night.[4] This behavior was typical of the communists: they always struck after midnight, catching everyone by surprise. The convoy finally took off and without any warning they were thus trucked to real camps, like "a consignment of pigs to the market."[5]

The trip usually took six to eight hours as the trucks moved slowly at about thirty to forty miles per hour. In some cases inmates were allowed to relieve themselves once on the side of the road. The convoy would stop in the middle of nowhere and one inmate would be allowed to go down to relieve himself; he had to come back before another was permitted to take his turn. In other convoys, since the guards would not let them off the trucks, the prisoners had to urinate in empty bottles or plastic bags. In some trucks, the situation got tense when a few inmates insisted on smoking in the enclosed environment despite the objections of others.

It was early morning when they arrived to the camp (usually a former South Vietnamese military installation). They were not only tired, but also hungry, thirsty, and very unhappy. They were assigned places to sleep and ordered to do minor things such as dig a well, repair living quarters, clean the yards, and pull out weeds. They gathered in the yard and were taught to sing revolutionary songs, which sounded strange coming from former enemies. The communist organization was loose in the beginning and the prisoners were allowed a lot of free time. A few talked tough and made fun of the young, thin, and poorly clothed *bo doi*,[6] although the majority remained cautious and reserved. The latter were afraid of being reported by "moles" who roamed around listening to all conversations.[7]

The prisoners were thrown some rotten rice and told to cook for themselves or given one bag of noodles for fifty people (the bag was only good for one person).[8] Not only was the food scare, but the pots and pans were also lacking. Luckily, each inmate had brought enough food to survive the first few days. Soon, the kitchen got organized and meals became regular although their quality and quantity still lagged behind the inmates' needs. The prisoners chatted with the *bo doi* and some even asked them to make a few purchases of food or drinks from the local market. The *bo doi*, who were happy at the thought of making extra money, bought the merchandise on the outside and sold it to the inmates.

As the days went by, inmates grew more and more restless. Hoping to hear something about an imminent release, they waited impatiently for any announcement. As the cadres simply advised them they had done well and would be released soon, their frustration increased. One month went by and they still found themselves locked up in the camps. They then began to worry. Although they did not know when they would be released, they refrained from acting up because they "did not want to hurt their chances of becoming a 'progressive man' and being released."[9] "Progressive" was the big word in the camp at that time because it was equivalent to being "reformed" (usually by working as informers), which in the mind of the prisoners meant "early release." Everyone worked to be acknowledged as a "progressive."

By three or four weeks, the prisoners ran out of money and food they had brought with them. Discipline was getting tighter. The *bo doi* began shunning the prisoners, avoided talking to them and were even ordered not to deal with them or buy them food. The illicit trade soon came to a halt. The meager daily food rations from the camps could not control the inmates' hunger. They began to have second thoughts about the whole process, became depressed and many slowly settled in for a long ordeal. They did not know it then, but all of them would languish in these and other camps for the next three to twenty-two years.

During that time, the officers' families at home began worrying about the whereabouts of their relatives as one full month had passed without anyone returning home. They traveled from one government office to the next, looking for information about their loved ones. A number of wives, frustrated by the lack of responses from the authorities, staged a public demonstration outside the Saigon police station. That night, the communist police rounded up all the demonstrators and "they were never seen again. Their children were left parentless ... and were encouraged to go into the jungle to the New Economic Zones."[10]

Truong Nhu Tang's mother was also inquiring about the fate of Tang's two brothers. He then realized that the directive announced on the radio was only "a ruse intended to mask the Politburo's real policy, which was vicious and ultimately destructive to the nation."[11] He went to Huynh Tan Phat, the Viet Cong president who took him aside and explained the thirty-day provisions did not mean the duration of incarceration would be limited to that period.[12]

The Saigonese then realized that the communists were good at playing with semantics and would give everyone the run around. They knew at that time that they would have to wait longer than expected, and that the prisoners would not be released until their captors set them free. All they could do was to wait and pray. Hai Thuan, a Viet Cong and one of Tang's coworkers was a southerner. He left Saigon in 1954 and went north to follow the communists. He had a son who was raised by his wife who had remained in South Vietnam. After coming back to Saigon in 1975, he realized his son had grown into a man. The latter became an ARVN officer and was sent to one of the camps for reeducation. He desperately wanted to save his son, but in spite of his long service to the revolution, he got the cold shoulder from the Politburo when he asked for his son's clemency. Feeling duped by the revolution, he killed himself and left a message asking for his wife's forgiveness.[13]

Tang was finally allowed to visit his brothers because of his importance in the government; he was then the minister of justice of the PRG.

"So we were chauffeured through the camp, trying hard to make out our loved ones among the clumps of dazed-looking prisoners." He caught a glimpse of his brothers who "were pale, thin, frightened, their eyes fixed in a glazed stare."[14]

He was not even allowed to talk to them. Thanks to his connection, one of his brothers was released four months later but the second one was still jailed in a northern camp nine years later at the time his memoir came out.

Gulags

The camps were similar in nature to the gulags established in Russia in the early twentieth century. Nothing had changed with the communists' ideology and technique. The CPV members had experimented with this method when they first took control of the northern part of Vietnam in the early fifties. Son Ha[15] reported that in 1954, after the communists' take over of North Vietnam, seven northern doctors who had served with the French legionary forces were sent to reeducation for two years. They were allowed to return home and practice for one year; afterwards they were sent back to reeducation camps for seven more years. Five out of the seven, who had forgotten everything about their profession by the time they were released, had to work as laborers on collective farms. The two remaining worked as orderlies in hospitals. They eventually became nurses and were allowed to practice medicine six years after their release.

After the fall of Saigon, the CPV members decided to use the same approach to deal with their southern adversaries. They called it *cai tao tu tuong* (thought reform or reeducation) with the yet unpublished goal of indoctrinating the South Vietnamese who had been exposed to "free or imperialist thoughts" with new communist thinking. But after reports about these camps were evaluated, it appeared the goals were simply incarceration, starvation, and torture. It had more to do with silencing political opponents than reeducating prisoners. Nguyen Cong Hoan, a communist representative who used his political connections, was able to see with his own eyes the "sullen, withdrawn prisoners doing hard physical labor" at camp T-50 in central Vietnam. He was not able to talk to them freely because he was escorted by the camp colonel.[16] He was also allowed to visit camp T-51, which was located in a remote area of central Vietnam. It took him five hours by motor scooter, then one extra hour by foot to reach the camp. There he found the prisoners "unusually quiet, emaciated, and obviously frightened." Even Nguyen Cong Hoan, the Viet Cong representative, had a "bad feeling about what was happening there."

Ginetta Sagan, a former anti–Vietnam activist after having interviewed "several hundred former prisoners, [and after reading] newspaper articles on the camps as well as various reports of Amnesty International" wrote in *Newsweek* magazine in 1982:

> The picture that emerges (from the reeducation camps) is one of severe hardship, where prisoners are kept on a starvation diet, overworked and harshly punished for minor infraction of camp rules. We know of cases where prisoners have been beaten to death, confined to dark cells or in ditches dug around the perimeters of the camps and executed for attempting to escape. A common form of punishment is confinement to the CONEX boxes — airfreight containers that were left behind by the U.S. in 1975. The boxes vary in size; some are made of wood and others of metal. In a CONEX box 4 feet high and 4 feet wide, for example, several prisoners would be confined with their feet shackled, and allowed only one bowl of rice and water a day. 'It reminded me of the pictures I saw of Nazi camp inmates after World War

II,' said a physician we interviewed who witnessed the release of four prisoners who had been confined to a CONEX box for one month. None of them survived.... Today there is no talk in Vietnam about human rights — only about the dictatorship of the proletariat and the need to suppress dissidents.

Prisoners were first screened at a major southern camp (Trang Lon and Long Khanh for the III Corps, Chi Lang for the IV Corps), which could contain 15,000 to 22,000 inmates each, then dispersed to remote areas for hard labor (Katum, Bu Gia Map, and northern camps). After serving their time (three to twenty years), they were brought back to a camp close to Saigon (Ham Tan) before their eventual release. The majority went through three to five camps during their reeducation period, while others were incarcerated in up to fifteen different areas. They were rotated from one camp to another at regular intervals,[17] every three, six, or nine months for security reasons. The moves were designed to separate different groups of inmates in order to thwart any rebellion or uprising or to move the more rebellious elements to high security camps. But at other times, the transfers appeared to have no clear reason at all. While the reasons might not be obvious to the prisoners or outsiders, decisions were usually based on evaluations of informers, group leaders, and camp commanders.

There were about forty such camps around Saigon alone to serve this large metropolitan area while scores of others were set up all over the countryside to handle the rest of the prisoners. And over the years, many more would be built to care for the growing number of internees. Overall based on some estimates, there were more than 1,000 camps scattered all over Vietnam. "There were more reeducation camps than schools. There were over 600 district reeducation camps, more than 100 provincial camps and more than 20 national camps."[18] Some sheltered a few hundred to a thousand prisoners, but others like the Trang Lon and Long Khanh camps housed more than 22,000 inmates each.[19] Each camp had three to five sub-camps with sections for criminals, officers of the old government, and anti-communists. The officers (political prisoners) were never sentenced and remained in the camps indefinitely.

There were two parallel systems of camps: one run by the military and the other by the police. The military usually controlled the camps located in the countryside, the camps deep in the forests, and the camps in remote areas of the highlands or in former South Vietnamese bases. The police, on the other hand, took care of jails in cities or counties and camps such as the Ham Tan camp, about 90 miles north of Saigon.

Three senior staff members (cadres or officers) ran the camps: the camp commander, the political commissar, and the logistics and supply director. Although bigger camps had a larger staff, the control rested on these three senior staff members who were supported by mid-level officers and soldiers or *bo doi*. Many camp commanders in turn had to report to the region commander and so on up to the ministry of defense. They ran their camps as they wished and accepted orders only from the Politburo and the minister of defense in Hanoi. They often ignored the local southern laws and rules.

The camp commander was in general a military officer while the political commissar, usually a party member and a northerner, had the role of enforcing the views of the party. In this divided leadership, whoever was the party member and, therefore, closely connected to the Hanoi regime, played a major role in the direction of the camp. Conflicts often arose when the commander was a southerner and the commissar a northerner.[20] Antagonism would at times break out: the commander would issue an order, which was counter-ordered by the commissar or vice-versa. The northerners seemed to have the upper hand in all the camps described, a condition, that the southern communists bitterly complained about.

Many camps were set up in remote and isolated areas in the central highlands or in territories previously controlled by the communists, such as close to the Cambodian, Laotian or Chinese borders. These areas were usually heavily wooded, surrounded by jungles or mountains, and infested by mosquitoes carrying malarial disease. The remote locations served as a deterrent to any prisoner who thought about escaping. Being hidden deep in the jungle and inaccessible to local traffic, the camps escaped the detection of the outside community, the press, and the local population. The communists could then carry out their punishment without outside interference or monitoring. They could also claim that these camps had never existed.

On the other hand because of their remoteness, these camps were not well protected from outside attacks by the Khmer Rouge[21] during their many incursions into South Vietnam. The prisoners and their wardens had to pull out of one camp in the middle of the night because of one such attack. The military commander was injured during the attack and transferred, not by a military ambulance but by a civilian bus, to a civilian hospital hundreds of miles away. He later had to undergo a leg amputation because it was the standard procedure in the communist health care system. Prisoners in the camp volunteered to fight against the Khmer Rouge, but their request was denied. A few days later, they were forced to carry ammunition boxes for the reinforcement troops, which came to retake the camp by force.[22] The whole scenario also highlighted the fact that no adequate medical facility was available in many camps or within a hundred-mile range of the camps. Thus any inmate who had the misfortune of falling sick usually died of lack of medical treatment.

Some camps were named after the town closest to them (Long Thanh, Thu Duc, Xuan Loc), while others did not have any name at all. One was simply known as camp 3721 (Bu Gia Map).[23] Others were set up in the middle of the jungles or mountains and carried an alphabet letter followed by a number. A number of labor camps in the Phu Yen-Cung Son districts in central Vietnam were labeled T-50, T-51, T-52, T-53, and T-54.[24] To make matters more confusing and misleading, many camps bore the same name. The Thu Duc camp (close to Saigon) had many sub-camps: some of them were located as far as Ham Tan close to Phan Thiet, some ninety miles away. The goal of this purported confusion, according to Tran Tri Vu, was to mislead people and to "give the appearance that there are less camps and less prisoners than they really are."[25]

In general, camps that were located in old military compounds were sturdier and in better shape and thus more livable than those built anew from scrap by the prisoners. The former were built with bricks or concrete following well-designed plans while the later were more primitive, often a wooden infrastructure covered with thatched walls and roofs and a dirt floor. Camps located in remote areas or in the middle of the malaria-infested jungles were the worst; they lacked everything from food, water, electrical power, medical supplies and access to medical care. Those built close to towns, rivers or ponds benefited from access to a variety of food and easily available source of water.

Some camps in old military compounds had a decent latrine system, which got plugged up frequently due to overuse from overcrowding and the use of jack-tree leaves instead of toilet paper.[26] The *bo doi*, who had lived in the jungles for so long, favored the use of tree leaves over paper for obvious economic reasons. And the inmates had to abide by their jailers' rules. Even in northern jails, prisoners were not given toilet paper. They shredded their clothes into small pieces (a few square inches) to clean themselves after going to the bathroom.[27]

The latrine system was primitive at best in other camps: either open-air holes[28] or one "bucket for a toilet for twenty to fifty cellmates."[29] Since inmates were not allowed to get out of their barracks at night, they usually used buckets for their nightly needs. New inmates had to sleep close to the bucket area, which was not only smelly but also crowded by the flow of people going back and forth to the bathroom. The combination of smell and noise kept many awake at night despite their fatigue. In many camps, the latrines were old, dirty, and in short supply. Since each section of 1000 men had only three rows of latrines, inmates had to get up at 5 A.M. and wait for the signal to use the latrines. Sanitation was terrible at the Suoi Mau camp: prisoners had to relieve themselves in ditches dug around the camp. These open-air holes attracted swarms of "blue flies that completely covered every tree and bush surrounding the latrines."[30] The blue flies were noisy, aggressive and usually larger than the regular ones. They spread infectious diseases like dysentery among camp inmates.

The large number of inmates necessitated the availability of an abundant supply of water mainly for health reasons. They could wash and clean themselves with ease in rivers or streams close to their camps.[31] Access to the rivers was sometimes limited for security reasons. In other camps, inmates were forced to dig wells twenty to forty feet below the ground to look for a new source of water. They were provided with only "a gallon of dust covered water for twenty cellmates."[32] All they could do was to clean themselves with wet rags and wait for the rain to come down to take their bath. Conditions became unbearable in these camps, especially when hot weather, lack of water, and overcrowding were present simultaneously. Heavily rationed water led to thirst, dehydration, and kidney failure especially for middle aged and elderly inmates. It also led to poor hygiene, food contamination, dysentery and rapid spread of scabies[33] and other skin lesions.

Mistreatment

All the camps followed the same routine with some local variations. In the beginning, prisoners were placed on strict isolation and contact with their relatives was forbidden. They were not allowed to see or write to them. This isolation period lasted from many months to a year in southern camps and up to three years in northern gulags. This process drove many inmates insane and created major emotional upheavals and familial conflicts.

In the first phase of the reeducation process, in addition to the nine-hour daily labor, they were indoctrinated for an additional three hours at night. They were taught seven or eight communist doctrines (chapter 11), followed by lengthy discussions after each session. They then had to criticize themselves and to admit in writing and in front of other inmates what they had done wrong according to the recently taught doctrines. They were, of course, all wrong for they had fought against the revolution. And during their whole incarceration period, the communists kept hammering down this concept until under the combination of hunger, tiredness, depression, and loss of strong moral values, they believed in earnest they were wrong in opposing the revolution. Under pressure, some even switched allegiance and in front of other inmates begged the party for forgiveness.

Work consisted of building new housing units for new inmates, clearing the forests, digging wells and canals, planting, harvesting, pulling ploughs, building bridges and roads, and doing anything they were ordered to do. It consisted of not only menial jobs, such as cleaning the latrines or the pigsty, but also dangerous ones like clearing mines (chapter 12). If there was not enough work to go around, they were ordered to move rocks from one place to another or cut down trees with worn out bayonets. A certain quota had to be reached; those who could not complete their work had to work extra on Sunday or had their meal rations cut in half. The work could be qualified as part of a normal boot camp had it not been associated with starvation (chapter 9), threats, beatings, executions (chapter 10), and thought reform (chapter 11).

It was not work that could be done leisurely in a joyful environment. The highly stressful atmosphere was induced by the *bo doi* who were always around to criticize, punish, berate and push them until exhaustion or death. Those who collapsed were thrown into jails and placed on half ration. The curtailment of food and water and the imprisonment often worsened the inmates' health and led to a certain death.

Inmates were told they were *nguy* (puppet) or the scum of the earth and were treated as such by teenaged *bo doi*. But in a society that boasted deep Confucian roots and that taught respect for the elders, such a behavior from the youngsters towards the older inmates was tantamount not only to disrespect, but also to a grave insult. It took away the last thing the inmates ever owned and cherished: their pride. It wounded them deeply; many became depressed and withdrawn while others attempted suicide. Many simply lost their humanity and will to survive. Many died of a combination of malnutrition, depression, and wounded pride.

Since they were considered by their wardens as traitors to the nation, they did not deserve to live; therefore, they were harassed, kicked right and left, beaten with gun butts, or killed at will. They were insulted at every turn. They had their food rations cut and were thrown into isolation areas at the slightest argument. In the end, there was not a single form of torture they had not witnessed or experienced. They were told over and over that had it not been for the high cost of bullets they each would have been shot a long time ago.

Many definitely felt their lives were worth close to nothing in this repressive environment. So they were on the defensive all the time, trying not to incur the wrath of the *bo doi*. They treated the latter with deference, calling them cadres, a title reserved for officers only. The delight of these teenaged *bo doi* caused an uproar among the cadres who were upset to hear the *bo doi* being elevated to the rank of cadres. In a regimented army, a grunt is a grunt and an officer is an officer. One cadre had even berated a *bo doi* for allowing inmates to call him a cadre. Once they were forbidden to call them cadres, inmates called these youngsters *Ong* (Mister), a title usually reserved in Vietnam for elderly people worthy of respect. And despite all the deference given to them, the *bo doi* continued to harass the inmates right and left.

The treatment of prisoners varied depending upon the location of the camps, proximity of towns or populated areas, and behavior of the staff members and the wardens. Although mistreatment was present in every camp, it was worse in some than others, especially in remote camps (Katum, or Bu Gia Map) where the *bo doi* felt they could freely harass the inmates with impunity. They terrorized them, subjected them to ruthless and endless rounds of punishment and torture, and sometimes threatened to execute them.[34] In these cases, inmates had no other recourse than to beg for forgiveness although they had not done anything wrong.

The cadres and *bo doi* used psychological warfare on the inmates, distorting the truth and sowing innuendos and suspicions that resulted in widespread confusion, resentment, distrust and fear among prisoners. Prisoners on one hand were told they were not detainees since they had not been arrested but had volunteered for reeducation. However, a slogan written on the blackboard of the wardens' meeting room read, "Vigilance! And more vigilance! We must absolutely not let any more prisoners escape from the camp."[35] Second, a cadre would tell a group of departing prisoners that they were moved to a better camp because they were "progressive." However, the same cadre would advise those remaining in the camp that the departing prisoners were bad, and therefore, had to be transferred to a higher security camp.[36] Inmates could not believe what they had heard and became suspicious and skeptical of whatever the officials were saying. Third, prisoners were often led to believe they would be released earlier if they worked harder[37] or were truthful in writing their biographies. In most instances, this did not turn out to be true because the power to release prisoners rested with higher authorities in Hanoi. They thus could work harder and harder without seeing any change in their status or treatment. Feeling cheated, many inmates took it easy and just did the minimum required of them. Fourth, in one camp in May 1977, rumors abounded about U.S. bombers attacking Cam Ranh Bay and Nha Trang prior to an imminent U.S. invasion.[38] All prisoners were rumored to be deported to the United Nations and forced to learn English right then.[39] When inmates asked their visiting families about the American attacks, they were advised no such attacks had taken place. Fifth, they were tricked into believing that opposition forces had revolted against the communist government and were encouraged to escape. When some did, they were ambushed by the *bo doi* and were killed outright.[40]

The wardens were cunning and cruel in their choices of trustees who supervised other inmates and prevented them from escaping. They always picked former high-ranking officers or officials to serve in these positions. If these people accepted the offer, they were viewed as working for the communists. They thus dishonored themselves in the eyes of the inmates. No one would ever talk or confide in them again. If they refused, they were sanctioned and remained in jail longer.[41]

The communists were also experts at playing one inmate against another and at recruiting informers (also known as antennas) to relay information, messages, and orders, and also to inform them of the mood, intentions and thinking of the prisoners. They recruited informers[42] from every group, big and small. Many antennas, on the other hand, with the help of the wardens acted so well that many remained unsuspected and masked for a long time. Some people were forced to become informers while others voluntarily gave out information to the wardens in exchange for a few perks: better food rations or the promise of an earlier release. In an environment where prisoners suffered from severe hunger, any bowl of gruel or swish could go a long way to induce an inmate to talk. Others were simply blackmailed into doing the job.

The danger was that all these reports were not always accurate; many were not only biased but also outright fabricated by the informers in an attempt to win favor from the wardens. No one knew how many prisoners had suffered unnecessarily from these false accusations: many had their sentences lengthened while others were sent to the northern camps for further questioning. The antennas not only betrayed their fellow prisoners, they also betrayed themselves: the communists used them over and over, then rotated them from one camp to another, and kept them interned longer.[43]

The first time inmates were allowed to write home was six or twelve months after incarceration or three years later in higher security and in northern camps. Even then, many letters were screened and never mailed out: many inmates saw piles of letters in storage rooms or garbage cans. When writing home, they were ordered to be concise and forbidden to give out the names and location of the camps. But cryptic notes had been innocently smuggled out: a request for sweaters indicated a northern location of the camp whereas the mention of mango, tangerine, or rambutan trees belied a southern camp. They were ordered to describe the camp situation in glowing terms: they were treated kindly, had plenty to eat, and were in good health.[44] Those who did not follow orders had their mail discarded. Usually the first few sets of mail were heavily screened and most of the letters were thrown into garbage cans. This process explained why many relatives remained completely in the dark about their relatives' whereabouts and health condition during all this time and why inmates waited in vain for a word from their relatives. This condition also led to tragic misunderstandings.

Wives who had not heard from their missing spouses for a long time thought they had died during the war. They then felt free to move on with their lives, sometimes remarrying or escaping from the country by boat.

It was only when overall economic conditions had worsened partly due to the U.S. led embargo after Hanoi invaded and occupied Cambodia that inmates were allowed to mail letters home more regularly and to receive packages from their families every six months. Since all packages were carefully screened at the camps, wardens realized they could benefit from this traffic by keeping any item (food or medicine) they liked. They then relaxed the rules and allowed inmates to receive larger packages more frequently.

VII

Southern Gulags

The majority of the camps were located in South Vietnam. Although they followed Hanoi's rules and regulations, they bore their own characteristics and particularities, which were dictated by the commanders and tainted by local flavors. The southern camps of Kien Giang, Trang Lon, Xuan Loc I and II, Hoc Mon, Buu Gia Map, Buu Loi, Da Ban and A-30, KaTum are reviewed in detail.

Kien Giang Camps

Former ARVN officers from the IV Corps were ordered to report to the Chi Lang camp near the city of Chau Doc where they were screened and scattered to camps near the Rach Gia and Ha Tien areas. These camps were located in the southernmost part of Vietnam (old IV Corps). Some were old military compounds converted into jails while others had to be built from the ground up by the prisoners. The newly built camps were primitive at best with a wooden structure and thatched roofs. There were just enough to protect the dwellers from the sun and rain. They were usually temporary in nature as inmates were moved rapidly to other inhabited areas to start the process all over again.

Biographies and Self-Criticism

During the screening process, inmates were categorized into various sub-groups: policemen, non-commissioned officers, commissioned officers, government contractors, public servants, politicians, and so on. Policemen and security agents were singled out, followed closely, or transferred to harsher camps.

Inmates were ordered to write their biographies in the morning. They had to do the same thing in the afternoon, and then again at night. Sometimes, they were awakened at 3 A.M. to write another version of their biography under candlelight.[1] They were forced to write their biographies over and over again. Each time, they were asked for more information about a certain period of their past. Concise reports were judged to be simplistic and were rejected outright. The work had to be rewritten many times until the wardens were satisfied with it. Inmates soon became confused, as they did not know what to include in the reports in order to satisfy their wardens. The latter, on the other hand, were not interested in the truth but what they believed to be the truth. They just wanted to intimidate the inmates and force them to confess their crimes. As long as inmates had reported killing a few *bo doi* in the past, stealing chicken and livestock here and there, working with the Americans and betraying the revolution, they were fine. If not, they were ordered to write and rewrite their report until they finally incriminated themselves.

In the end, each prisoner wrote twenty or thirty reports, if not more. As a result, many vaguely remembered what they had written in the first and subsequent versions of their reports. The *bo doi* checked and rechecked carefully the different versions and once they detected any discrepancy, they brought the inmates in for lengthy questioning until they were satisfied.

Some prisoners were wise enough to simplify their reports by putting only the essentials and sticking to one version. Many others described their career path in detail, including all the battles they were involved in and the number of enemy soldiers they killed. These "confessions" later served as acknowledgements of their wrongdoings. In their desire to be left alone, prisoners "had accused themselves of the most serious offenses they could think of."[2] They did not want such harmful remarks as "attempt to hide past offenses" or "unwillingness to show repentance" to be added to their records. These remarks, they knew, were equivalent to death sentences.

But instead of being rewarded for their truthfulness, the prisoners were severely punished and moved either to higher security or northern camps, which were considered to be stricter in discipline. In the end, by acknowledging their "crimes," they incriminated themselves further and, as a result, remained in the camps longer than other inmates. Many never saw freedom again because of the "blood debt" they owed to the revolution, languishing in the camps until they died.

Having acknowledged their crimes, they had to stand up in front of the other inmates, analyze their mistakes, criticize themselves, and ask the party for clemency. In a camp close to Hiep Tam town, every night at the self-criticism session, each group had to pick one person — preferably the laziest one — to be punished by confinement in the conex. In the end, everyone in the camp had to "taste that torture at least once,"(3) roasting during daytime and frozen at night in the conex.

The harassment was not only limited to inmates, but also extended to family members. The latter were either denied visits for trivial reasons or granted visits only after paying bribes or doling out extra favors. In these remote and isolated camps, the camp commander and his wardens ruled supreme and got away with anything. The beautiful wife of a former Green Beret captain was forced to have sex with the guard chief each time she wanted to see her husband. She was warned that if she refused, he would be "singled out for special treatment."[3] She finally consented under pressure but became pregnant after a few encounters. The captain, who later became aware of his wife's dealing, killed himself in shame and desperation by biting his tongue.

Gulag Labor

After the screening process came the labor part. The goal of the wardens was to put inmates to work (the harder the better), even non-productive work such as moving rocks or starting rice culture on arid soil. They were asked to transform virgin territories and forests into arable lands, although no one had ever checked whether the land was fertile enough for culture or not. If the result was unfavorable, they were simply moved and forced to perform the same work in another area. Inmates were used as readily available workhorses: two or three prisoners were assigned to pull a plough while another worked as a conductor. They had to perform the assigned job no matter how hard or menial it was and whether he was an intellectual or a plain soldier. Under that system, everyone was equal and had to do the same work.

Once the job was completed, they were moved to another forested area to start the same process again. It was not uncommon for many inmates to be shipped from one camp to another. They were divided into teams assigned to a specific job (i.e., building housing, working in the fields, digging wells, tending the gardens, clearing mines or serving in the kitchen). They had to endure the hot and humid weather, monsoon rains and mosquito bites, in order to cut down trees with dull knives and to level the ground with whatever tools they had available. They had to build decent housing for their wardens, build fences around the camp to prevent inmates from escaping, and dig wells to obtain drinking and cooking water. They then leveled nearby areas to plant vegetables and rice to supply their meager rations.

Everything had to be done by hand since only light duty tools were available. In many places, prisoners resorted to using worn out bayonets, instead of saws, to fell trees. When water was not available, they dug their own wells forty to sixty feet deep with the help of just a few shovels. The work took forever, but inmates had plenty of time on their hands. Inmates also dug irrigation canals by hand. The hard manual labor of the late seventies was reminiscent of that of the twenties or thirties when machinery was not available.

They had nothing to shield themselves from the hot tropical weather with temperatures fluctuating between 100 and 110 degrees Fahrenheit. They used available material to cover themselves: straw, paper, even their own shirts. Since water was not readily available, sunstrokes were fairly frequent. As a result of heavy manual work, workers developed large calluses on their hands and feet. Cuts were frequent and became infected easily because of lack of medications. Prisoners protected themselves by putting any herb or plant they could find in the forests on the cuts. The majority of the wounds, however, healed spontaneously, although a few became badly infected and led to sepsis and death.

Because of lack of fertilizers, prisoners were advised to use the slash and burn technique to get a quick good crop. They burned down the trees and bushes over a large area. The ashes temporarily provided a good milieu for culture. However, after two seasons, the monsoon rain rapidly washed away the topsoil, causing severe erosion and rendering the land unusable for agriculture. The communists then told visiting western delegations, who came to investigate human rights abuses, that the erosion was "caused by American defoliation."[4]

Latrines were open-air holes about one foot deep and prisoners would wait "to catch our excrement in a big ladle."[5] Animals' dung and human waste were thus collected for use as fertilizers. This practice, which was only used in North Vietnam in the pre–1975 years, was forced onto South Vietnam and became one of the most contested legacies of communism in the South. In other areas, a latrine was simply a platform built on the edge of a pond where catfish were raised. Prisoners would squat over a small circular hole carved out of the floor of the platform. Human wastes were thus delivered as food for the scavenging fish, which "fought wildly for their meal, leaping out of the water."[6] In this camp, grass was used in place of tissue for cleaning purposes. Prisoners were lucky if they were allowed to consume the same fish they had daily fed with their wastes, thus completing the natural life cycle.

Food and Medicine

Prisoners were given two bowls of rice soup each time at lunch and supper. No breakfast was provided in many camps: inmates simply went to work hungry each morning. Meat was available only once a year on the anniversary of the revolution, and even then only one pig or cow was allocated to every 300 to 500 prisoners. At another camp, the regimen consisted of "salt or dried fish with rice and hardly no vegetables." The severe hunger induced by a poor diet caused severe muscular wasting, weight loss and nutritional disorders, which led to eventual leg swelling and beriberi. In the end, inmates just felt weak most of the time and had no energy to do any work.[7] Hunger pains and associated nightmares kept them awake all night long. The next morning, they were so tired that they were unable to go to work. As a result, they were thrown into a conex for punishment and starved again. The vicious cycle never ended. Repeated starvations led to cachexia and slow death by exhaustion and fatigue.

In a camp near Ha Tien, the guards overworked the prisoners and allowed them to sleep only five hours each night in order to wear them down so that they did not pose any threat to them. Prisoners grew corn, lettuce, and cabbages but were not allowed to eat the vegetables as these products were destined for sale at local markets and the revenues went into the pockets of the cadres and *bo doi*.

Inmates thus had to steal everything from edible plants to crickets in order to supplement their meager rations.[8] They ate "crickets and lizards raw"[9] on the spot in order not to be caught by the guards. Those who were caught stealing and eating without permission were severely punished. Huynh was "kicked in the stomach" and thrown out of the hut into the pouring rain because he was suspected of eating without permission. All night long, the rain came down hard and pounded him like "a thousand needles pricking his skin."[10]

To supplement their daily food rations, prisoners turned to unusual sources of food; they became adept in catching anything that flew or moved (i.e., flies, worms, rats, snakes). Some camps rapidly became "rat-free camps of the socialist world." If they were lucky enough to work in the fields, they could hunt for wild berries, green leaves or forage for cassava or sweet potato, which they again consumed raw.

The poor quality and poor processing of food caused disabling diarrhea (dysentery) among inmates and sent them to camp clinics that lacked everything from physicians, intravenous fluids, and medications to laboratory and X-ray machines, where they ended up receiving only supportive care before succumbing to their diseases. In most camps, the only medications were aspirin and quinine. Every single medical problem was treated with these two medications. Death thus became a certainty when prisoners suffered from a mine injury. In another camp, the nurse would prescribe the "use of herbs or leaves" or would give anti-malaria pills for everything from a headache, diarrhea, cold, or flu.[11] In many camps, there was not even a first aid kit except for an occasional bottle of iodine.[12]

Trang Lon Camp

Trang Lon camp was located in Tay Ninh province (South Vietnamese III Corps), about one hundred miles west of Saigon and only a few miles from the Cambodian border. Its characteristic landmark, the Mountain of the Black Virgin (Nui Ba Den), was visible on the horizon. It was originally an American fire support base with its own airfield. After the 1973 Paris agreement, it was turned over to the 25th ARVN division and was known as the Trang Lon camp. After May 1975, it changed hands once more and became a prison fortress for unsuspecting South Vietnamese. On June 28, 1975, from various locations in Saigon, convoys of Molotova trucks slowly lumbered toward Trang Lon, carrying their first batches of ARVN officers/captains and other workers.

The once clean, crowded and amenity-laden camp appeared deserted, ghostly and run down in mid–June 1975. The wooden barracks with their torn and ragged roofs sat empty and silent. Abandoned trucks, empty shell cases, and military gear were scattered all over the camp. Prisoners were directed to the unkempt barracks that rapidly filled up with new occupants. Military convoys, one after another, brought in untold numbers of prisoners who rapidly took over the vacant barracks. The area soon became so crowded that at its height, it housed more than 22,000 junior officers.[13]

An area of 15 × 5 meters (45 × 15 feet) held 120.[14] Once confined to the camp, they were first strip-searched, then their money and valuable objects (such as jewelry, pens, watches, rings) were confiscated as "a token payment of unpaid debt to revolution."[15] A few inmates cynically remarked that CPV members "first strip us of our material possessions; next they will try to strip us of our pride and dignity; and eventually our very souls."

Even the wardens became overwhelmed in the beginning by the sheer number of prisoners and let them roam around for a while. They were then assigned to do latrine work, clean and fix the poorly maintained barracks and their roofs, clear or weed the surroundings of the camps, or carry water for cooking and cleaning. They were assigned the job of tearing up the runway of an old airfield near the camp with only sharp wooden sticks[16] or axes in the Hiep Tan camp.[17] When they could not do the work, they were criticized for their "bad spirit." They tried again to twist steel rods with the same wooden sticks but to no avail. Again they were criticized for their bad spirit. The *bo doi* then changed teams, mixing different groups together with no success. After laboring in a similar fashion for about a month, they were finally given a blowtorch to cut rods to use to beat on concrete. Time went by and not much got accomplished because of the lack of equipment.

Soon prisoners were subdivided into regiments, battalions, companies, platoons and squads. And the system became more organized. At the end of the first ten days, prisoners restlessly waited for their release from the camp as the communiqué had previously suggested. As time went on, they were advised they would be kept in "reeducation" camps for some time and had to work to "earn" their own release. Those who, according to the revolution, were "reeducated" would be released sooner. The majority of prisoners slowly realized that they had been duped by the communists and became angry or depressed. They, however, were resigned to the worst and soon no one was talking any more about release, but only about survival. For many, the Trang Lon camp turned out to be just a transit camp and a gateway to other camps scattered all over the country.

Inmates had to participate in political sessions during which they were constantly reminded that they were criminals for having worked against the fatherland and for having helped the ruling class. They were told they owed a lot of blood debt to good people who had fought against the Saigon government.[18] Inmates forced themselves to pay close attention to the boring discussions in order not to fall asleep in the middle of the lectures. At the end of the sessions, they were randomly quizzed about the topics discussed, and those who could not remember them lost their food ration.

Each prisoner in the beginning received 350 grams (about three quarters of a pound) of rice a day with some salt, which they had to cook on their own. The "made in China" stamped rice bags that had been transported south during the war via the Ho Chi Minh Trail for the Viet Cong's use now served as food for the new inmates. This was "red rice" used only to feed pigs and poultry in the South.[19] Having been stockpiled, probably for quite a long time in hideouts in damp forest areas, it had mildewed and was definitely rotten with "white tiny worms squirming around among the grains." For lack of a better product, the inmates forced themselves to eat the rice in spite of their revulsion. After being on this diet of rotten rice and salt for three weeks in a row, many developed bowel problems from constipation to dysentery.[20]

As the camp became reorganized, the personal cooking made way for a communal life. Rice was cooked by a group of prisoners on duty in the kitchen and brought to each barrack in huge containers. For supper and lunch, they were given a bowl of rice in water. "Swill is what Americans called it." They were so hungry that they fought for every bowl of swill: "every man watched carefully that he got as much as the others."[21] Fights broke out whenever a person felt cheated. In many camps, the *bo doi* walked away when fights occurred. They were happy to see inmates fighting against each other, thereby demeaning themselves. In others, they stepped in immediately to reestablish order and to send the involved inmates to solitary confinement. As the incarceration progressed, hunger became more acute and inmates looked for ways to obtain extra food. One prisoner noticed that pigs were fed white rice while inmates barely had enough to eat. He was so hungry that he stole and ate the rice reserved for pigs. He then asked for permission to take the "decayed cabbage leaves" the *bo doi* left for the animals to cook for supper later. From that time on, he managed to work close to the pigsty in order to get his share of rice.[22]

Biography Sessions

Then came the biography sessions. Everyone had to write down his own biography from childhood to the fall of Saigon. Family details (maternal parents, grandparents) were also included. Those who did not remember the details, forgot the circumstances, or did not give enough details were ordered to put in more details until the wardens were satisfied with the final product. Lieutenant Luong, a former recruiting officer, was ordered to write one biography after another, not because he had committed any major crime, but because he "had two wives both living under the same roof" under the old regime.[23] Things became worse when he claimed to have grandparents who had concubines. He was ordered to expand his account, which became as thick as a book.

The prisoners were surprised to hear one day that a few inmates, labeled as "progressive," were released only a few months after their incarceration. This knowledge pushed them to work harder in order to be regarded as "progressive." But they soon realized no matter how hard and how long they had worked, they were still in the camps many months later. It was clear to them that those who were released earlier were in fact communists "planted in the groups to encourage prisoners to report truthfully."[24]

Everyone had to write legibly as scribbling was not permitted because it "was a crime of the bourgeoisie."[25] Those who had bad handwriting had to work hard to improve the legibility of their writing. No one was found to be faultless in the eyes of the wardens. Anyone who had worked with the Thieu government or the Americans in the past had fought against the revolution and, therefore, was guilty for some reason or another. If they did not kill any communist, they were responsible for not having tried to stop the war. This explained why physicians or pharmacists were also sent to the camps for two and a half to three years. Many had previously treated wounded Viet Cong soldiers at a time when the country badly needed their expertise. One former paymaster had to declare that he had increased bonuses to his own soldiers as an incentive for them to kill more communist soldiers. Another physician had to plead "guilty to the crime" of having successfully operated on General Phu for an eye ailment in the past. He had cured the general, thus allowing him to continue his career of killing more Viet Cong. The physician had thus "missed the opportunity of making himself worthy of the Revolution." An artillery lieutenant pleaded guilty of firing 44,000 rounds of 105mm artillery shells at Viet Cong units in three days, killing and wounding 27,000 Viet Cong soldiers, notwithstanding the fact that it was logistically impossible for one battery to fire 44,000 rounds of shells in three days.[26]

Any self-implication was rapidly accepted, although it sometimes defied logic. Some prisoners, therefore, made the mistake of providing detailed information about their past, hoping to earn favors from the wardens for being upfront, straightforward, and repentant.[27] These "self-confessions" were later used by the wardens as proofs that the prisoners were "real criminals" and deserved long-term incarceration, although many of the confessions were fabricated under the pressure and threat of food withdrawal or isolation. Prisoners were forced to write one version after another of their biography, and all these versions were compared to one another. Any discrepancy between these versions required further documentation or explanations to the wardens.

Faced with unending starvation and misery, two prisoners in a camp broke down a few months after being incarcerated. The first one challenged the guards to shoot at him. The guards tackled him, but he continued to shout anticommunist slogans and continued to try to run away. They shot him. His body, ridden with bullets, fell heavily on concrete.[28] The second one, a pharmacist, appeared to be depressed after writing his confession. He collected all the gunpowder that was lying around the camp and made it into a pile. He sat on it and burned himself to death after saying goodbye to his friends.[29] The air was filled with a fishy smell of burned human fat.

After having completed their biographic and lecture sessions, the second stage of their reeducation process began. Many prisoners were simply shipped without explanation to remote camps where they were forced to do hard labor. Others were encouraged to move to a labor camp to repay their debt. The cadre told them they had to do hard labor in order to be granted release and those who went first would be the first to be released.³⁰ Many volunteered but later realized that they were not released earlier than anyone else. On another occasion, the cadre tricked the inmates into moving to Bu Gia Map, a malaria-infested area, by suggesting that houses with electricity and plumbing had been built for them and tractor plows and bulldozers were also available. But when they arrived at destination, they faced the most impenetrable and virgin jungle they had ever seen. There was no trace of lodging, electricity or heavy machinery. They had to sleep on the ground and suffer from cool weather and mosquito bites while they built their own camps. The box number of the camp was 3136.³¹

Xuan Loc I and II

These camps were located in the III Corps, in Long Khanh province close to Saigon. Prisoners were first sent to the Trang Lon camp for screening then scattered to other camps like Xuan Loc I and II. The latter were divided into fifteen sections of about 1,500 prisoners each. Due to overcrowding, each prisoner was allotted a 60 cm (two feet) sleeping space on a cold damp concrete floor. A 5 × 7 meter room held fifty prisoners.³² Regulations were strictly enforced and body and bag searches were conducted unexpectedly: anything sharp or of value was confiscated.

This large population led to strict water rationing: each inmate was only allowed three cups per day. The lack of water resulted in outbreaks of infectious diseases. Inmates just washed themselves with wet rags during the dry season and bathed only when it rained. The downpour caused thousands of adults to rush outside like madmen to savor the freshness of the rain.

Medical Problems

The worst medical problem faced by the prisoners was an outbreak of scabies that had been acquired during their incarceration at the Trang Lon camp. The overcrowding and the closeness of the sleeping areas along with poor sanitation contributed to a rapid spread of the disease. Since medications against this condition were not available in the infirmary, inmates used whatever medicines they had brought with them to fight it. One person caught snakes with his bare hands, then removed and swallowed their gallbladder uncooked as a protection against scabies;³³ he somehow never got scabies. Others were advised to rub their skin with guava and cassia leaves before bathing. This form of therapy did not help either and soon almost everyone in the camp caught the disease.

The scratches soon became sores, which grew bigger as they were scratched. Left untreated the sores became infected causing disabling pain, smelly drainage and low-grade fever.[34] Prisoners were unable or afraid to move around because of the pain. The simple rubbing of clothes against the inflamed areas caused excruciating pain that brought tears to many brave souls. They were finally given permission to write home to ask their relatives to send in medications. The medicine was sold on the black market in many southern cities. The medicine was left over from the pre–1975 years. With the influx of western medicines in the form of antibiotics and steroids, the sores dried up and crusted. The inflammation disappeared and inmates were able to put their clothes on and walk normally without pain.

Medical treatment in the camps was delivered by a nurse and was rudimentary at best. The infirmary had only Chinese-made anti-malarial medication.[35] There was nothing to combat diarrhea and dysentery. If a patient were complaining of toothache, he was ordered to go to the kitchen to get two spoonfuls of salt with which to rinse his mouth thoroughly. As for fever, the patient was given one clove of garlic that he had to "pound to a pulp, then [stuff] up his nose."[36] In the beginning, those who could afford it paid the *bo doi* nurse to buy for them medications, sugar or dry food from the outside. The vitamins and sugar tablets did wonders for their malnourished bodies. As the transactions became conspicuous, the nurse was caught and transferred to another unit.

Hoang Xuan Trung, a professor of sociology at the university of Can Tho, was injured during an explosion at Long Khanh reeducation center. Attempts to remove shrapnel from his leg were performed twice without anesthesia by a nurse right in the camp. The knife was dipped only in hot water for sterilization. Other prisoners had to hold the patient down while the nurse cut on him. Trung fainted during each procedure because of the pain. He could have been transferred to the Long Khanh hospital, which was located only one and a half miles away for care but the nurse chose not to. The wound became infected and the patient was scheduled for an above the knee amputation. He refused any further operation, developed sepsis and then committed suicide as a result of constant pain.[37]

One prisoner tried to take apart a detonator, but it blew up on him ripping open two of his fingers. Somehow the nurses who treated him let the wound get infected and he ended up having to have his right hand amputated. He was so fed up with life that he wanted to commit suicide.[38]

The Bo Doi

Inmates had plenty of time to observe their guards. They noted that the latter, usually teenaged northerners, slowly imitated the southern way of living. They started wearing wristwatches and carrying small radios, which they played at maximum volume. The inmates borrowed their radios so they could listen to the news from the BBC or VOA. The *bo doi* also picked up the habit of smoking and soon they fell in love with foreign brands of cigarettes. In the beginning, they squatted uncomfortably on the ground to take their meals as they used to do in the jungles. They later had inmates repair chairs, benches, desks and tables they used at work and make new furniture sets for their personal use.

A *bo doi* revealed that life was difficult in the north even during the postwar period. As rice production fell short of the demands, northerners had to mix forty percent potatoes and cassava roots to their rice[39] and many families ate rice only once a day. Between harvests, all they had to eat for months was cassava or sweet potatoes. He also mentioned that the main goal of the incarceration was to keep the ARVN soldiers in custody while the government proceeded to abolish the old regime.[40]

Four distinct features characterized the *bo doi* who guarded the camps. First, they tried openly to obtain money to purchase things they dreamed about such as wristwatches, radio sets, fountain pens, sunglasses, and cassette recorders. They bought and sold items to needy prisoners for a profit. Some even stole metal sheets from the camp roofs to sell at the market.[41] One *bo doi* pilfered two bags of rice and sold them to the villagers.[42] A quartermaster was searched and found to have 3,000 dongs and a gold watch as savings, while his salary was only six dongs a month.[43] A military truck driver, who was supposed to deliver five bags of kernels and two bags of rice to a camp, kept one bag of rice for him to "keep the black market going."[44] The study monitors joined in the rackets to squeeze money out of the inmates. Each inmate was allocated several dongs monthly by the state to buy food to supplement the rice. Some of the money was used to buy vegetables grown by the study monitors and even by the inmates. The money was then deducted on the grounds that "inmates don't need what they can grow"[45] and set aside as "government fund." At the Bu Loi camp, a *bo doi* shot deer in the nearby forests and sold the delicious venison at cutthroat rates to the inmates. The Bu Loi camp commander had a nice collection of bicycle parts such as pedals, spokes, chains, and so on ... enough to assemble several bikes. They were all bribes from inmates' relatives. Chinese relatives of a prisoner even gave him a house in Saigon.[46]

Second, the bo doi in general cared very little about politics and did not hide the fact that their side was plagued by internal conflict between northerners and southerners.[47] The battalion commander at Xuan Loc II was a southerner while the political and camp commander came from the North.[48] The two were often at odds with each other, but the political commander always had the final word being the eye and ear of the party in the camp. This rivalry within the communist military system left the southern *bo doi* and cadres upset at their northern counterparts. In another camp, one *bo doi* mentioned that the northern soldiers "told us what to do. They held all the positions higher than us."[49] The camp commander, a southerner, once complained, "the stupid northerners are still my boss. I can't do a damn thing."[50]

Third, they engaged in extravagant destruction mostly as a result of ignorance. They destroyed a whole block of newly built houses just to get the corrugated metal sheet needed for the roof of the meeting hall.[51] They took apart electrical transformers to get the many colored wires, which they used to weave shopping bags. Vehicles that were slightly damaged were torn apart to provide steel for the smithy, rubber for sandals, aluminum to make various articles for daily use. Expensive items intended for collective use were made into cheap small items for individuals.[52]

Fourth, the *bo doi* were like parrots. They regurgitated everything they were taught. They came from the same mold, and behaved according to the same model.[53] Some cadres talked about a North Vietnamese pilot "turning off the motor of his fighter plane to ambush an American bomber in the clouds" and they took all that to be gospel truth.[54] Brother Ten talked about MiG-21 fighters flying over the American B-52 bombers and shooting at them, forcing them to come down within the range of the SAM-3 missiles.[55] The inmates just laughed at these explanations. According to them, the cadres must have been brainwashed and stupefied by the party and the state. They led

> lifeless lives, having been transformed into Pavlovian dogs to serve a barbaric tyranny built on a barbaric doctrine. That a human body is reduced to mere physiological functions and deprived of thought and judgment is the saddest thing on earth.[56]

Hoc Mon Camp

Dr Tran Xuan Ninh, a former pediatric surgeon at Saigon's Children Hospital, witnessed the behavior of the detainees at the various camps he had been secluded. According to him, deprivation at the Long Khanh camp brought out the most primitive human instincts in the fight for survival: "proud men of rank and of good social standing were suddenly reduced to fighting like animals over petty things like paper, toothpaste, pencils, tobacco."[57]

VII. Southern Gulags

Under desperate conditions, he found that men turned against their previous values, their past, their families and friends. One young physician who came from an anticommunist family broke down under the pressures at Suoi Mau camp. Upon graduation from medical school, he was brave enough to volunteer to join the airborne corps and worked tirelessly to save the injured. In the camp, under pressure, he suddenly repented against all "offenses committed against the revolution." In his self-criticism essay, he even denounced his own parents as his enemies.

Another physician at the Hoc Mon camp became the wardens' devoted informant. Although he had been a well known leader of a Catholic political organization in the pre-1975 years, his turnaround behavior stunned everyone. He lost all the respect of his fellow inmates who shunned him. He later had to turn to Buddhism to cope with his loneliness.

A doctor in the same camp reported to the warden that an inmate, under a high fever delirium, had cursed the names of Uncle Ho and Prime Minister Pham Van Dong. The guards came and dragged the patient to a conex container across the road from where Dr Ninh was detained. They beat the delirious prisoner with iron chains from dusk to about 11 P.M. They later brought the corpse to the "medical station" for certification.[58]

On the other side of the coin, there were also stories of great heroism at the Hoc Mon camp. A captain recounted the story of "the Red Flag on St Peter's cathedral" on certain nights. He made sarcastic remarks about the communist regime and was finally moved to the Katum camp for disciplinary reasons. A former Tank Corps lieutenant read his self-criticism essay (after the first ten brainwashing sessions) in front of everyone, enumerating all the military medals he had earned and the number of Vietcong he had killed.

Prisoner Vo Van Tung of the T4 Hoc Mon camp wrote to Prime Minister Pham Van Dong asking for the release of all reeducation detainees on the grounds they had not done anything wrong. He said they should be treated as prisoners of war and should receive a fair trial. As a result of the letter, he was thrown into a conex, ordered to write a self-criticism, which he adamantly refused to do. On Christmas Eve of 1976, the prisoner's conex was sprayed with bullets. He bled excessively from a leg fracture. Not only was he not taken to the infirmary for care, but he also had to languish in the conex in pain from a gunshot wound and a broken leg. He only survived the incident thanks to the care of his fellow inmates who surreptitiously slipped antibiotics to him to thwart infection; his bone, however, never healed. When he was finally allowed to return to the camp he was not given any assistance by order of the *bo doi*. It took him a full day to drag himself out of the container, across the road and the courtyard to his barrack.[59]

A former ARVN paratrooper in the same camp bravely decided to ignore the commands and orders of the wardens. For punishment, he was subjected to all kinds of torture from which he emerged physically broken but still unrepentant. He was lucky and strong enough not to die from his injuries and was in the end released from the camp. He ended up resettling in the United States. A less strong-willed prisoner would have died long before in the camp.

Bu Gia Map and Buu Loi Camps

These two camps and their many sub-camps were located in the highlands (former II Corps) where the weather was usually cool or cold and misty. The area was isolated and appeared mysterious behind the veil of thick forests. The jungle was impenetrable due to dense vegetation that had grown rapidly during rainy season. The mountains were inhospitable due to the scarcity of food, ruggedness of the land, and the malaria infested forests. Only tribes of Montagnards lived in these areas as the South Vietnamese were turned off by the inhospitality of the region. Although the camps were very close to the Cambodian border, escape was not easy if not impossible through the rugged mountains and dense jungles. A few trips in these areas caused everyone to come down with a high fever.[60] Moreover, the border was patrolled by Vietnamese border guards with dogs.[61] Even if an escapee were able to foil the border guards and reach the Cambodian side, he would face instant death in the hands of the Khmer Rouge.

Their first task was to build a shed to store rice, which would be eaten by termites if left on the ground.[62] The only tools available to them were roughly forged machetes with iron handles. Equipped with these blunt tools they climbed the mountains, chose their trees, and began their work. It took them a long time to sever a trunk. Even after it was cut, the tree refused to fall, being held back by lianas that had wound around the foliage. Prisoners had to climb up the tree to chop the foliage off. They then pulled the tree down and took their work back to the meeting area.

Cold weather at night and hunger made life difficult and miserable in these isolated mountain areas. Many prisoners woke up in the middle of the night because of hunger pains. They then felt the morning chill that bit on their skins and bones and made them shiver. Unable to sleep, they then sat with their arms around their knees and a blanket wrapped around their shoulders until daylight. The lack of food wore them thin. Their bodies were in tatters. So were their minds. They were so tired after being awake all night long that they could barely go to work the next morning. They dragged along and had a hard time keeping up with the whole group. They then had to walk barefoot in the jungle on stony mountainous ground and through thorny bushes. They had not been supplied with any new shoes or clothes since they entered the camps. Bruises and cuts were common. Some could not put weight on their feet. The number of sick inmates increased rapidly. Many became depressed. While clearing the forest, one desperate inmate decided to build a pyre for himself. He then lit it and jumped in the middle of the blaze, burning himself to death.[63]

Mountain jungles were infested with leeches and mosquitoes. Clouds of mosquitoes swarmed around all warm-blooded animals and humans, darting into any open orifices: mouths, noses, and ears. Inmates had to use a makeshift net to cover their heads and faces to protect themselves from the insects. Work in the forests was dangerous for their health. Bamboo shoots gathering trips were also known as "blood donating trips." Mosquitoes were not the only dangerous creatures in the forests: leeches were everywhere. They crawled through all kinds of clothing or socks to reach the skin where they started sucking on the prisoners' blood. They even dropped on inmates' heads from tree branches. Many detainees became ill due to loss of blood that was further compounded by poor nutrition.

Prisoners were advised to build their own camps. Despite the fact that they were living in malaria-infested forests, they were not given any net or blanket to protect them from mosquitoes. Almost everyone slowly became infected with malarial disease. As a result, inmates either died from full-blown malaria or suffered from chronic recurrent malarial attacks.[64] "In constructing their camps, they dug their own graves."[65] Many thought the camp, strategically placed in a malaria-infested area, was overtly used for extermination of the prisoners. In one instance, a prisoner was tied to a pole and left outside for two weeks during which time he acquired malaria.[66] Other health problems plagued the prisoners, including diarrhea brought on by drinking the polluted water.

Despite all these hardships, only eighty-seven out of more than 1,000 inmates in one camp had been released after three years of incarceration and more than a dozen had escaped. Group torture was seen on one occasion: fifty prisoners were tied-up, forced to kneel down in the yard under a hot baking sun after being "beaten relentlessly" by the *bo doi*[67] for staging a hunger strike to protest the regime of hard labor and insufficient food. They were then sent to regimental headquarters for further treatment.

A new group of 300 prisoners arrived to the camp wearing odd looking clothing made from sandbags for military fortifications. They were found to be "officers with the rank of major in the former army." They looked old because of their odd clothes and the treatment they had received.[68] They were evidence of the harsh treatment reserved for "reactionaries."

In the middle of the night, forty inmates were called out, escorted to the brightly lit yard, and marched away in the darkness. They were never heard again. They had all been "former security agents, military policemen, and persons who had worked in the propaganda apparatus of the former regime."[69]

When wives were finally allowed to visit the prisoners, they were lodged in small huts outside the camps because of lack of hotels and the remoteness of the camps. They remained around the camp for a few days and had to do the usual washing and cooking. *Bo doi* were seen snooping and masturbating themselves while watching the women wash in the rivers. Guards at the Bu Gia Map camp used the occasion to come out at night and rape the women.[70] The women were afraid of reporting the assaults for fear of causing retribution on their husbands. One night, one of the women let the attacker come close to her and stabbed him in the face with a pair of scissors she had laid by her side for protection.[71] When Nguyen Ngan reported the assaults to the camp commander, the latter denied knowing of any such incident. One of the commander's officer later admitted one *bo doi* had been sent to the local hospital for an eye ailment. No more assaults were reported for a while. A few months later, Ngan realized attacks against women were happening again, but this time away from the camp while they were heading home. The visitors also reported they were robbed on a deserted stretch of Highway 14 leading to and from the camp.[72]

Da Ban and A-30 Camps

While military personnel in and around Nha Trang (II Corps) were immediately jailed, Lu Van Thanh as well as other teachers, civilian engineers and doctors were urged to attend a three-day indoctrination course on April 7, 1975 (Nha Trang fell three weeks before Saigon). They were allowed to teach the remainder of the school year. In the summer of 1975, they were forced to attend a month long indoctrination course followed by a three week refresher course in August during which they wrote their biographies and confessed of their crimes against the revolution. They were then blacklisted and dismissed from their jobs.[73]

As intellectuals, they were deemed harmful to the revolution. They were jailed on April 25, 1976, and transferred to the Da Ban camp. They were neither judged nor sentenced although their families were notified they would be incarcerated for the next three years. Located thirty miles northwest of Nha Trang city, the Da Ban camp was designed to house 1,000 inmates. It comprised three areas: A was reserved for camp supervisors, cadres, and soldiers,

VII. Southern Gulags

B contained several rows of thatched houses for inmates, and C served as work and storage areas.

They were divided into groups of fifty to sixty persons, led to a nearby forest and ordered to cut down the hundred-year-old trees with picks, hoes, axes, and bush hooks. No saws or heavy machinery were available. Thanh's group comprised of six doctors, two engineers, and forty-seven teachers. The guards constantly yelled and screamed at them each time they slowed down. Around lunchtime, they were ordered to bring the timber back to the camp where they had lunch: two bowls of rice and a bowl of vegetables. They walked back to the forest at 1:00 P.M. and returned at 5:30 or 6 P.M. They made the trip twice a day and Thanh estimated they had covered 4,000 miles during the first five months. Each night was reserved for a self-criticism session during which they evaluated themselves based on their work, study of communist rules, progress toward being responsible socialist person, and adherence to camp rules and regulations. They worked eight hours a day, seven days a week.

One of their duties consisted of gathering animal and human wastes and mixing them with soft soil using their own hands to make fertilizers to grow vegetables. Another job was to transport big trunks of precious wood they had harvested in the forest back to the camp. Each trunk was about three feet in diameter and fifteen feet long. After lifting the trunks across mountains, they rafted them singly along rivers and streams, which could be as narrow as three feet or as wide as sixty feet. They pushed each trunk before them, either riding on it or guiding it through each turn. The swift current and cold water in many of these rivers made the job not only difficult but also dangerous. At any time, they risked being knocked out or crushed by the big tree trunks. They also had to grow rice, pull the plough in place of buffaloes in a field eight miles away from the camp to thresh corn, grind paddy, and transport the sixty pound rice bags back to the camp.[74]

Under these hard working conditions, many elderly inmates died of malaria, diarrhea and fever. A 70-year old former hamlet chief also died in the camp. Young prisoners, unable to handle the pressure, tried to escape but were shot to death.[75] On August 10, 1977, many detained were led to believe they would be released, only to find out later they were transferred to the A 30 reeducation camp.

A-30 was among the larger camps in South Vietnam. Located 70 miles north of Nha Trang, it held at its peak more than 4,000 inmates, mostly non-commissioned officers to colonels. They were locked in their buildings at night where they had 18-inch-wide space for sleep. 90 to 100 detainees shared a 13 × 6-yard building. Those considered to be reactionary were housed separately in a disciplinary cell bearing the number 13. All detainees went to work at 5:30 A.M. and returned to the camp at 5:00 P.M. The total number of cadres and guards was 140. Their daily ration was less than one pound of rice daily with two sweet potatoes or cassava and a small bowl of vegetables. On such a poor regimen, many inmates fainted at work.[76]

The 1977 monsoon season hit the camp hard. Inmates were rushed to the fields to recover as many crops as possible: pick up the wet corn, lift the potatoes and cassava coots, and cut the rice. They were then locked in their buildings while torrential rains flooded the river then the camp. Despite their screams for help as the rising water reached their beds, they remained locked until Col. Dai, the province security chief, finally gave the order to move them to higher grounds. When the flood was over, the aftermath was terrible: the dispensary was filled with sick people suffering from colds, pneumonia, and fevers. The patient load so overwhelmed the nurse that inmate physicians had to be relieved from their physical labor and reassigned to the dispensary to participate in patients' care. The rest of the inmates had to work from dawn to dusk to clean up the damage, repair the buildings and replant the crop.

The camp was riddled with examples of physical abuses and corruption. Inmate-lieutenant Vinh was repeatedly kicked for walking slowly while carrying a bunch of cassava trunks. He was not only near sighted, but the field was also slippery and the winds stronger than usual that day. Inmate-captain Tien spent two months in a torture room, with his legs in a ferret and one hand tied to a shackle hooked in the wall. Four times a day, he received boot kicks and was beaten with sticks all over his body. Four Catholic priests were confined to a special room in a restricted area. And an inmate-lieutenant commander was shot to death for criticizing the arbitrary policy of the camp and for trying to escape. A sick inmate was repeatedly kicked for being late to a roll call in the dispensary.[77]

Col. Dai was known for releasing young inmates from rich families who were charged with attempting to leave the country illegally after securing five to ten ounces of gold. Major Tran, the camp leader, granted weekend leaves to inmates in exchange for "donations": TV sets, radios, oil paintings, sofas, armchairs, and so on. Two teachers were released after offering one ounce of gold each.[78]

Katum Camp

This was one of the camps prisoners would only talk about with fear in their eyes. It was the Auschwitz equivalent of the Vietnamese gulags. It was located in the middle of the dense forests of Tay Ninh, 90 miles northwest of Saigon close to the Cambodian border (former III Corps). The area was formerly the command center of the Viet Cong in South Vietnam. This was where the recalcitrant, "hardheaded" prisoners and those who owed blood debt to the revolution were sent for punishment, not rehabilitation. Hardheaded only meant antirevolutionary. The prisoners were people who refused to believe in the communist theory.

Katum was a large camp housing about 10,000 prisoners. Barracks were more run down than those at Trang Lon camp. The many towers and barbed wires built by the inmates themselves gave it an appearance of a concentration camp. Guards patrolled the barbed wire and the moat. Any ripple seen on the surface of the water was the warning signal someone had attempted to escape. This was a good security system and escapes were rare. Wild animals (i.e., tigers, bears, wild boars, snakes) roamed in the surrounding forests making any escape not only impractical, but also dangerous. Numerous communist posts guarded the eastern side and controlled the rare access roads to the camps. To the west was Cambodia. A westward escape was possible, although no one knew what would happen to the escapee in Cambodia since the Khmer Rouge were not friendly to the Vietnamese at that time.

The system at Katum was well regimented in the beginning. Prisoners had to wear POW uniforms made of gray material with wide red stripes up and down. "Dangerous" prisoners had their heads shaved for easy spotting. Soon the uniforms wore out and prisoners used sandbags or rice bags to sew makeshift shirts or pants. The latter, of course, fell apart in the rain and during hard work. Many people ended up with skimpy rags that, in the end, even exposed their private parts. Each barrack had its prisoner-leaders. The cadre called them "progressives," but the inmates knew them as "point-men" because they pointed to others to denounce them.

The wooden floor of the barracks had been removed to upgrade the wardens' houses. Prisoners, therefore, slept on concrete or on the ground. The cadre woke them up at 5 A.M., six days a week for songs and exercises. There was no breakfast at Katum because the point-men had volunteered to "donate the food to socialism" a long time ago, while prisoners were starving to death.[79]

Every morning one prisoner had to guide a short lecture about how good labor was for everyone. They then went to work, which consisted of clearing the ground and cutting down trees around the camp to make escapes difficult. Prisoners had to design their own tools. Some used old bayonets, which were very dull, to "beat trees to death." Others had to move rocks. The worst job was clearing minefields. Prisoners got killed everyday because they did not handle mines the right way. There were no bandages for wounds, which were simply packed with dust. They tried to stop the bleeding by pressing the wound. But when their hands got tired and they let up on the pressure, blood squirted again and the injured prisoner died.

They broke at noon for a half an hour lunch. A pot of swill was brought in for forty-five prisoners who had to divide the food among them. They fought aggressively for each bowl of soup because everyone was hungry. Those who could not fight or were not fast enough were bound to starve and to die of malnutrition. They got their second swill at 5 P.M. and there never was any meat. From 6 P.M. until midnight, they were criticized for their work. The point-men were given some quotas to fulfill: "so many trees or rocks in a week." If the quota was not met, the group had to do extra work on Sunday, which was their day off.

If a full ration was "two small bowls of swill" a day, those who were punished had to survive on half a ration for the next four days. No prisoner could survive on these meager rations for a long time without becoming exhausted and weak. As their work suffered as a result of their exhaustion, they were again punished and assigned to the "shit detail." The job was to remove fifty-five gallon drums of prisoners' wastes and to spread them every day on the ground where the cadres grew their vegetables.[80] The job was not only nasty, but also dangerous because of the potential for infection. The smell and sight made them sick and ruined their appetite; the abrasions and cuts on their hands became infected. Although the communists could claim they did not kill the inmates with their own hands, they had intentionally let nature, starvation, and excessive hard work decimate scores of them. This was an example of socialist Darwinism: the fittest survived while the weaker ones perished like flies.

Do The Long's Story

Any war or any concentration camp has its own hero and its own tale. This was also true of the Katum concentration camp. Upon graduation from medical school, Do The Long[81] served his country by enrolling in the Marines. Following the fall of Saigon, instead of surrendering to the communists, he took to the jungle in an attempt to start a revolutionary army. He was later arrested and sent to the Katum camp in April 1976 for crimes against the state.

He walked barefoot in the camp and wore pants sewn with a piece of cloth taken from a rice bag. His bare chest exposed dark brown skin and a thin, malnourished body. He felt utterly sad about his misfortune. He went from being a medical doctor in a formerly strong military army to a ragged, dispirited, and lonely prisoner in the middle of the jungle. His treatment at the camp further dampened his feelings of misery. He could not confide to anyone in the camp because any word or comment could be reported to the *bo doi* and could result in disastrous consequences.

In order to survive in the camp, he had to supplement his meals with toads, tree-worms, and rats. As a former Marine, he was knowledgeable about the surrounding topography as well as the edible plants and fruits. He knew how to find fresh water from streams. He was always thinking about escaping, but chances were minimal in the Katum camp, which was guarded by numerous communist posts on the eastern side and bordered by Cambodia on the west side.

Long and his friend Binh tried to save one or two sweet potatoes once or twice a week. They dried them off in preparation for a future escape. They got extra food by tutoring the *bo doi*. The latter were in general uneducated and none of them was able to add numbers having more than two decimals. One of the *bo doi* thought that once he had learned the basics, he could enroll into a college course by correspondence. Having fought for the revolution for some time, he knew the party would be supportive of his efforts and grant him a position of principal in a small school. Long became a palm reader and a love letter writer for the uneducated *bo doi*.

They got acquainted with a female *bo doi* who took them under her wing. She asked them everything about Saigon and the pre–1975 South Vietnamese women. She had heard that Saigon was big, cosmopolitan and had a lot of cars. She had also heard that women wore beautiful *ao dai* and lipsticks and had their nails painted. She heard that people ate a lot of meat. Her biggest dream, she confided to them, was to visit Saigon at least once in her lifetime. She soon commented that she was ready to leave Uncle and the party to follow a puppet soldier. From then on, the two puppet soldiers had plenty to eat, courtesy of Le thi Gai. On one occasion, she brought them some leftover rice, which was certainly a welcome relief from the sweet potatoes and the swill they had to consume everyday; on another occasion, she even gave them fruits and cookies.

They wondered how such a friendly and sweet woman could be a *bo doi*. They learned she had enrolled in the army at the end of her sophomore year in high school with the promise that once the war was over, she would be sent to the Soviet Union for further training. A lot of women were sold on these promises. She told them there were many deserters in the North. The latter just separated from their group while moving on the trail and went into hiding in the forests. They would occasionally come out to steal food from the trail station. They sometimes mingled with the Montagnards. Many died of starvation, illnesses or from attacks by wild animals. The only way women could avoid the draft was if they were pregnant. With her right hand, Le Thi Gai made a big curve in front of her belly. Once pregnant, they were not eligible for service. She was asked how girls could get pregnant since all the males had been sent to the South. She explained that in the north party members and old men were a national resource.

One day, Long and his friend overheard a heated argument between *Gai* and a *bo doi* to which *Gai* was apparently engaged. The *bo doi* was upset that *Gai* had spent a lot of time with the two prisoners and had barely talked to him. He reminded her the party had sanctioned their relationship and would report her to the commander if she kept seeing the prisoners. She challenged him to go ahead. On hearing that exchange, the inmates knew they were in trouble. They thought there was nothing worse than the wrath of a jealous mate.

As predicted, they were both sent to the forest to do hard labor the following day. There was no more teaching or writing love letters, and no more extra food. As life became harder, they thought more and more about escaping. They joined three other ARVN captains and carefully drew plans for an escape. Then suddenly, *Tam*, one of the captains, received a one-week leave to see his family. His dad as well as the rest of the family had moved to an NEZ. While working in the fields, he stepped on a mine and blew himself up. What was unusual about this leave was that rarely did the communists ever grant a leave. Many prisoners had similar family problems and no one up to that point had been granted a leave of absence. Two weeks after his return to the camps, *Tam* was called in to report to the office for questioning for three days in a row. What happened in the office remained secret between *Tam* and the *bo doi*. At noon on the fourth day, he was unexpectedly released from the camp.

At 4 A.M. the following morning, the prisoners were awoken by a group of *bo doi* who stormed into the room with their AK-47s fully cocked and told them they were looking for a stolen K-54 gun and a magnetic compass. The two captains, Long and his friend, were thrown into five by two by two foot tiger cages. The cage was so small that they could not even sit down or stand up; all they could do was to lie down with both feet raised. They were taken out of the cages daily to be interrogated and beaten, then shoved back into their small dwellings. Sensing death close, they started praying. Never in their lives had they prayed so intensively.

Gai was the only distraction and hope during this period of hell. As the nurse of the camp, her duty was to care for the prisoners' wounds. When she saw the gaping wounds, she just cried and mumbled, "They had to be animals to beat you men like this."

Then one day, on the eve of the lunar year 1978, they were brought before the tribunal for judgment, with the camp commander as the judge, the assistant commander as the prosecutor, and one *bo doi* as juror. There

VII. Southern Gulags

was no lawyer representing the accused. With this type of justice, they were ready to accept a death sentence. But the camp commander stood up, read the charges and said:

> On the occasion of this solemn holiday, you are free to return to your camp. But remember, you must not say anything about the interrogations and the beating. Everyone knows here that we want to use you as examples so everyone in the camp is clear about the treatment reserved to those who steal military gear. If you say anything about what has happened, you will go back to the cage.

They were all surprised by the sudden change in attitude of the staff and later found out that *Gai* had used her political clout to protect them. She told the tribunal that the prisoners had made major progress in their thinking, and that none of them had taken the gun or the compass. They thanked Gai. They did not know how to express their deep gratitude.

Two months after the *Tet* festival, around April 1978, the two remaining captains in the group of five were moved to other camps; the transfer effectively killed any attempted escape. Long and Binh were also separated and the only contact between them was through *Gai* who risked her career, life, and safety to inform them about what was going on in the camp. What motivated her to play this role was unknown to them. They could only think that there were "good and bad people" everywhere and *Gai* turned out to be a "good person" from the other side.

A few mornings later, there was a call for an emergency gathering of all the camp prisoners. This could only be for two purposes: either to account for the number of prisoners or to announce sanctions against some prisoners. They were advised that someone apparently had escaped overnight. In the end, everyone was accounted for, except Long. He was nowhere to be found. Peace and quietness soon settled on the camp, and everyone seemed to have forgotten about the escape incident. Three weeks later, a *bo doi* told Binh he had seen the remains of Long and asked him to identify them.

With the permission of the camp commander, *Gai*, the *bo doi* who had discovered the body, and Binh went into the forest to look for the truth. It took them half a day to make their way through the dense forest to the isolated area. The body was decomposed to the point that it was difficult to identify it. The body also had suffered from the ravage of wild animals as well as ants. *Gai* kneeled down to take a close look at the body and started crying, "That's him. That's Long," *Gai* wept inconsolably. "This backpack is mine. I have given it to him. This handkerchief, too…. And, this ring, I have brought it to him."

Twenty-one years had elapsed since that time. These were twenty-one long years during which Binh had kept the tale of Dr. Do The Long, his hero, to himself. He just wished he could meet again the two most important people in his life. The first one was Dr. Long. But wherever he was, he must have been happier than being in a camp. The other person was *Gai*, this *bo doi* who used to sing glorious communist songs when they first met her proved to be one of the most angelic persons on earth. She had brought them food, compassion, and companionship during these difficult years in the camp. Without her, their stay in the Katum camp would have been hell on earth.

VIII

Northern Gulags

Camps in North Vietnam were in the beginning reserved for high ranking officials: lieutenant colonels and above. The latter were thought to be dangerous core, which had to be debriefed and watched closely by the Hanoi government. Later even lower ranking officers, from lieutenants and above, were also shipped to northern camps if they were suspected or simply perceived to be antirevolutionary. Working with the Americans or just being a former South Vietnamese policeman also entitled a person to a trip to a northern camp. Many generals and high level officials in the Southern government were shackled and flown to Hanoi first under heavy security. The rest, colonels and below, however, were loaded on board aging freighters and shipped north.

Camps were first located in a few northernmost provinces of Vietnam, near the Chinese and Laotian borders, but then sprang up all over North Vietnam. There were camps in the provinces of Hoang Lien Son, Ha Nam Ninh, Bac Thai, Vinh Phu, Tuyen Quang, Thanh Hoa, Nghe An, Quang Ninh, and others. There were 82 camps scattered in the province of Hoang Lien Son alone and roughly 300 colonels were interned in camp 2, close to the village of Yen Bay.

Son La, Lao Kai, Ha Tay, Nam Ha, Yen Bai, Nghe An, and Vinh Phu are reviewed in detail in this chapter through personal accounts of those who were interned there.

Son La Camp

Captain Vuong Thien spent one year at Long Giao camp in the Long Khanh province (south) before his transfer to the Son La then Yen Bai camps (north) and finally to Nghe Tinh (central Vietnam).[1]

Long Giao, which was an American camp before becoming the headquarters of the 18th ARVN division in 1973, became an internment camp for South Vietnamese military personnel after 1975. Since water was severely restricted due to the presence of a large inmate population, prisoners had to collect rainwater coming down the gutter for washing and teeth brushing during the rainy season. During the dry months, they had to dig new wells to search for new sources of water. Even at 60 feet below ground, they were only able to find a little muddy water, which had to be set aside so the mud would settle at the bottom of the container.[2] That water was then used for brushing and washing.

The rice distributed for consumption was moldy after having been stored in the jungle for many years. It was poorly processed and contained grains of sand. The ration contained the usual swill, vegetables and a few morsels of dry fish. Prisoners became weak after a few months of this regimen but still had to go through the same reeducation process as in other southern camps.

One year later, Thien along with 1,000 other inmates were crammed into the cargo haul of a boat heading north. The trip took three days and they subsisted on military Chinese dry rations, which consisted of green beans, sugar, vitamins and wheat flour in a compressed form. Drinking water was distributed twice a day. Once a day, the *bo doi* pointed a water pipe toward the cargo haul and sprayed down below as if they were washing cattle. Inmates had to relieve themselves in gasoline containers, which overflowed on the second day. When the ship swayed, the wastes splashed on everyone's trousers and shirts.[3] They had to protest loudly before they were allowed to dump the wastes overboard. They finally arrived in Hai Phong, then transferred to a train that took them to Son La close to the Chinese border.

The jails were built by the French years ago and were either covered with straw or tile roofs. They met many South Vietnamese soldiers who were caught back in 1971 in South Vietnam during Lam Son 719 operation. The latter were marched to North Vietnam on the Ho Chi Minh Trail and finally interned there.[4]

Thien was then transferred to a newly built straw camp one mile away from the main camp along with 250 other prisoners. The weather in Son La was always foggy, damp, and cloudy. The sun appeared at noon only to disappear again around 3 P.M. behind the tall mountains. Every day they were divided into groups of five and led by a guard to the mountains to cut bamboo trees to make fences and to build new housing units for the cadres. They had to climb high in the mountains to get the right material as the trees close to the camp had been previously cut. Sometimes they had to go to two or three different mountains to find the right material and then had to haul it back to the camp. If they did not have to gather bamboo trees, they had to work in the fields, pulling on the plough while another inmate directed it. They had to cut down trees to make place for new fields where rice, potatoes, corn, peanut, and yams would be planted.

The temperature in Son La was about 20–30 degrees Fahrenheit in winter compared to a balmy 60 degrees Fahrenheit in the south. Since southerners were not used to the cold weather, they had to lie on hay placed on the ground and burn wood to protect themselves from the cold. Even in this setting, they felt the bite of the cold weather. Meals consisted of corn, sweet potatoes, and self-grown vegetables. Prisoners were so hungry that they ate raw vegetables or sweet potatoes they stole from the fields, or anything that moved including crickets.[5] The lack of adequate nutrition caused inmates to become weaker with time and many died of malnutrition. Others were shot for arguing against being overworked and a few were jailed in dark rooms for insulting the cadres.

Lao Kai Camp

At the end of the war, Dr. Hiep, a flight surgeon captain in the ARVN, tried to escape by boat with his family.[6] After a two-week journey in the South China Sea, they arrived in Singapore but were denied asylum and chased away. They ended up returning to Go Cong, South Vietnam, where they were taken prisoner. After spending one year at the Chi Hoa jail in Saigon, Dr. Hiep was transferred by boat to Lao Kai, North Vietnam, close to the Laotian border.

At the camp, he met a group of Special Forces commandos who were captured back in 1962, some fourteen years earlier, when they were parachuted into North Vietnam to do spy work. They had been treated as missing in action and considered dead by the southern government and their families during this whole period. Being experienced with camp regimen, they advised the newly arrived prisoners not to try to escape because the camps were heavily guarded and surrounded by tall mountains and forests. And secondly, they were told once the villagers spotted a stranger, they would stop whatever they were doing to apprehend him in order to get a reward from the state.[7]

Prisoners had to do the usual chores, such as cutting down the trees, leveling the ground, or working either in the fields or in brick factories. There were, however, two unusual jobs in Lao Kai: one was picking up tea leaves and the other was building bamboo houses. Tea trees were planted on the steep hillsides of surrounding mountains where huge forest trees were cleared to provide maximum sunshine on the tea trees. The uneven and steep terrain made harvest of tea leaves difficult. To complicate matters, hornets used to build nests at the base of the tree. Any attempt to forcefully remove the tealeaves would disturb the nests and cause an armada of bees to fly out and bite the unsuspecting and careless prisoners.

The other job was to prepare lattices of bamboo to make the walls of houses. These bamboo trees had long intervals between the nodes and were indigenous to the northern mountainous regions. Bamboo trunks were cut one meter long each, and the nodes were crushed but not broken. The trunks were flayed open longitudinally, flattened, and used to cover the roof and sidewalls of the huts. Termites loved bamboo trees and destroyed the material in no time, necessitating constant repairs.[8]

Each camp had a maximum of ten units: K1-10. Hiep was in K1, while the commandos were in K4. Each unit was composed of twenty groups of 100 prisoners each. The second Lao Kai camp, Phuong Quang, was located close to the Chinese border. It housed the famous dissident poet Nguyen Chi Thien, author of "Flowers of Hell":

>Work till you drop or ropes will tie you up,
>Though sick, don't moan
>Or rifle butts will poke your back.
>You will resist? Beware
>Dark cells and irons crushing feet.
>Hunger and thirst we know as plain routine.
>We'll take a chance and even eat wild roots.
>…At night we all lie dreaming of some meat-
>Many by day will grab potato peels.
>Who can suspect that deep within the wilds
>The Party's hiding tens of thousands of men
>And killing them with schemes of every kind,
>All cruel, vicious, dastardly tricks?
>…Some men with piteous bodies and bad lungs
>That spit out TB blood still go to work.
>…O Marx, you old son of a bitch,
>Is this the paradise you promised once?
>Even sick, dying men can't be excused-
>Let 'em stand in the rain and get soaked through….
>   Nguyen Chi Thien[9]

After one year of hard labor, Dr. Hiep was allowed to work in the infirmary. The medicine cabinet was modest. One patient with active tuberculosis was treated only with a weekly calcium infusion instead of the usual triple antibiotic treatment. Two other patients died of TB.

During the 1978 Vietnamese-Chinese war, prisoners were moved to K3 of Tan Lap camp in the province of Phu Tho. They took a motorized wooden boat to navigate on the Lo then the Hong (Red) River. They were transported on communist Zin trucks and thrown into rooms full of lice where they suffered for a month. Dr. Hiep was then moved to the infirmary located at K5, the main unit of Tan Lap camp. There were a few unfortunate deaths, among them that of a South Vietnamese Supreme Court judge who died of sepsis from a leech bite sustained during his work in the fields.

The overall health of the prisoners was deplorable.[10] Patients transferred from other sections suffered from severe malnutrition. If the condition was not associated with mental depression and if the patient was immediately fed with a well balanced diet, he could rapidly recover. However, the inmate who had malnutrition associated with depression usually refused food; this self-starvation process further aggravated his condition and led to a certain death. A commando was brought in on a stretcher in a depressed and irritable mood. His eyes were closed and he also refused to eat, drink, or be treated by the communists; he rapidly went downhill and soon expired. His prognosis was poor even if good treatment and medicines were available. And not much was available at the K5 infirmary.

Although the majority of inmates died of malnutrition and lack of medications, Dr. Hiep had recognized a few patterns, which could be linked to their lifestyle. Old policemen and officials, who were usually sedentary, succumbed mostly from illnesses such as heart disease, stroke, cancer, or malnutrition. Old soldiers, on the other hand, died from work injuries: falling from a mountain, being crushed by a tree trunk, or being swept away by flooding rivers. Young and fairly healthy commandos, on the other hand, usually sustained violent deaths, which although rare were due to ingestion of tree roots, which they thought was ginseng. These roots caused severe parasympatholytic effects resulting in mouth dryness, accelerated pulses, fever and madness, which resulted in instant death.[11]

Mental illnesses, which could be lumped together as a postwar syndrome, were frequently seen in this group of patients. Incarceration, long-term separation from their families, loss of pride and self worth, and harassment by jailers were the main contributing factors. Inmates became depressed and usually remained in their rooms, although a few who became psychotic started running around the infirmary courtyard insisting on meeting their family members. This is an under-reported and, therefore, under-treated medical condition that is frequently seen in Vietnamese veterans from both North and South.

Although precipitating factors of the postwar syndrome might be different for the soldiers (incarceration, loss of self-worth for the southerners and pure neglect or loss of moral values for the northerners), the cause of this mental illness appears to be similar for both groups: the letdown from a long and brutal conflict. Bao Ninh, a North Vietnamese soldier, wrote about a brutal war "that warps soul and personality." The cessation of the conflict, instead of ushering an era of joy, happiness and reconciliation, brought with it new hardships. A "new war" started to impose socialism in the South. There were economic woes from war ravages, new hostilities with Cambodia and China, expansionist colonialism, and so on. New wars meant more sacrifices after a quarter century of war. New wars also meant no time for healing the minds as well as the wounds. "There is no new life, no new era, no hope for a beautiful future."[12] Ninh then became bitter because like other veterans, he felt neglected. There "had been no trumpets for the victorious soldiers, no drums, no music."[13] As he realized he had been used during all this time and made a huge sacrifice for nothing, he became depressed, drowned himself in alcohol and turned violent.[14]

Hysteria could also manifest itself in form of paraplegia. Dr. Hiep noticed many patients were suddenly unable to walk although they had no evidence of muscular dystrophy or neurologic deficit. Others became blind or deaf, or both without any reason. This condition could last one whole year, then as suddenly as it came, it disappeared without a trace. Most of the patients recovered fully without incident. A similar condition had also been noted among the Cambodian refugees who came to the U.S. after the war. About 150 middle aged women who had been victims of the Khmer Rouge suddenly lost their vision while they were in the United States although all their eye tests came back normal.[15] It appeared as though their brain was so "shell-shocked" or traumatized by the horrors that it did not want to see anything more.

Dr. Hiep was freed in November 1979 after four years of incarceration, three of them in the north. He emigrated from Vietnam and arrived in Canada in 1981. His case exemplified the arbitrariness of the treatment in communist Vietnam: as a physician, he never was in a sensitive position to harm the DRV and had probably not killed any northern soldier, but still was sent north for a three-year reeducation in addition to one year of confinement in the south.

Ha Tay Camp

Col. Tran Van Phuc was first jailed in the South for a total of 14 months. At the Long Thanh camp, a former orphan village, Phuc and other prisoners had to study the basic socialist lessons and revolutionary songs, clear the compound of weeds, and write their biographies. "The communal toilet was a hole in the ground with boards arranged for seats."[16] He was then sent to the Thu Duc reeducation camp before his transfer to the Ha Tay camp in the North.

Col. Phuc was interned in the same camps as Tran Van Tuyen, a renowned lawyer, a former South Vietnamese senator, a deputy prime minister, and a vocal critic of the Thieu regime. As a South Vietnamese senator, Tuyen enjoyed political immunity and used it to the max. He was one of the "third force" politicians in Saigon who advocated dialogue with the Viet Cong and neutralization of South Vietnam. We all know now that this plan would not work because right after the fall of Saigon, Hanoi blatantly discarded all "third force" politicians as well as Viet Cong. After 1975, the same communists he had sought to include in the Saigon government sent him to the Thu Duc camp where they humiliated him, berated him, and called him a puppet. He tried to explain his position during various camp discussions but was simply ignored. They later sent him to the Ha Tay camp and continued to shun him. Soon it was noted that he behaved like a distraught person. He often paced the front yard of the camp alone with a sad and sullen face, emitting long sighs. He was found dead in his bed one morning and thus became the first casualty of the Ha Tay camp. Some said he died of a brain hemorrhage while others said he committed suicide. He was buried with a simple tombstone marked "PCM" (Phan Cach Mang: anti-revolutionary).[17] His family was only notified about his death three or four years later. This case exemplified the differences between the Thieu regime and the totalitarian communist regime: while the former was soft on Tuyen and granted him his full constitutional rights, the SRV had no problem hard handling him and even driving him to death.

During the daytime, prisoners had to work as cooks, gardeners, farmers, blacksmiths, carpenters, and so on. At night, they were locked in their barracks and forced to study propaganda newspapers. They were fed two meals for a total of 300 grams of rotten rice along with salt and boiled vegetables. Rice was sometimes replaced by cassava, potatoes, or *bo bo*. The meager ration was not enough to keep them healthy, as they needed at least twice that amount. The hunt for extra nutrition yielded edible weeds, berries, grasshoppers, frogs, earthworms, and crickets that had to be "quickly consumed raw" before the guards discovered them.[18] Due to lack of food and hard labor, inmates' health declined rapidly right in front of the guards' eyes. They soon were unable to perform their job because of their trembling hands and shaky and swollen legs. Many prisoners just withered away and rapidly died of malnutrition or lack of medicine. The only medication available in the camp was *xuyen tam lien,* which was prescribed for all illnesses, including flu, cough, fever, and headaches. The dark green, bitter, and ineffective pill was made from the heart (*tam*) of lotus seeds (*lien*).

It was only when inmates showed evidence of visible physical decline and mental deterioration that the communists allowed them to write home to request items like medicine and food. All packages were sent to a PO box number where they were inspected. Money, foreign magazines, and salt were confiscated. The rest was turned over to the inmates who were delighted to receive food and news from home for the first time in three years. Craving sugar, one inmate used toothpaste as a substitute. He took pleasure in sucking the whole tube and in the process hurt his stomach. Another ate a whole kilo of dried sausage by himself in one sitting and ended up sick.

After harvest time, inmates had to turn over the thick and heavy soil while others pulled the plough. They then weeded the paddies by pushing the weeds with their hands and feet deep into the mud through leech-filled water. They worked under freezing conditions, planting the winter-spring crop. They experienced pain and numbness while struggling in the icy mud. They felt a second episode of pain when the numbness later subsided. Despite working in difficult conditions, they also had to suffer the ire of the *bo doi* if they did not finish their work in time.

In the middle of the night, guards stormed the rooms and selected inmates who were dead tired, taking them away to undergo intensive sessions of severe interrogation. These inmates had worked in the past for intelligence services, security agencies and police forces in the southern government. These sessions lasted many days after which they returned to the camps "dazed, silent and uncommunicative."[19] The intensive and repetitive questionings, most likely under severe pressure and even torture, no doubt drove many of them insane. Prominent Saigon figures and high-ranking ARVN officers were also interrogated for months yielding a "voluminous archival records" for the Hanoi officials.[20] Since many of these confessions were obtained under torture, it is unlikely they were very accurate and truthful. Inmates would probably tell theirs captors and torturers whatever they wanted to hear. Once they were subjected to this intense and personal scrutiny, not too many of these high officials were known to have survived; they somehow died for one or another reason.

Between 1978 and 1983, many unexplained, sudden deaths occurred in the Ha Tay camp. "Col. Phan Duy Quan of the 9th Infantry Division died in his sleep. Col. Nguyen Van Hoc of military countersecurity died while eating dinner, as did Col. Nguyen Van Ton and Col. Ton That Dinh. Col. Phan Khac Tuan of the Bureau of Military Training died from eating spoiled food."[21]

Nam Ha Camp

Colonel Phuc was moved to this camp in 1982. Guards were in general compassionate as most of them were older and behaved with proper dignity. For the next five years, each day was the same as the preceding one. After twelve years of imprisonment and hard labor, Col. Phuc suffered from severe mood swings ranging from optimism to deep despair and depression, especially when a few inmates began to be released. His hopes for an imminent release were dashed when he heard the news that previously released prisoners were picked up again for more interrogation and investigation during which they suffered "brutalities," then returned to the camps.[22]

Fatalities continued to grow in the camp. "Professor X. died of a stomach ulcer and another inmate died of leukemia. General N. passed away from prostate cancer, Col. PH from tuberculosis, and Col. H. and general Q. from strokes."

Alerted by reports of mistreatment and torture in the camps, Amnesty International and other delegations were finally allowed to visit Vietnam on fact-finding missions. Nam Ha and Ha Tay became the showcase camps in the North for these foreign observers. Camps were always spruced up during these periods: toilet areas were cleaned and made sanitary, living quarters were put in perfect orderly condition. Sick patients were sent to other hospitals; half of the prisoners were sent away to give the impression that the quarters were not cramped and the rest were not allowed to speak to the delegation members.[23]

The largest delegation came to the camp in early February 1988, thirteen years after the fall of Saigon. By that time, the majority had been released and had returned home. But the fact that a large number of prisoners still remained incarcerated at that time underscored the vindictive nature of the Hanoi regime. The communists would never forgive or forget.

During the thirteen years Col. Phuc was imprisoned, his family also suffered "indignity, humiliation, fear and deprivation of their own being impoverished by the new regime." His wife, a former schoolteacher had to complete a five day reeducation course before returning to her teaching job. She then had to work for former janitors who were elevated to supervisory positions. The pay was meager, forcing her to do extra work as a seamstress to make ends meet. Col. Phuc's children were blacklisted and not allowed to study beyond high school. They had to peddle books and newspapers on the streets to bring extra income home.[24]

Yen Bai Camps

Colonel Huynh Van Chinh was first jailed at the Vinh Long prison in South Vietnam. More than a hundred prisoners were packed into each cell, which was built for 40 people. His house, car, and belongings were confiscated and his wife and children were evicted. The communists took whatever they liked. They seized people's valuables but did not record them. "For every ten measures of gold they took, they only reported five to their superiors. Of the five they reported, they substituted half with fake gold and kept the rest."[25] In August 1975, all officers were transferred to the Long Giao prison, near Saigon, where they studied communist lessons. Col. Chinh was moved to Suoi Mau-Tam Hiep reeducation camp where he witnessed three inmates being shot to death for trying to escape.[26]

In June 1976, he was sent to the North. Yen Bai, a mountainous region near the Chinese border, was well known in Vietnamese history as the site of an uprising by nationalists against the French in 1930. The area alone was home to roughly eighty camps with mailboxes from AH1 to AH80 and an inmate population of 15,000 to 20,000. Yen Bai camp 1 was especially crowded as it had to accommodate a total of 400 colonels. Each prisoner was, therefore, allocated half a meter wide space to lie down at night.

Col. Chinh's job was to carry away the wastes of other inmates to be used as fertilizers. The job was so repugnant and unsanitary that he and his friend both lost their appetite at meals.[27] Another colonel had to lead buffaloes to the fields in preparation for fieldwork while generals were kept near the camp to gather tea leaves and to prevent inmates from escaping. The other inmates had to cut down trees or work in the fields in harsh weather. The daily routine was hard labor, for everybody, without exception under difficult working conditions. From 1976 to 1979, inmates were allowed to write home only a few times a year, but could not receive any visits from their relatives. The isolation dealt a big psychological and emotional blow to the inmates. Many became depressed as a result.

At 3500 meters in elevation, the weather was so cold that no one dared take a bath. The water in mountain streams was as cold as ice. Southerners, who were used to a tropical climate, could not handle the cold and the rarefied air of the high mountains. They did not even have adequate clothing for this type of weather as they were told to pack only for a thirty-day reeducation and did not expect to be sent north. Due to poor hygiene, they were infested with lice, which in turn caused itching and scabies.

Meals consisted of two bowls of soup and boiled vegetables twice daily. Later, inmates were able to supplement with some jicama they had planted since their arrival to the camp. This meager regimen left them hungry all the time and hunger pains tortured them and kept them awake at night. They had to consume any wild vegetables and berries they could find to satisfy their hunger. The berries were consumed raw and caused twelve men in a camp of 500 to die of food poisoning. From 1976 to 1979, they were fed *bo bo* (black wheat) sent to Vietnam as cattle feed, first in form of flour, then as unprocessed grain (1977–1979). The husk of the grain was so tough that elderly inmates whose teeth had deteriorated because of malnutrition could not chew it. They had to crush the grain with improvised mortars and pestles[28] before being able to consume it. But once the grain had been dehusked and discarded, there was not much left to eat.

Two months after their arrival in the North, four colonels tried to escape but were caught by villagers while trying to cross a river. They were brought back twenty-four hours later after being severely beaten. Four holes were dug in the ground just deep and wide enough for them to stand in. The holes were covered with planks and dirt as though they were buried alive. They were shackled all the time and were let out to relieve themselves. The escapees suffered from daytime heat and nighttime dampness and cold day after day. A short time later three prisoners confessed and were sent to hard labor while their leader was beaten, strangled and hanged.[29]

The only medication available was a small, bitter pill called *xuyen tam lien* made from the heart of lotus seeds and used as a remedy for everything from diarrhea, flu, infection, stomach pain to cancer. Since the medicine was obviously not effective, prisoners turned to western medications sent in by their relatives in the South. Traditional medicine such as moving a flame over the abdomen to drive out the illness was also used. Many patients, therefore, died of curable diseases like dysentery because of lack of medicine.[30] Lieutenant Colonel Sang moved his bowels 20 to 30 times a day, until he was completely dehydrated. When he could not walk, he crawled; when he could no longer crawl, he dirtied his own bed. He soon died from complete exhaustion and dehydration.[31] The situation stabilized somewhat when inmates were later allowed to receive packages and medications from their families. Local villagers, aware of the presence of modern medicine came to the camps asking the inmates for cough and cold medications.

Col. Chinh met some villagers who wore long French coats and saluted them in military fashion. He discovered that they were non commissioned officers in the French army during WWII who were exiled to Yen Bai since 1954 by the communists. They remained in exile 30 years later. Another nationalist who refused to move south in 1954 was also sent to this remote area.[32]

Col. Chinh was transferred back to the South to Xuan Loc camp Z30-A. There he encountered a well known architect who had been jailed for being part of the dissident national restoration movement. He refused to submit to the communists despite pressure and threats. They called his family in to take care of him but he refused to see them. The guards finally threw him in a cell, chained his legs, and slowly tried to starve him to death.[33] Col. Chinh was released in 1988, almost 13 years after his incarceration.

Nghe An Camps

These camps were located near the Laotian border. Built a long time ago by the French for the detention of Vietnamese nationalists and now run by guards from the Public Security Agency, they were considered to be the worst camps in the North. When inmates realized the guards were brutal like the KGB of the Soviet Union, they rapidly became depressed and terrified.[34]

They were lodged in old brick buildings that were unusually cold in winter and hot in summer. They did not have the right clothing to protect them from the harsh weather and were thrown into crowded small rooms: 80 men in a six by twelve meter room or 150 to 200 men in an 8 × 24 meter room. Following any infraction, they were locked in a small cell without light where they remained shackled on one leg for 10 days or more and given only half the food ration.

For beating the company leader who was found to be an informer, all the inmates from this company were punished and had to work seven days a week. They were sent to the fields earlier and returned to the camps later than anyone else. Agricultural work was hard in this arid region, which was considered the poorest in Vietnam. It consisted of pulling the plough when buffaloes and oxen could not even do the work. The soil was so rocky and poor that fertilizers (mainly human and animal wastes) were needed for every crop. For punishment, inmates were forced to carry fresh wastes to fertilize the fields with their bare hands since bamboo sticks and gloves were forbidden.[35] To compound the problem, they were not allowed to wash their hands or take a bath afterwards and had to eat with their dirty hands. They were not even allowed to rub their hands on the ground or on leaves to eliminate the odor of the wastes. After a few agonizing days and knowing they could not win under these circumstances, they gave up resistance and were again allowed to wash their hands.

Under this inhumane treatment, one colonel became depressed. His ulcer acted up causing abdominal pain. He could not use the medications sent by his family since they had been confiscated. The pain, the work, and the worry worsened his depression. His weight dropped from 75 to 40 kilos.

As his work became more and more erratic, his fellow workers and jailers criticized him for being unfit and for holding them back in their work. Unable to endure the stress, he attempted suicide twice by taking cloroquinine, an anti-malarial agent. He got sick but did not die from it.[36] In 1981, he suffered from appendicitis and had to be operated on, following which he developed severe, disabling diarrhea.

Lang Son Camp

Col. Thi (not his real name),[37] a former commander of the Thu Duc Military Training Camp, was jailed in a camp close to Saigon for more than a year before being shipped to the North along with others around October 1976. When they arrived at Lang Son, they had to walk uphill to their final destination close to the mountaintop. They felt wobbly and many fainted due to lack of nutrition and fatigue. They were also not used to the rarefied mountainous air, having lived all their lives in southern low-lying areas. After an overnight rest, they felt invigorated and continued their uphill march. At their destination, each prisoner was given four five foot long pieces of wood along with a plastic sheet to use as a makeshift tent. The rocky mountain ground became their bed and the plastic sheet their roof.

They were divided into various groups. Some had to set up the kitchen area and prepare food while others cleared the ground. The rest went to the forests to gather the necessary trees and branches. They had to build everything from scratch. Everything had to be improvised and handmade. All the basic building materials were derived from the nearby forest. The work went on for three long months during which they had to fight against harsh weather and a hostile environment. Once the housing units were completed, they were told to build a wooden fence around the camp.

Two teams were sent to the forests and ordered to bring down twenty foot long (about six meter) bamboo poles. Armed with only two pocketknives, each team of three prisoners faced the daunting task of cutting down six large bamboo trees. One prisoner wondered out loud how to cut down six long bamboo trees with two pocketknives. The first team went to the designated area and was lucky enough to find a dozen readily cut bamboo trees that were laying on the side of the road. They helped themselves and slid the trees downhill to the camp.

The second team, however, was not as lucky. The dull knives just chewed on the tree trunks instead of cutting them and it took the prisoners a long time to transect each tree trunk. The tree then refused to fall down being held by its foliage that had intertwined with that of nearby trees. To bring it down, the prisoners had to pull, tug, and twist the trunk that remained stubbornly stuck to the other trees. Sweat was pouring off the men's foreheads while indescribable words filled the air. One prisoner finally had to climb on the tree and cut the branches one by one in order to free it. The work seemed to last an eternity. The men were completely worn out when they finally returned to the camp. The trees were later used to build the camp gates.

The guards ordered them to keep on cutting the trees and to sell them to the villagers. On full section of the hill soon became denuded of trees and the ecologic damage was obvious when rainwater rushed down the denuded slopes and eroded the soil. The villagers got upset, came to the work site and threatened to kill the prisoners if the latter did not stop cutting down the trees.

The frightened prisoners abandoned the project and turned to growing vegetables, fruits, and even rice. They had to dig the hard mountain soil, level the ground, plough the fields, plant the seeds, harvest the rice plants, and water the vegetables. The excess was then sold on the market. While some prisoners tilled and ploughed, the job of collecting water buffalo dung fell on a few of them. Because of lack of chemical fertilizers, buffalo dung and even human wastes were used to fertilize the fields. This was common practice at that time in North Vietnam. It was heart wrenching to watch a former ARVN colonel or general following the water buffaloes with a bucket in his hands ready to collect their wastes. Here and there, the once powerful colonel or general had to bend down, scoop the dung with his bare hands and drop it in his bucket. Soon the prisoner smelled as bad as the contents of his bucket. The sight of a high ranking officer collecting dung brought tears to many prisoners. The animal wastes were then brought back to the camp where they were dried and later used as fertilizer. Human wastes were also collected and treated in the same fashion.

Sanitation as well as food and nutrition in the camps were poor. Food was available but was severely rationed. Under a regimen of two bowls of soup a day, everyone became malnourished. Over a period of time, chronic fatigue set in and they became dizzy, pale, lost weight and developed leg swelling. On many occasions, they developed dysentery, a severe form of diarrhea that was a result of poor food processing and/or food poisoning. They continuously ran to the bathroom until they fell down from exhaustion and had to be carried to the infirmary. Vegetables and plants fertilized by animal or human wastes were easily contaminated with bacteria and led to epidemics of dysentery in the camps. Sick prisoners were treated at the camp's clinic. Since there were not enough nurses available, Col. Thi and a few other prisoners were recruited to take care of the patients despite their lack of formal medical training. Many patients died from these common, preventable and treatable diseases because of lack of adequate medical treatment and failure to transfer to regional hospitals. However, thanks to the epidemics, Col. Thi and his friends did not have to do heavy duty work for at least six weeks.

The cadres asked the inmates to craft for them wooden furniture: chairs and tables, then hutches and drawers. Since many of the latter were former engineers, woodworking was simple compared to building bridges or fortifications. They gathered wood from the forests, then cut, trimmed, leveled, and connected different pieces of wood together to produce beautiful pieces of furniture that later adorned the guards' rooms. The guards were amazed at the quality of these fine products. They had never witnessed or envisioned that such esthetics, material comfort, or stylishness could exist in this world. These qualities were unknown and unheard of in a communist society, which was only geared towards war. They were so excited about the fine woodworking that they requested more furniture to be made and taken to the market for sale.

The guards were rather poor and their salaries meager. They lived in housing units only slightly better than those of the prisoners. Under the communist system that despised material well being, everyone's dream was to own three things: a watch, a radio, and a bicycle; this was their version of being "rich." With the profits generated from the sale of furniture and wood, they bought bicycles, watches, and radios for all the camp workers, from the commander to the simple soldier.

Vinh Phu Camps

During the war, North Vietnam had successfully played both the Chinese and Soviet cards to its advantage. It received military and financial aid from both countries. Leery of its big brother China, it sided with the Soviet camp after the war. China felt threatened by this new coalition. It had to face the Soviet Union on its northern and western frontiers and North Vietnam on its southern flank. In 1978, political and military tensions erupted between the Chinese and the North Vietnamese. After Vietnam invaded Cambodia, the Chinese decided to teach the Vietnamese a lesson by invading North Vietnam. Vietnamese troops thus faced two simultaneous wars, one in Cambodia and the other at the Chinese border. Local people living close to the borders were relocated farther inland. Re-education camps were also moved out of the conflict area and relocated in the Vinh Phu province near Hanoi. The prisoners had to build new camps from scratch and restart their routine in other places.

During all this period, the whereabouts of the prisoners and their camps were classified as state's secrets. The prisoners' families did not know whether their loved ones were still alive, healthy or suffering from any illness. They knew less about the location of the camps. Having not heard from the prisoners for many years, they lived in agonizing fear and worry. Rumors had it that many had died from unknown illnesses, although not a single family had received any official notification from the government. No one had been allowed to visit the inmates.

Then one day, the government, probably under pressure from international organizations, allowed the prisoners to write home. All the letters were censored before being dispatched. Prisoners were only allowed to mention that they were alive, well and being re-educated. They had to mention that they had received the best medical treatment and that they were well fed and well treated. This of course was totally untrue. But the prisoners had to comply with the orders otherwise their letters would be held back. The return address was a zip code related to a specific camp. Families were elated to receive news from their loved ones for the first time and to know that they were still alive, although each letter contained only one or two paragraphs. Families wrote back but it took them another year or two before they were allowed to mail one or two pound packages to the prisoners. The incoming mail was also censored before being delivered to the prisoners.

By chance, a woman in the Vinh Phu area was asked to relay a message from one of the prisoners to his family in the South. That woman had acquaintances in Saigon and did her job. It took the will, bravery, and perseverance of a southern woman who decided to track the whereabouts of her husband to unlock the location of the camp. She took the train to Hanoi, went to the Vinh Phu area, and did her own detective work. She walked straight to the camp and asked to see her husband. The guard got angry and asked her how she knew about the camp location. She responded that she found the camp by placing together rumors and asked to see the camp commander. The guard contacted his supervisor and after a lengthy deliberation, the woman was allowed to see her husband. Once the location of the camps was known, the rest became history but not without further harassment and much more red tape. After many years of arduous, complicated, and repeated requests from the families and stonewalling from the government, the prisoners were allowed to receive visits from their families.

In the meantime, the prisoners continued their hard labor: working in the fields, cutting trees, or making furniture. They were asked to make a twelve foot riverboat but could not figure out how to make one without steel, nails or hammers. The guards told them to dig a hole in the ground the size and shape of the boat to be built and to weave bamboo rods along the borders

VIII. NORTHERN GULAGS

using the ground as a mold. Once the boat was completed, they dug it out of the soil and applied natural glue on the outside of the boat to make it impermeable to water. A few benches were added to the boat, which was then ready for use. The guards were thrilled with the final product and admired the work and the ingenuity of the prisoners. They later asked them to build a few more boats: a fifteen foot and then a twenty foot boat.

Having heard the inmates had some western medications, a villager approached Col. Thi one day and asked him for a few pills for his wife. She apparently had been so weak that she could not even move around. Thi thought he would get himself in trouble if he gave her the wrong medications, so he gave her husband a few vitamin pills. The villager carefully held the precious pills in his hands, went home and gave them to his wife. The next day, he came by and told Thi that his pills were doing wonders on her and that she was stronger than yesterday. Thi gave him two more pills. The following morning, the villager came by with a large smile on his face. He was excited that his wife had recovered and was able to walk, talk, and smile.

The news of the miracle pill rapidly spread around the village. All the villagers soon looked for Mr. Thi to ask him about the pill. Thi sympathized with them and gave them his remaining pills. It turned out that these villagers were once well-to-do business people in Hanoi. After the communists' take over of North Vietnam, these city dwellers were deported to these new "economic zones" where they were sequestered for the last two decades. They barely survived from the land and the county they lived in did not have any factories to provide them with jobs and extra income. They were so poor that they did not even have access to physicians, good nutrition, vitamins, and medications. Thi felt sorry for these people who had suffered so long and so much under the communist regime that had diverted all the riches of the country to finance a war of aggression against the South.

South Vietnamese women who wanted to visit their husbands jailed in the north faced difficult bureaucratic problems. Obtaining a travel permit from the south to the north was a nightmare. In the beginning, the police in South Vietnam would only issue travel permits up to Hue in central Vietnam about 800 miles north of Saigon. In Hue, they had to apply for another permit for the remaining 400 miles that separated Hue from Hanoi. Otherwise, they had to hide from the authorities if they wanted to travel on their own. When they arrived in Hanoi, they had to take another train to Vinh Phu, which was located in the highlands and walk another three miles before reaching the camps.

The trip took three full days, and the most affordable way to travel was by trains that were packed to the gills. Getting a train ticket to either Hue or Hanoi was difficult due to seat limitation. Only a limited number of trains serviced the reunification line between Saigon and Hanoi. Soldiers and government officials, of course, had first priority on these trains, and the remaining seats were sold on first come first served basis.

In Hanoi, visitors were warned to be careful with their personal belongings, bags, and jewelry. Around that time, pickpockets were roaming around town and train stations, preying on strangers. They knew of the value of gold and had their eyes on necklaces or bracelets, but strangely enough they did care about diamonds, for the latter were still rare and unknown to the northerners. One teenager went straight to a southern woman who was wearing a gold necklace, yanked it off her neck, and swallowed it. The youngster then walked away. The woman screamed but to no avail. The Hanoians were not much help. They just stood there and watched. They had too many problems of their own to worry about petty theft, which was common after two decades of war. And there was no proof about the theft, unless someone forced the youngster under an X-ray machine.

The women were advised about reporting the theft. They went to the police station and claimed they had lost all their papers during the robbery. The police issued new permits allowing them to return to Saigon. From Hanoi, they took a three-hour train ride to Vinh Phu. They then had to walk uphill along a river to the camp while their bags were transported by boat since there were no other means of transportation. The river was so shallow in certain areas that the flat bottom of the boat rubbed against the riverbed, making transportation of passengers by boat impossible. On their arrival, they had to inquire about the whereabouts of their husbands since three different camps were located within the same area, and the prisoners could be transferred from one camp to another without notice.

Thi was advised about his wife's visit. The guard pulled him aside and asked him to recite the 100 rules of the Communist party before he was allowed to see her. Since he could only remember the first three or four rules, he did not know what to do. He recited the first three rules then stopped. The angry woman guard exploded and berated him for not wanting to be re-educated. Thi calmly explained that he knew all the rules by heart, but he became so excited when he saw his wife that he forgot everything. The guard thought for a moment then allowed him to see his wife for fifteen minutes.

At this first meeting, they could not say much because they were under the watchful eyes and ears of the guard who was sitting at the head of the table. His wife told him that everyone in the family was in good health and that his second son had gone to Dalat for further studies and that he liked it there. Thi did not know why his son would go to Dalat, a resort town with no major college, but he did not want to pursue the matter further. He told her he was feeling well and reminded her to take good care of the children. She then asked the guard if she could leave a few items for him.

This concluded the fifteen minute visit. It took Mrs. Thi two long months to plan for the trip and acquire the necessary permits, and three whole days to get to this remote area. For all this hassle, she was allowed to see and talk to her husband for fifteen minutes. But it was better than nothing. She knew for sure he was alive, although he was just a shadow of the past. She at least could hold his hands, which were covered with thick calluses. She remembered that he did not have these deformities when he was in the South. She thought that he must have worked a lot with his hands. She did not fail to notice how thin and malnourished he was or how wrinkled and sun tanned his skin is. Overall he had lost most of his teeth, his vigor, and had aged considerably within the last few years. A few tears slowly rolled down her cheek. She could not do anything else but weep loudly as her husband was taken back to the camp.

It would be another six months before she returned to the camp. She had decided to make the trip to the north twice a year to see her husband. In between she had to work in order to save money for the next trip. On her second trip, she noticed the presence of a new guard who let the couple talk without hanging around. Rumors had it that some of the prisoners' wives had complained directly to the ministry of defense about the intransigence of the first woman guard who was then replaced. It turned out that she had a brother who was killed during the war in the south, and that she herself had been injured on the trail and from that that time had borne ill will against the prisoners and their wives.

Mrs. Thi had brought her husband a few sticky rice cakes, which were his favorite food. But when she unwrapped them a bad smell came out. She knew the cakes were spoiled because of the heat and lack of refrigeration. She threw the rice cakes in the river and saw them drifting downstream. A few prisoners who were heading toward the couple saw the rice cakes in the shallow water. Without saying a word, they immediately jumped into the water, grabbed the cakes, split among themselves and ate with delight and without a second thought. A surprised Mrs. Thi wondered why the prisoners would eat spoiled food. Thi explained that they had been hungry for so long that they did not care anymore. They would eat anything in order to fill up their stomachs. They did not have the luxury to throw away any food because there was not enough to go around in the camp. They ate what they could and whatever was available. In spite of it, they had hunger pains most of the time, but had learned to disregard their feelings a long time ago.

He then enquired about his second son who went to Dalat. She told him that he had escaped by boat with his uncle but did not want to talk about the escape in front of the female guard. She mentioned that lychees were available in the north. They were so sweet that she bought three kilos and planned to bring them to her husband. On the train, however, torn by the sight of hungry local children begging for a few lychees, she decided to give everything away. Although the local people advised her not to, she did not care; she could not turn her back on the hungry children. She also found that the north had no tropical fruits like mangoes, rambutans, and jackfruits. She had bought a few mangoes in Nha Trang on her way up to the camps and when the Hanoians saw the mangoes, they went wild and begged her to sell them at three times the regular price.

Thi then told her the story about the cars. One day the guards asked whether any of the prisoners knew how to drive. Everyone raised his hands since each of them had driven a car once before. They then asked for twenty volunteers to drive cars from the regional center back to the camp. Again everyone volunteered for the job, of which twenty were chosen. But they also wondered why such a small camp would need that many cars.

The next day, they were taken to the regional center for some business dealings. At the end of the day, they were shown, instead of cars, twenty oxcarts to pull home. Each oxcart was heavy enough for one man to pull. They struggled long and hard, but managed to pull all of them back to the camp. It was late by the time they arrived at the camp. The kitchen was closed and the rest of the prisoners had dined and gone to bed. The twenty volunteers were definitely tired and worn out. On top of that, they had to go to bed hungry. They were so upset that they could not sleep and ended up swearing all night long. They thought they would be allowed to drive real automobiles, and this was the reason they volunteered for the job. They swore licensed drivers were not needed to pull these oxcarts as anyone could have done the job.

The government, after so many years of tightly controlling the movement of the prisoners, finally loosened its grips. Although inmates had to remain in the camp at night, they were free to go to the village during daytime to peddle their products to the villagers. After unwrapping the packages sent to them by their wives, they gathered all the multicolored rubber bands that were used to hold the packages together (tape was not available in Vietnam). They then gave the rubber bands to the village children who were delighted with the presents. The children had never seen these rubber bands before and wore them around their wrists like valuable bracelets. They were also given pencils and notebooks, which the children proudly showed to their parents. The prisoners also gave the villagers a few meters of fabrics, which had been sent to them by their families. They had found out that, although villagers were allocated two meters of fabrics per family per year, most of the time government stores had run out of fabrics a long time ago. The prisoners felt bad that the villagers and their families had to wear worn out clothes because of the inefficiency of the factories, lack of care, and the ineptitude of the communist government.

The prisoners were asked to make daggers for their jailers. They soon found a way to make the blade, yet did not know how to fashion the handle. They then asked their jailers if they could provide them with buffalo horns. The jailers brought in a pile of horns with which they made handles for the daggers. And soon, each jailer proudly carried a dagger with a buffalo horn handle on his side like a prized trophy. The news spread fast. Even jailers from other camps were asking for their daggers. A mass production of daggers ensued and soon the whole county ran out of buffalo horns.

Thi had been passing blood rectally for some time and as result had been feeling weak. He thought his hemorrhoids were acting up and did not pay much attention to this problem until he fainted one day. He was taken to the camp clinic for observation. X-ray machines were not available, however. Luckily the bleeding stopped spontaneously and he was able to do some work a few days later, although he was still weak. Since medication was not available at the clinic and on the advice of his friends, he treated himself with herbs he gathered in the nearby woods. He felt lucky he did not have any problems afterwards. Years later, he had another bleeding episode and was lucky enough to be in the United States at that time. He was taken to the emergency room and was found to have a bleeding stomach ulcer that was resolved with medical treatment.

One spring came and left. Then another spring ... and another one.... It had been ten years — ten long years — since the prisoners were first taken into custody in Saigon then shipped north. Having endured untold ordeals, Col. Thi and his compatriots were just a shadow of the past: they had not only lost weight, but their teeth had also fallen out, their skin was covered with thick calluses, their hair was gray, their joints arthritic, and they all had aged beyond recognition. But they considered themselves fortunate to be alive. They hung in desperately waiting for an eventual release order, which would set them free. Their only hope was to be reunited with their families before incarceration, punishment and starvation took their final toll on them and wasted their rapidly waning strength.

One by one, they were given their release papers. They shared their joy with the villagers, who, touched by the generosity of these strangers, decided to give them a farewell party. The villagers banded together to bake and cook a magnificent meal for the soon to be released prisoners. Thi took note of the addresses of the villagers with the thought of sending them gifts in return.

Once he arrived home in Saigon, thanks to the income generated by his wife who turned out to be a good businesswoman, he sent each northern family a few meters of fabrics, vitamins for the adults, and rubber bands, pencils, and notebooks for the children. The villagers did not write back, but did let the remaining prisoners know how deeply they appreciated Mr. Thi's gesture and that they would always remember him.

Mr. Thi, on the other hand, just wished the government could do a little more to improve the well being of its people. The latter did not need much: maybe a larger ration of rice and meat, a few meters of fabrics, and freedom to travel. They were not difficult to please.

Comparison of Northern and Southern Camps

Inmates in northern camps were different than those sequestered in southern camps. The first group was composed mostly of middle aged or elderly high-ranking officials who had spent a long career in the ARVN or GVN while those in southern camps were younger and had spent less than five or ten years in the service.

The older northern inmates had more medical problems, such as heart, lung, and kidney problems, diabetes, and hypertension, than the southern inmates. They used to be chain smokers and heavy drinkers and many led a sedentary life. Although many of them had a borderline health status, they did not receive any medical screening and care in the camps. Actually there was not even a good dispensary in any of these camps for the communists lacked a good health care system. In spite of this fact, the knowledge and skills of many inmate-physicians went unused because they were incarcerated.

Having been in the leadership position for some time, the northern inmates were used to order, control, and having people do the work for them. In the camps, however, they faced a different situation. They had to obey orders given by young and immature wardens and perform manual and what they felt was "dishonorable" work, such as collecting dung or pulling a plough. They were also not treated decently according to their age and rank and felt hurt as a result. The descent from a high position to a lower one within a period of a few months was so traumatic that many never recovered from it. They suddenly lost all their prestige and rank, were stripped of their yang, and tumbled down to the lowest rank of society. They wore rags in the camps, a problem that had never happened to them before, washed their own clothes, and were ordered around like simple soldiers and not officers. They were told not to answer until or unless they were addressed. They did not have any "aide de camp" to solve their basic needs. Above all, they felt they had lost their dignity. This situational change was unbearable to many and caused them to become depressed.

They also remained in the camps longer (on the average ten to fifteen years) than southern inmates (three to eight years). In the beginning, many were not released even when they became sick, so they just died in the camps, away from their families. Only a few and elderly inmates were released early whey they became gravely ill. The earliest high-ranking official to be released was Dr Vu Ngoc Hoang, general and chief of the ARVN Medical Corps. He spent five years in confinement in the north and was released only after intervention by the French government (his wife is a French citizen).[38] This incarceration was two years longer than the usual time spent by an army physician. The longer incarceration exacerbated many more medical illnesses in this elderly population.

The cold weather and the rarefied air of the high mountains were especially harsh for these elderly inmates who were used to a low land, tropical climate. Farming under these conditions and on frozen ground was extremely difficult and taxing on the cardiovascular system. Northern jails were not heated and inmates had to huddle together to protect themselves from the cold. They were never told they would be shipped north and thus had not brought adequate warm clothing. As a result they developed scabies, which spread rapidly because no one dared take a bath with icy water. The chance of dying from pneumonia was too high.

Lack of medicines was notorious inside as well as outside northern camps. Even if they had money, they could not buy any western medicines outside the northern camps while medications were frequently available on the black market in the South. They were only allowed to have family visits in 1979, four years after their incarceration. Without such visits, they not only could not receive supplemental food or medications, but also missed their relatives badly. Physically and mentally, they did not adapt well to all these adverse conditions.

Northern inmates felt they were treated more harshly than their southern counterparts. Inmates, in the North as well as in the South, were forced to work in the fields and pull ploughs. Although pulling a plough was by itself strenuous work, that job turned out to be much more difficult in the northern icy or rocky grounds than in the soft and muddy southern fields. And this type of work was much harder on an elderly northern inmate than a young southern prisoner. Overall, for the same type of work, the energy expenditure was much higher and the work more exhausting in the North than in the South.

Older northern inmates were physically, mentally, and emotionally less fit than their counterparts in the south. Natural conditions were also much more adverse in the North than the South. At the northern Thanh Phong camp close to the Chinese border, the mortality was so high that Hanoi had to close the camp. "When you got sick, you died. There was no medical treatment. We ate only rice and some vegetables we picked from the jungles."[39] If the southern *bo doi* appeared to be cruel but unsophisticated, the northern wardens were cunning and knowledgeable. They knew how to break the inmates, play with their morale, and bend them to their will without even beating them. They, however, could be ruthless and cruel because "they considered themselves exiled too. For them it was the end of the world. They were desperate. Their food was little better than ours."

Overall the combination of hard work, cold weather, lack of food and medications, the presence of lice and their harsh treatment "destroyed them and killed them slowly day by day."[40] All these factors adversely affected their health and contributed to the reported high mortality in northern camps.

IX

Starvation

Food, especially rice, was the most important item in the camps. It was so important that when an explosion rocked the Long Khanh camp and destroyed many buildings, the first thing the *bo doi* did was attempt to salvage as many rice bags as possible. They neither cared about the burning buildings nor the injured inmates who were lying in their own blood on the ground. One inmate who happened to be around the storage area and helped move the rice bags to a safe building was one of the first and rare ones to have his sentence commuted. When a typhoon hit central Vietnam in November 1977, inmates at A-30 camp were rushed to the fields to pick up the wet corn, to lift the potatoes and cassava roots, to hastily cut the rice, and to carry them at full speed to the warehouse. In the aftermath of the flooding, their rations were further cut down and reduced to rotten corn and cassava. They were then forced to work from dawn to dusk, even on Sundays, to make up for the damaged crops.[1]

Food could not be found anywhere in the camp except in the storage areas where it was vigilantly guarded day and night. The *bo doi* and cadres knew its importance and used it as a weapon with unequaled brutality and efficiency. They doled out the minimum amount required to survive, but no more than that. And that minimum would be further reduced or even withheld at the slightest infraction.

Food Rations

Rations in the reeducation camps were based on a value of 0.25 dong per diem. An example of the weekly menu follows:

1 day — rice with salt.
1 day — rice with fish sauce.
1 day — rice with pork.
1 day — rice with fish.
3 days — rice with vegetables.

The above menu was typical for all the camps. Meals were cooked by the inmates under the supervision of the *bo doi* who watched them closely to prevent any stealing. They were served twice a day, at lunch and supper. The regimen did not provide enough calories and nutrition for the prisoners who were subjected to hard labor. A laborer handling heavy work would require 3,000 to 4,000 calories per day to remain healthy. The above meals barely provided 1,000 calories a day. In addition, vitamins were not available due to lack of fresh fruits and vegetables. With a daily caloric deficit of 2,000 to 3,000 calories, one could see how inmates could rapidly lose weight in a matter of a few weeks. This condition was further aggravated by the fact that the Vietnamese are small people with not a lot of bodily reserve to spare. This explains why many inmates deteriorated rapidly in the camps: they either became very lean and thin or swollen from head to toes from beriberi. They soon lost their hair, their bones became brittle, their teeth decayed rapidly, and their wounds rarely healed well. It also explains their constant hunger and their aggressive search for extra nourishment in and around the camps. Without that meager supplemental nutrition and the food provided by their families, many more would have died.

There was neither bulk nor nutrition in the above menu. In the beginning, food was mainly gruel or "swill" with a few morsels of dry fish or vegetables. The swill, being mostly liquid rapidly melted away in their stomachs and made them feel hungry again a few hours later. Although lacking in taste and flavor, it was gulped down rapidly for lack of anything better. In other camps, red rice was served with salt water or fish sauce along with a small amount of vegetables. When fish sauce was missing or ran out, it was substituted by salt water. Inmates would dip the rare pieces of vegetable with salt water pretending it was fish sauce and swallow them with rice. This regimen could not be called substantial by any standard.

Food rations varied from camp to camp depending upon the number of inmates, food availability and whether the food could be grown locally (vegetables, sweet potatoes, cassava) or shipped from regional centers (rice, fish, meat, sugar, fish sauce). Since some camps were more self sufficient than others, inmates in those camps received a larger daily ration. However, since most camps were located in isolated, arid and forested areas, additional cultivation yielded only marginal quality food (yams or cassava) that added bulk but yielded minimal nutrition to the daily rations. But anything was definitely better than nothing and all the prisoners knew it well. At the Bu Gia Map camps, prisoners were able to grow large fields of cassava and benefited from it. But, in a poor, war ravaged and bankrupt country, not a lot of food, either quantitatively or qualitatively, was available. Although vegetables, cassava, sweet potatoes, and peanuts were immediately available for consumption, rice culture on the other hand required many years of intensive work to meet the demands of all the prisoners in the camps.

In one of the camps on the island of Phu Quoc, a few inmates were given "500 grams of uncooked rice and small portions of vegetables and dried fish"[2] although that amount could range from 200[3] to 700[4] grams daily. In most camps, however, the average ration was less than 300 grams per day: two small cassavas for breakfast and a single bowl of rice for each main meal.[5] In the beginning, prisoners were fed "red" rice, which was usually fed only to pigs and poultry. It was "dirty, moldy and partly rotten."[6] It was processed so poorly that it was mixed with sand and contained tiny, wiggly worms. This rice came from the reserves the Viet Cong had stored for many years in the jungles during the war. It was also fed to inmates housed in the Saigon jails.

During the first year in the camps (1975–76), each prisoner was allocated 16 kilograms of uncooked rice per month. In the second year, the ration was cut down to 12 kilos with flour, corn, cassava, sweet potatoes, and *bo bo* substituting for rice. If the inmates grew more vegetables, their daily ration was proportionally cut; if they grew less, their ration became larger. When rice became scarcer, inmates were fed "one meal of rice and one meal of sweet potatoes a day. After that, rice was mostly replaced by wheat flour. For every three meals of wheat flour, they were given one of rice."[7] Mildewed cassava and *bo bo* grains later replaced the rice. *Bo bo* was an imported grain used to feed horses. It was as large as a green bean and could even be tasty. But once consumed, it could not be digested and caused severe abdominal cramps until it found its way out.[8] Having nothing else to eat, inmates learned to chew it well and eat it sparingly, in small amounts. Elderly inmates in the northern camps had a tough time consuming *bo bo* because most of them had lost their teeth as a result of poor nutrition. Since cooking did not make the husk any softer, they had to find a way to crush the grain before consuming it.

They were also given cassava (manioc) as a substitute for rice. They each received one and a half kilos of cassava a day. After peeling and cooking, only half of that amount was edible. Anyone receiving old cassava went hungry for that meal because it was as hard as a piece of wood and thus no longer edible. On many occasions, they were given corn in place of rice. In northern camps, the corn was usually young and barely edible. The edible part was about one fourth of its total weight. Therefore, unless they wanted to remain hungry, they had to eat everything including "the corn cobs."[9] In one camp, the cadre deliberately created a food shortage by storing pumpkins and cassava roots and releasing them only when they were half rotten.

Fish was available once a week. In the beginning, dried fish, which had a longer shelf life, was used and later replaced by fresh fish. But fresh fish tended to spoil easily in hot tropical weather without refrigeration. On occasions, the *bo doi* carefully screened all the food at the time of delivery and returned any spoiled material to the providers. Conscientious cooks would discard these rotten fish even though they further decreased the bulk and caloric level of the food.[10] Uncaring ones would dump everything in the cooking pans. The end result was a rich looking but inedible meal. Fresh fish were available in the Mekong Delta and thus served more frequently in southern than remote northern camps. In one camp, the *bo doi* "never failed to seize part of the provisions for their own use ... and selected the fattest fish for their table."[11]

As far as meat was concerned, no major source of protein was available. One cow was killed annually, usually during the Tet Festival, to feed 300 to 500 prisoners. One pig was divided between 200 to 300 and in one instance up to 1,000[12] yielding only a few morsels for each of them. Since it was almost impossible to divide meat in such tiny portions, in many camps the prisoners just tossed the chunk of meat in a large container and made soup out of it. They fought for every little morsel of meat they could get, and those who were slow to get in line did not get anything at all. In some camps, the wardens would stand by and watch the prisoners lose their dignity in their fight for food. In others, they walked away, letting inmates fight one another. And when fights became violent, the instigators were rounded up and sent to discipline cells or conex.

Meals were gulped down in less than five minutes since there was nothing to chew. Most meals were liquid. A few inmates took their time thinking they could control hunger better by eating slowly and trying to savor it although rice mixed with salt water had no taste at all. Mealtime was thus not a particularly happy time. Besides fighting for food, there was nothing to chat about or discuss. And the less they talked, the better it was for them. Nearby lurked an unknown "antenna" ready to report what he had gathered during these discussions. This was a race for life and these rations provided only the minimum needed to survive. Without them, they would surely die of starvation. With them, they hoped to prolong their ordeal a bit longer.

"This ration is not to keep you alive but enough to put off your death for a while. So try and make it go down. The longer you delay your death, the better chance you will stand you'll stand to see spring blossom."[13]

IX. Starvation

Hunger

Hunger was so pervasive that inmates thought about food all the time, day and night. In an environment where food was restricted and controlled by the *bo doi*, the only way to get ahead was to forage in the fields for cassava roots, grains, berries, and even grass or to hunt for any insect or reptile they could find. They tried any kind of plant they judged edible. And many were poisoned after trying unknown fruits. They were no different than prehistoric men looking for food and trying to survive in an adverse environment.

In the North, inmates developed severe constipation after eating wild banana. The excess tannin in wild bananas led to constipation then severe dysentery and death because of lack of medication. Twelve men in a camp of 500 died as a result of eating wild fruits and vegetables.[14]

> Most of our free time was spent trying to get more food. Not unlike animals, we only thought of eating ... eating. There were days when we could not find anything edible to cook at night. Going to bed with an almost empty stomach, which kept rumbling over and over, we could not sleep.[15]

The communists knew the value of food and used it to their advantage. The best way to punish, besides isolation, was to withdraw food. Hardheaded inmates were usually placed in isolation and given a half ration. Food became a weapon used to control the prisoners. They soon learned they had no legal right to a daily meal; they had to earn it. Those who worked hard, followed the rules, or showed signs of rehabilitation were given their daily rations. On the other hand, any inmate who did not meet his quota or disobeyed orders was stripped of his meal. And the poor fellow who was unable to work because of weakness caused by poor nutrition was further penalized by the loss of his ration.

A prisoner could cry or beg for leniency, but in the end he had to go to bed hungry. At night, he was tortured by hunger pains, which kept him awake or caused him to have nightmares. He was weaker the next morning and still unable to work. Slowly he fell behind, was further punished until he could barely crawl out of his bed and finally had to be brought to the infirmary for care. However, because of lack of medical treatment and care, he would slowly wither and die of starvation and malnutrition.

When the cadres used their power of withholding meals, all the prisoners towed the line. There was no bigger deterrent to opposition than starvation. A hungry stomach would turn wolves into lambs.

> In a communist prison, the first blow they will deal you is hunger, and it also turns out to be a death blow. A bite of food means more than a bite of food — it bears the full weight of existence. A prisoner who considers the likelihood of survival must consider his ability to find and eat anything.[16]

Hunger was so pervasive it made inmates do strange things. They fought for or positioned themselves to get the last drop of soup or rare morsels of meat. They watched the food handlers carefully to make sure all the portions were equally divided among them. One spoon more or less could cause a fight to erupt. On many occasions, rice that spilled on the ground was rapidly grabbed and consumed by inmates. In their fight for survival, many lost their manners and reverted to their basic instinct. Those who were not fast enough or did not fight lost out.

A few would do anything to get their hands on an extra bowl of rice and turned to reporting their roommates for any illegal activity or unwise comment about the communists. They became the much feared and despised "antennas" for the wardens. Others volunteered to clean the pigsties in order to steal the rice reserved for pigs. The *bo doi* valued the animals so much they fed them "white" rice while inmates were only fed "red" or coarse rice. One inmate had to dig a well for another in exchange for sugar cubes. The inmate was given one cube for the first meter of well, two cubes for the second meter, and so on.[17] The average remaining inmates were resigned to receive their meager daily food ration.

Others competed to serve as cooks. Kitchens were the only places loaded with food in the camps but also closely watched by the wardens. Stealing food in the kitchen (rice, cassava, or even a cabbage) became a usual pastime for a few. It not only satisfied their hunger, but also their quest for revenge against their captors. When they cook a large amount of rice, a layer of burnt rice would always deposit at the bottom of the pans. In the beginning no one liked that crusty burnt rice because of its sour taste and its toughness on their brittle teeth. But once inmates became hungry, they longed for anything. The burnt rice soon became a highly sought commodity. Those who worked in the kitchen stole part of that rice before it was distributed to every unit. On other occasions, they would make arrangements for another inmate to collect the garbage in which they had thrown a good cabbage or anything edible. The garbage collector would fish out the goods at the dumpster site, take them to the camp to divide them among his friends.[18]

> In the forced-labor camp, the overwhelming, all-encompassing reality was hunger. Even he who had always been a spare eater, he was always hungry, let

alone the active and vigorous, younger men. Everyone was hungry all the time, so hungry that all they could ever think of was food.[19]

To satisfy their hunger they had to learn to eat anything that crawled, such as lizards, centipedes, mice, birds, grasshoppers, and snakes.[20] Many became expert in the art of catching snakes, mice or rats. It required a lot of ingenuity and dexterity to build a trap in camps where no hardware or tools were available. It required a lot more skill to catch a rat with one of these improvised traps.

> Rats were a popular source of food. These huge sewer rats were briefly singed over a fire and then skinned.... I had to gut the rats with my fingers, yanking off and tossing away the head and four paws; then spicing the remnants with my five-spice powder, salt and lemon grass, I barbecued the carcass.[21]

Rat meat was barely edible but it was a good source of protein for the starved inmate. One inmate found a mouse's nest built in a bamboo hole along with four or five newly born, still red mice. "He picked them up, stuck them on an improvised stick of bamboo, and ate them raw right there." Others found small frogs, the size of a thumb, in nearby ponds and ate them. Any insect, besides providing additional protein and a change in the daily menu, could serve as a substitute for meat. "They ate live crickets, first pulling off their spiny legs, then popping the crickets in their mouths."[22] Although not everyone was lucky enough to catch these creatures and not everyone was brave enough to swallow them raw, desperate inmates did desperate things. They ate whatever was available in order to survive, even if that source of food was limited and not renewable. Once they had hunted down all the living creatures in and around the camps, they had nothing else available to eat.

"There had been some lizards — of the gecko variety — running around when the men first arrived, but after a few "field operations" by the humans, they might as well [have been] considered extinct."[23]

In a few southern camps, the fields were often separated from the camps by a barbed wire fence. Inmates who were hungry would crawl underneath the fence and go hunting for cassava roots or sweet potatoes in the darkness of the night. They worked mostly by touching and feeling as any light would have alerted the *bo doi* of their presence in the fields. They uprooted the cassava plants to get the edible roots then replanted them in an upright position so that the wardens would not be aware of the theft. They then brought the roots back to the camps to cook.

This hunt for food was not for everyone, but only for the most daring inmates. It was a risky business. Suspicious *bo doi* watched the fields carefully and aggressively hunted down all the thieves. They could randomly shoot at any moving person in the field if he failed to surrender at the first summon or beat any inmate who was caught stealing before sending him to disciplinary cells. They at times stood watch in the fields and caught the inmates on the spot. Even if an inmate were successful in stealing a few potatoes or cassava roots, he could be reported by an antenna and not enjoy the success of his fieldtrip.

If the prisoners were lucky enough to work in the fields during daytime, they could steal vegetables, cassava roots, sweet potatoes, or berries in the South and peanuts, cassava, and sweet potatoes in the North. With sweet potatoes, they could eat "both the vegetable and its young leaves"[24] while medium young earn corn was consumed raw in the fields. They usually acted alone, each person trying to fill up his belly as fast as possible, although at times they were more thorough and worked as a group in order not to be caught. A few would feast on the corn while a couple stood watch and later they would switch. Although many were careful not to leave any trace behind, a few were careless, throwing cobs or leaves on the ground. They got caught as a consequence.

Overall, inmates stole roughly ten percent of the crop, but they rarely took rice from the fields, for uncooked rice was not digestible. Wardens watched the "high quality crops" (i.e. peanuts) closely, as they could be destroyed by insects or stolen by inmates. To prevent insects from eating peanut seeds, the *bo doi* "put them in a concentrated DDT solution." Although peanuts mixed in this solution smelled strong, inmates stole and ate them anyway.[25] Short of that, a prisoner could resort to chewing grass. One inmate "managed to pick handfuls of that grass, wash it in a stream and chew on it ... until there was no juice left, and he would discard the fibers and stuff his mouth with some more fresh grass."[26]

Inmates would hide stolen crops (corn, beans, cassava) in many places in their bodies before returning to the camps. They wrapped the items compactly in a piece of cloth and hid the packet in their buttocks or in shirts with double lining. They usually carried a container of water with them to work and later used the container as a hiding place after dumping all the water out. They sometimes hid beans or corn in their boots, then carried the boots on their shoulders while walking home barefoot. Although they loved to bring their "catch" back to the camp to cook it and savor it at their leisure, this was not always possible due to regulations. Therefore, on many occasions they had to consume these items raw,[27] most often on the spot with utmost secrecy. For being caught stealing and eating without permission, they had to "stand at attention before the cadres to be reviled, abused, and ordered to write confessions."[28] They were beaten[29] or simply placed in solitary confinement with their regular rations cut in half.

One day, an inmate killed a six meter long snake and brought it back to the camp. The men in his platoon had a big feast. The platoon leader called him to his office and told him his platoon's ration would be cut for the next two months because it had too much meat that month. As the inmate inquired about the decision, the cadre told him he had eaten too much snake meat recently and the snake belonged to the government.[30]

Cooking in the camp was not easy. In the beginning, it was simply forbidden in many camps. A few prisoners did it anyway, surreptitiously and at great personal risk. A few fellows would stand watch while others dug a hole in the ground, dropped in a few twigs and cooked whatever they had caught, sometimes snakes or geckos. By cooking in the ground and sitting down in a circle around the fire,[31] they were able to prevent the sparks of fire from being detected from outside the building. They also had to rapidly vent the smoke.

Cooking supplies had to be hidden most of the time, otherwise they would be confiscated.[32] Later, the *bo doi* simply turned a blind eye on the cooking business and everyone started cooking outdoors under a tree.[33] They did not have cooking pans, but plenty of Guigoz aluminum cans (a highly prized item) they could use. They usually cooked rice, vegetables, cassava, and ate it with dried meat or fish sent from home.

The lack of food caused severe physical disabilities. First of all, everyone lost weight and became emaciated. They seemed to lose all their energy. They walked slowly with eyes sunken in their sockets. Their legs showed only bones and skin for all the muscles had atrophied. Persistent malnutrition caused their teeth to fall out. Many soon became edentulous. One inmate had shrunk from 140 to 90 pounds and his hairs had grayed after only one year in the camp.[34] Ben Cai's weight fell from 150 to 100 pounds.[35] After four years of incarceration, a 140-pound engineer became a ghostly 89-pound male.[36] Forty percent of the inmates became disabled with severe muscle wasting, paralysis or rheumatism. Two men in a group of 30 died of exhaustion and malnutrition. Some groups had more deaths while others had less.[37]

Second, a malnourished body was unfit to fight off diseases and infections. Not only was the inmate weak, but his immune system also refused to work. "A mere cold could confine a person to bed for several days, not to speak of a case of malaria. Some people did not recover even after a full month."[38] A cut sustained during work would not heal for a long time, slowly becoming sore and often infected.

Third, they developed metabolic disorders unique to malnutrition. They could lose their eyesight because of lack of vitamin A or break their bones because of lack of vitamin D. They often exhibited signs of beriberi secondary to lack of vitamin B1 and as a result their bodies became swollen from head to toe. Longer periods of malnutrition could damage their hearts by adversely affecting heart muscle function. Some inmates experienced heart failure and died as a result. This disease, which had been completely eradicated in the western world a long time ago, could only be seen in third world countries, reeducation camps, and jails where malnutrition was prevalent. The reappearance of these walking skeletons and swollen bodies conjured images of the Nazi Holocaust of decades past.

Family Support

The food shortage became so bad prisoners were finally allowed to receive food from their families. The quantities allowed were small in the beginning then slowly increased with time. Frequently requested items included rice, salt, sugar, medicine, and dried meat or shrimp, which would keep for a long time. Sugar was sorely missed as it could serve to boost the strength of these malnourished inmates. Dried meat was the most prized item as it could be stored for a long time. Everyone was also hungry for meat. All the packages sent in by the relatives were screened by the *bo doi* who kept any item they liked. The leftover was given to the inmates. In many camps, rice that was sent in was confiscated as the *bo doi* felt it could foster an inmate to escape.

It was only years later that families were finally allowed to visit their relatives in the camps and bring in food and money. They themselves had become so destitute that many could not even afford to make the trip no matter how dearly they loved their husbands, brothers, or sons. Many were unskilled housewives whose jobs in the pre–1975 years were to take care of the household and children. Once the breadwinners were jailed, wives and children had to work for a living or were sent to a far away economic zone. They peddled anything from food and fruit to clothing for a few *dong* while their children took care of themselves by selling newspapers and begging or foraging through garbage cans. In the worst scenario, they could labor, day and night, in an economic zone for two bowls of rice a day. Under these circumstances, it was no wonder they could barely make ends meet in the new society, which openly discriminated against southerners[39] and relatives of inmates of the reeducation camps. They were all labeled as either class 14 or 15, at the bottom of a supposedly classless society. This alone pointed to the real intent of the party.

For those who could make it, the trip to the camps was hazardous because of the camps' remoteness, absence of adequate roads, and lack of safety of the countryside. The distance between Saigon and Bu Gia Map camp was more than 200 miles through hilly country, roads filled with potholes or mined by the warring factions, and damaged bridges still not repaired after the recent war. They first had to take the bus to Phuoc Binh, a village located about twenty miles from the camp, stopping at all the big or small communities along the way. By the time they arrived at the village, it was already too late to go to the camp for safety reasons. They stopped overnight at the village and had to "sleep on the stalls in the market as there was no inn and take turns watching the luggage."[39] The next morning they tackled the rough, narrow, and deserted road from Phuoc Binh to Bu Gia Map camp, which wound through heavily forested areas. Visitors often fell prey along this unsafe stretch of road to bandits who robbed[40] or raped[41] them in broad daylight. Even a *bo doi* fell victim to these attacks when he biked alone on that road. A few bandits came out of the woods, mugged him and stole his bike. He had to walk back to the camp fuming with anger and enlist the help of a few other *bo doi* to hunt down the thieves. The journey to northern camps was much worse as the roads were uncharted. Maps and information were lacking and permits were difficult to obtain. Camps were hidden in secretive and hilly areas (see chapter 8).

Once they arrived at the camps, they had to face hostile *bo doi* who could simply deny the visits for unexplained reasons, harass, or even physically molest them.[42] If the visit was granted, the inmate was notified and allowed to meet his family in an enclosed area outside the perimeter of the camp. The *bo doi* then screened all the packages brought by the prisoners' relatives. They spread all the items on the table and went through each one, confiscating anything they liked: dried ground meat, dried bread, and packages of instant noodles.[43] They gave the rest to the inmates. This was an official version of a "cut" in the transaction. The *bo doi* benefited as much from the visits as the inmates.

On other occasions, they just returned many items to the relatives without any valid explanation. While meat was unavailable in the camp, a cadre returned a package of dried meat to a prisoner's wife with a haughty communist statement such as, "There is no shortage of meat here."[44] The frightened relative did not know what to do except quickly grab the package and stash it away. Without dry meat, the inmate sorely missed the chance to build up his strength and add some variety and flavor to his meals.

Nguyen Cong Hoan, a communist legislator, wrote about an event at the Bu Gia Map camp:

During the New Year holiday (*Tet*) I came to visit a cousin at Nguyen Ngan Dien camp. I personally witnessed a scene in which an old mother who had brought a bottle of fish sauce for her son was viciously insulted before everyone and then denied permission to see him. The old woman went down on her knees, but her plea was ignored. When the prisoners were allowed to line up to receive their packages, the cadre loudly asked them, "Do you need fish sauce here?" All the prisoners shouted back, "No, we have quite enough fish sauce here!" The truth was that far from having any fish sauce, they did not even have salt."[45]

Because of hazardous road conditions, inmates' relatives were allowed to stay overnight in small huts built by the inmates outside the camps. Profiting from the occasion, the *bo doi* hid "in the bushes along the stream to watch the women bathe in the evening, masturbating as they stared."[46] They also came to their huts at night to molest the visitors.[47] A woman who woke up in the middle of the night watched as a stranger furtively snuck into her hut, approached and start fondling her. She used a pair of scissors she kept on her side to stab his face. The stranger, caught by surprise, escaped after letting out a loud yell. A few days later, an inmate representative who had raised the question of relatives' molestation by the *bo doi* learned one of them had been sent to the local hospital for treatment of a stab wound to the eye. In other camps, the "progressives" (mostly inmates turned informers) were given "permission to force themselves on the women visitors as a reward for progress in reeducation."[48]

Despite these dangers, relatives kept flocking to the camps, bringing with them food, compassion, and love while uplifting the inmates' spirits at the same time. Although the majority of women stuck by their jailed husbands during these difficult times, marital problems did occur. During a visit to the camp, a colonel's wife blamed him for all her suffering under the communist regime by not letting her escape abroad earlier. Stung by her criticisms, he withdrew within himself, became depressed and attempted suicide twice.[49] Captain Ben Cai's never knew why his wife did not visit him at the camp. He learned after his escape that she was living in the open with his former Jeep driver and even had had his baby.[50] One woman after seeing her dispirited husband in the camp a couple times went home, divorced him, turned over her children to her in-laws and eloped with a cadre. There was also the story of a colonel who was interned in a northern camp. His wife left without informing him, asked a neighbor to care for her daughter and went on with her own life. The little girl had to peddle things for a living instead of going to school in order to save enough money to pay a visit to her father at the camp one day. The two cried profusely at the meeting, the father for having been deserted by his wife and the daughter for having lost a mother and the chance for an education. Following his release after eight years of incarceration, he vowed to catch up on the lost time and to give his daughter a good education. He home schooled her and taught her all the basics. When they finally came to the United States under the Orderly Departure Program, despite his daughter's lack of formal training she was deemed academically fit to enroll in a university from which she later graduated.

Supplies brought in by relatives became the lifeline for the inmates. This is not to say that they had plenty to eat; on the contrary, they were still starving in spite of these rare visits. Relatives on the other hand faced tough economic times outside the camps and had to scrap every *dong* and sacrifice a lot in order to buy goods to bring to the camps. And there was only so much a person could carry to the camp on each trip. But there was no question that without these supplies many more inmates would have died of starvation during their long incarceration. Nevertheless, only a few inmates kept all the food for themselves. Many shared it with their friends. And when the latter got their food, they paid the favor back and everyone had something new to eat once in a while.

In 1979, as regulations were relaxed at some camps, a few *bo doi* "bought a pig, killed it and sold the meat" to prisoners. They also sold tobacco and alcohol.[51] At the Bu Loi camp in the highlands, one *bo doi* went hunting in the woods, killed a deer and then "sold the delicious venison at cutthroat prices."[52] Of course, not everyone could afford to buy these goods, although they were available at a few camps. Times had certainly changed, for in the beginning the *bo doi* were strictly forbidden from socializing with the inmates. The socializing between the two groups was an anathema to the revolution: "As revolutionaries, they must not associate with inmates, the counterrevolutionaries."[53]

By 1980, after five years of imprisonment, the inmates were still trapping rats for food and getting by with a marginal intake. In one camp, food was so scarce that one *bo doi* even led them to a villager's field close to a camp to steal corn.[54] The *bo doi* did not fare any better. They had to "supplement their rice with flour" donated by France. That "gift from France to the people of Vietnam" ironically was exclusively reserved for the *bo doi* while the prisoners' main staple remained *bo bo*.[55]

Guigoz-Canism

A strange phenomenon had occurred as a result of food shortage: the emergence of the so-called "Guigoz-canism." In the camps food rationing forced the inmates to live close to the standard of "humanoids who had discovered fire (i.e. they were allowed to boil or broil whatever they could forage as foodstuff)."[56] Without that accommodation, the majority of them would simply not have survived the rigor and destitution of the camps.

Reeducation, which was supposed to instill prisoners with "the spirit of collective ownership," instead heightened their instinct for survival and drove them to become more individualistic. Survival became one man's fight because group formation was discouraged in the camps. The first thing the *bo doi* did was to separate and isolate friends by relocating them to different groups or camps. In order to survive in this adverse environment, inmates learned to be self-sufficient by storing food and cooking it at their leisure instead of waiting for their regular meals. The tool that gave them this freedom was the Guigoz aluminum can. The 20 cm-high (8 inches) and 8 cm in diameter (3 inches) can was made in Holland to store powder milk. It was larger than a Nestle can and turned out to be the most precious appliance in the reeducation camp. It was light and could be easily carried around or hidden away. It served as a container and was large enough to hold a little more than one meal. A few prisoners were ingenious enough to insert two pieces of wire for handles in case they needed to use the can as a cooking pot. Soon every single inmate tried to get one of these convenient cans.

The prisoner could store his twice-daily meal in the can and eat it later at his leisure. He could also keep food that had been scavenged in the field during daytime. "A fistful of greens grabbed from the wilderness, some wormy potatoes picked in the fields, a few grains of rice gleaned from the ground ... a snake killed on the way to work"[57] ... or whatever edible were dropped into the can to be furtively or leisurely cooked later. The can became the inmate's lifeline: a meal was readily available whenever he wanted it and thus he did not have to worry about having hunger pains at night. He soon became so attached to it that he could be seen "living in mute isolation hugging his Guigoz can." The following verses described that close relationship:

> When I was a soldier
> My gun was my wife
> When I was in the camp
> My wife was my Guigoz can...
> She was tiny and cute
> A faithful wife...
> ...Formerly a mother from Holland
> She brought her milk to newborn babies
> Today on the road to reeducation camp
> She followed me to hard labor
> Like a shadow behind a man
> Like a foot linked to a leg...

IX. Starvation

...One evening
The cruel bo doi
Spied on her and took her prisoner
Along with many of her friends.
I was found guilty of cooking.
Then the crude hands of the bo doi
Stripped her of her silvery coat
Eviscerated her,
Crushed her with his sandals,
Abruptly ending a beautiful life
Then tossed her in the dumpster...
...O Guigoz can
So tiny and so cute
A faithful wife...
...How much I missed thee...[58]

Every night in the camps, the inmates were lectured about the classless society with no exploitation of man by man. They were told that outside the camp, people had a good life and were enjoying the socialist society. But once the class was over, instead of following the concept of socialist collectivism, each inmate rapidly returned to his room to cook himself something to eat. He was thus ushered into the "new socialist life not with collectivism but with Guigoz-canism: an unwholesome individualism spawned in an environment of black despair as a counter to the morbid collectivism enforced by the communists."[59]

Once released home, the former inmate was surprised to see that everyone outside the camp was also using a Guigoz can to store food for lunch before going to work. There was a lot of red rice, vegetables, but no meat. Life had become so hard in the late seventies that everyone had to fight in order to survive. He then realized that "the whole country had turned into a huge prison camp where all inmates were doomed by hunger and misery to fight and squabble over each meal."[60]

He also noticed that while all cans were equal in capacity, their contents varied greatly. He learned the lesson the hard way. One day at a construction camp, the man in charge of heating the Guigoz cans for the board of overseers at a construction site fell and spilled all the cans. The hungry eyes of the workers were surprised to see the spilled contents: a thin layer of rice substitute on top, a thicker layer of white rice, and the rest was just meat and fish. In a poor society, only the top comrades, the director, the political commissar, the engineer, and the manager could afford such a fancy meal. On the other hand, the poor people subsisted only on rice and vegetables.

To paraphrase Lenin, "Tell me what you hide in your Guigoz can — I'll tell you what class you belong to in the classless society."[61]

Tuong[62] philosophically concluded: "Under communism, people must renounce the wish and desire to live happy and fulfilled. The one endeavor left for everybody is to hustle and eke out a livelihood less wretched than that of his or her neighbor."

Executions, Tortures, and Confinements

Documentations about tortures, confinements, and executions abounded in the literature about the camps. Any former camp detainee had either witnessed or suffered from one form of torture or another: some were exposed to rain, immersed in cold water or forced to live in unhygienic conditions; others were struck, beaten, kicked, or chained or tied to others; some were put in solitary confinement, or forced to endure mock execution; others nearly drowned, were sleep deprived, forced to do hard labor, and so on.[1] If higher authorities did not order them, they at least condoned them by looking the other way. They did nothing to stop or minimize these activities. They also did not investigate nor discipline the wrongdoers. At most, a brutal *bo doi* could be taken off duty for a few weeks or months only to be later returned to his former post where he continued to harass or take revenge on the inmates with impunity.

Tortures and Beatings

Torture and cruelty were common in the camps.[2] First, punishments were administered in a random and arbitrary fashion as if the *bo doi* were given *carte blanche* to do whatever they liked in order to control the inmates and keep them in order. There was no uniformity in the sanctions. Second, not only was the guilty inmate punished, but on many occasions the platoon or company also suffered the same fate. Third, sanctions included beatings, solitary or group confinements, shackling or other methods of restraining, as well as withdrawal of food. Each camp seemed to have invented its own method of torture or confinement. There were about as many ways to confine or torture an inmate as the jailers could think of. Fourth, the duration of a sanction was variable and left to the whims of the *bo doi*: a prisoner could be shackled and isolated for a few days, a week, or sometimes longer for a similar infraction. The treatment was, therefore, not uniform but extremely varied. This accounts for the difference in the reporting of treatment at different camps.

Threats and intimidations were common in the camps. One cadre in the A-30 camp gave a 30-minute briefing before and after the daily work in addition to regular instructions. He stated:

> All of you are teachers, engineers, and officers who would have been shot to death at the very beginning if I had been allowed to. Now it is time for you to demonstrate your ability to work; you must work very hard; there is no break time at all. A half-hour for lunch is enough....
>
> Ten straight hours (of work) a day, no more, no less. I will shoot anyone who does not adhere to my rule. Your fate is still in my hands although the party and government have forgiven you. You people have committed crimes in the past; now it is time for you to pay....[3]

For having rebelled against the inmate-leader and informer, all inmates in one company in a northern camp were forced to work in the fields longer than the rest of inmates. They were sent to the fields earlier and came back later than any other group. For punishment, they were ordered to scoop fresh human wastes with their bare hands to be used as fertilizers.[4] They were then denied the use of wood or bamboo sticks to handle the wastes and were not allowed to wash their hands or bathe afterwards. They had to eat and sleep with their dirty and smelly hands. The following day, realizing they would not be allowed to wash their hands on return to the camps, they decided to wipe their hands on leaves or on the ground while heading home. They were shouted at when they started to fall behind. After one week of such treatment, they gave up resistance against the cadre and company leader and were allowed to wash again.

Beatings happened so frequently that they appeared to be the norm. Prisoners were beaten "whenever the guard felt like it"[5] and wherever he had the urge to do so, either inside the camps or in the fields, and often without a good and obvious reason. Guards used anything at their disposal: sticks, whips, or gun butts and in many instances even their own hands or feet. Fairly trivial infractions, such as talking or not getting in line fast enough, could precipitate the beatings. There were cases where prisoners were "brutally beaten because they had stopped to rest"[6] during work or on their way back to the camp or because they were suspected of stealing a few peanuts. One inmate was kicked in the stomach. He "shriveled up like a snail" and was thrown out of the hut into the drenching rain where he stayed until the *bo doi* let him in.[7] Another was kicked in the spleen and died soon after. As detainee missed the roll call at the dispensary of the A-30 camp by a minute. A guard grabbed him, "slapped his face, gave him several punches, whipped him down, and then kicked his chest and abdomen with his combat boots."[8] He remained unconscious on the ground for more than fifteen minutes before being taken to a nearby bed.

One inmate in another camp described the following scenario:

> My hands were bound behind my back and my feet are tied. They beat me twice a day with their bare feet and hands. They kicked me in the head. They beat me until I could not move anymore. They did this before each meal for seven days.[9]

A room made of brick and equipped with a big wooden fetter, shackles and iron-covered sticks was built for reactionary elements in the A-30 camp. Captain Tien who spent two months in that room confided:

> I was forced to lie down on my back with my two legs in the fetter, and my left hand was tied overhead to another shackle hooked to the wall. I ate my only daily meal with my right hand and I was allowed to go out once during the day for about ten minutes. Four times a day, especially at night, I received boot kicks and was beaten with sticks all over my open body, without a cry, as ordered.[10]

Inmates were not only beaten, but also dragged in the dirt, insulted, and spat on. For wearing glasses (a sign of education for the *bo doi*) and despite being a mechanic, one prisoner was labeled as a traitor. The cadre beat him up and had his left thumb tied to the right toe and the right thumb to the left toe all behind his back. He was then dragged in the dirt like an animal. And all the prisoners "lined up, spat on him, and called him traitor."[11] If they did not, they would have been labeled as a "sympathizer to the traitor" and would be dealt with severely. On another occasion, one guard who had never seen people wearing glasses until he came in contact with southern inmates angrily remarked that inmates did not show respect to him when they removed their hats but not their glasses in his presence. He ordered them to remove their glasses. The elderly inmate-leader, who wore glasses because of his astigmatism, had to comply, but by doing that, he was unable to call out and read the names of the people in his company assigned to go to work.[12] The company was thus stuck at the gate for a long time before being allowed to move forward.

Mass beatings took place in one camp. The cadres made twenty-four prisoners beat each other for not having reported an escape. They kept hitting each other until they could not move their hands anymore. They were then sent to the guillotine center and left in the sun for a whole day. When the escapee was caught, he was immersed in a barrel full of water. The *bo doi* then beat on the lid of the barrel with a stick for a full minute before taking him out. The only thing the escapee knew was blood was "coming out of his eyes, nose, ears, and mouth."[13]

Besides the regular shackles, inmates' toes or feet could be tied together with ropes. These restraints were cheap and available in any camp. They could cut blood circulation or erode the skin over a period of time causing infections, bony exposures, and limb loss. The *bo doi* were expert in the art of torture and had invented numerous torture-positions:

1. The Honda: With the prisoner's hands and feet tied together, he was hung and beaten.
2. The Auto: The prisoner was tied "butterfly style," with thumbs tied together behind his back. One arm was put over the shoulder and the other pulled around the trunk of the body.
3. The Airplane: In case of the single airplane, the prisoner's left wrist was tied to his right ankle behind his back. In the double airplane, the left wrist was tied to the right ankle and the right wrist is tied to the left ankle. In these two positions, the inmate could only lie on his side. He could also be tied to a pole, standing or lying down, or sitting on concrete for various periods of time. As a variant of this form of treatment, the thumb was tied to the great toe.

Inmates released after such a treatment were often unable to walk.[14]

Women inmates shared the same fate as men. Being either former military personnel or government officials, they were jailed in special camps and also beaten.[15] They slept on the ground in many camps without covers or mosquito nets.

Priests were especially targeted because they were believed to be anti-communists. They were thought to have bad influence on the inmates and, therefore, were held in isolation away from other groups. Four priests died in one camp after a year and a half of incarceration.[16] Four other Catholic priests were confined in a special room in the A-30 camp. Meals were brought to them twice daily and the door of the room was opened only during mealtime. No one was allowed to have contact with the priests.[17]

Confinement

Rules were strict. Any infraction, even the smallest, was dealt with harshly usually by flogging, withdrawal of food, or isolation. One prisoner was confined to a two by two by four foot cage for simply buying noodles from one of the guards.[18] Another prisoner had to kneel at the camp gate under the bright sunlight the whole day for saying hello to his friend.[19] A physician prisoner who was caught trespassing the boundary of two camps was beaten, flogged and left unconscious in the sun for a whole day. His wife who happened to visit him that day argued against the severe treatment. She was jailed on the spot for "subversive language" despite the fact that she did not express any political view. In another camp, prisoners were left standing for an hour in the dark so they would be bitten by mosquitoes while listening to the *bo doi*'s invectives and threats.[20]

If a prisoner offended a guard, he was first disciplined then shipped away to a special camp, usually to the Katum camp. If he stood up to the guards, he was sent to the "discipline house" (conex) where he was chained, starved and isolated for weeks or months in a row. Three or more inmates could be chained at the ankles in the same conex at the same time. One respected Vietnamese sculptor was kept in the discipline house for "more than eight months."[21] The simple fact that he survived the ordeal was simply a miracle.

The places of confinement could be an empty well,[22] a "discipline cell,"[23] a disciplinary cage,[24] a four by two by two foot bamboo "tiger cage,"[25] a "guillotine center,"[26] a conex container,[27] or even ditches dug around the perimeter of the camp.[28] Whatever was available in the camps could be used to build a torture chamber.

Since an empty well was a fixture in many camps, it was conveniently used as a jail: the guards just dropped a ladder, forced the inmate to go down into the well and simply pulled up the ladder. The inmate was fed and allowed to relieve himself once a day, but otherwise was left in the well until the sentence was completed. The discipline cell, a smaller version of the well, was a "square hole measuring two by two yards and was three yards deep. The hole had a foot and a half of water in it. There were a lot of mosquitoes."[29] There, prisoners fell prey to mosquitoes, which bit and kept them awake all night. They could not even rest unless they wanted to get wet or sit down in the cold dirty water.

The *bo doi* were also expert in building tiger cages as they had experience with this form of treatment during the war. The disciplinary cell was a two by four by three yard bamboo cage, which could house a maximum of six prisoners. In the middle of the cage ran a bar with three holes on each side allowing each of the six prisoners to have one foot locked.[30] The smaller "tiger cage," depending upon its size, was used for isolation of one or at most two inmates.

Other prisoners were sent to the "guillotine center," an open area in the courtyard where they had their right thumb tied to their left great toe and their left thumb to their right great toe behind their backs. They were then left in that position all day long under the bright sun or all night long in the dark to become prey to blood sucking mosquitoes. After being treated in this manner, they were dead the next morning with their "face sunken, pale as a banana leaf from blood loss."[31]

Conex containers were hollow metal containers used for transporting goods or military hardware overseas. They were relics of past American intervention in Vietnam. They had been discarded in a corner of the camps and became the famous jailhouses of the communists. They were free and required minimal maintenance. The *bo doi* drilled holes and ran pipes through the conex. Prisoners who challenged the camp system or were found to be rebellious were shackled to the pipes with handcuffs behind their backs.[32] The absence of air vents in these steel containers rendered the atmosphere suffocating. When the tropical sun shone on the conex, the temperature heated up and the conex became an oven. The severe heat during daytime dehydrated the prisoners, causing heat stroke with subsequent mental confusion and disorientation. In some camps, they were kept awake all night by an electric light that came on after sunset while in others they just lay in total darkness. As they were constantly locked in the conex, they had to relieve themselves in improvised containers. They were given meals once a day, but were sometimes too ill or too weak to consume them. Therefore, not too many inmates survived a lengthy stay in the conex.

Captain Ben Cai stayed in total darkness in such a conex for over a month as there was no light inside his box. He was fed once a day and allowed to relieve himself once a day. He was thirsty as a result of the heat, and then was starved by the limited daily food rations. He was taken out for interrogations at anytime of the day but especially at night when his physical and mental resistances were at their lowest level. Then they threw him into a cell of an old jail built by the French and left him to rot there for a year.[33]

In the Ben Gia camp, inmates were confined in ditches, called "living graves," dug around the perimeter of the camp, but visible from the watchtower. The ditch was seven to eight feet long but narrow and camouflaged by bushes and shrubs. Inmates could sit but not lie down in it. They were fed a bowl of rice and water once a day.[34] They had no contact with anyone except those who fed them. Many became malnourished or died as the result of this treatment.

X. Executions, Tortures, and Confinements

Summary Executions

Many executions were made on the spot without due process while others were just bureaucratic formalities. In other situations, the accused was a priori guilty and the commander was simply there to read the verdict and witness the execution.

As one inmate fought back after he was caught escaping from a camp, the soldiers simply "[bayonetted] him right through the mouth to the back of his neck."[35] On another occasion, a few guards became "jealous of those who had received bribes" from two prisoners and "threatened to call for an investigation. To get rid of the evidence, the bribe-takers terminated their victims"[36] and set it up to look like the prisoners had tried to escape.

When prisoners became rowdy during a meeting in one camp, the "feared and fawned upon chief of the labor camp, a very clever and cruel person" had no qualms about pulling out his gun, "pointing it at the middle of the prisoner's head and pulling the trigger."[37] The sudden execution of a random prisoner immediately reestablished order in the camp. No one wanted to be the next person to be shot.

Executions were part of the deal in other camps as well. At the Minh Luong camp, forty-four prisoners were waiting for the execution call at one time. Twice a week, loudspeakers blared the names of the convicted (without any trial), then "an account of offenses against the country, a conviction, and a death sentence — never a defense or a last rite." All the crimes enumerated were the same for all prisoners who were led to the forest. Eleven pistol shots. Then it was over. This was typical communist expediency. One prisoner in the camp murmured, "No laws, no reasons, no mercy."[38] This simple and ruthless process explained why there usually was no any open dissention under a communist regime. Neither was there an openly reported blood bath since all these executions were done in the middle of the jungle and out of view of the media. With little or no trace left of the executions and without any documentation, the government could claim it knew nothing of such executions.

Random shooting was also reported. In one camp around 5 P.M., ten inmates were called out and told to go to work. They were led away and shot dead. As this became more typical, the inmates realized they would be shot if they were called to work in the afternoon. In another camp, a deranged *bo doi* used to shoot, without obvious reason, inmates who went to the bathroom.[39] When the camp director found out about these incidents, instead of punishing him, he just sent him to another camp.

One night in January 1976, a lieutenant inmate cut the camp wires like a sapper, got out of the camp, put on a *bo doi* uniform he got from a bribe, and walked away. A guard caught him because he did not know the password. He was brought back to the camp, tied to a pole, gagged, and shot to death the following morning in front of many prisoners.[40] Nguyen Ngan witnessed two similar executions at Trang Lon camp. Major Ho and Second Lieutenant Loi were shot to death by firing squad while trying to escape on September 13, 1975.[41] In another camp, three young officers were sent out to cut wood. They attempted to escape but were caught. The next morning, all three were sentenced to death by firing squad. One ARVN colonel's nephew-in-law, Lieutenant Chien, was shot and killed while attempting to escape from the Hoc Mon camp.[42] Two inmates who attempted to run away from the A-30 camp were shot to death while any detainee who "made a silent protest or complaint about the dictatorial policy in camp would face the firing squad."[43]

In a Bu Gia Map camp, prisoners were tricked into escaping by rumors spread by the cadre.[44] They were ambushed and three of them were wounded first then shot to death as suggested by the presence of multiple bullets in their heads.[45] Since they had tried to escape, they were not even given wooden coffins for burial.

In another camp, three prisoners who were caught trying to escape were executed in March 1976.[46] At the Suoi Mau Camp, Ben Cai recounted the story of two prisoners who attempted to escape. A mine blew one up killing the first man who crawled through the fence and the other was shot to death right on the spot.[47]

Nguyen Manh Con, a writer, was shot at Xuyen Moc camp for having gone on strike in an attempt to gain his freedom. Nguyen Xu Dich, retired lieutenant colonel, was shot to death at Vuon Dao camp after having been incarcerated in a dark cell for four months and then held in a conex for two months.[48] There were probably many more executions that were not reported.

In the Dinh Thanh camp in central Vietnam, more than 200 prisoners were taken away, then bound together in groups of nine. They were marched away in the middle of the night. Two and a half hours later, the "prisoners were slaughtered by fire from rifles and submachine guns."[49] The valley was declared off limits to everyone. Relatives noticing the smell of decomposed bodies and the sight of swirling vultures above the area came in and found their loved ones still tied together all shot in the face.

A former ARVN militiaman who did not report to camp lived under the Cau Dai Bridge. One day, he saw 30 prisoners shackled together with massive angle irons. They were marched to the bridge and then toppled into the river where they instantaneously drowned.[50]

> The extreme cruelty and barbarity of these killings were part of the communists' plan to terrorize the population. Beheading, stabbing, denial of

proper burial—such practices, reminiscent of those of ancient emperors, were no more lethal than others, but they did serve to outrage and humiliate the victims' families. When the communists, as they sometimes did, beheaded the corpses of those they had just massacred, they knew that any relative who came by for the bodies would view such a death as particularly shameful, and that the memory of it would remain with those families for generations.[51]

"Extra judicial [without minimal guarantee of due process of law] execution is the most extreme and irreversible form of repression."[52] This form of sham trial and execution was fairly common right after the fall of Saigon. It was a form of communist revenge against their former enemies and represented the "bloodbath" many westerners were talking about.

First, the accused had no legal protection and no rights to appeal. Minimal or sometimes no investigation was needed because the official had the final say. If he felt that the act was wrong, it was wrong. No one could argue against it. He made the law and also executed it. Therefore, abuses of the law were common and frequent. Second, the tribunal was composed of people who had no legal experience, such as the military management committees or the people's court. Third, charges were usually vague and flimsy. People were urged to come forward and denounce any "wicked element" of the community. Anyone who refused to come forward could himself be accused of conspiring against the state and the people, being anti-revolutionary, or collaborating with the accused. And in order to protect himself, a person unintentionally or under pressure was forced to make false accusations. Since the nature of "wickedness" was not defined or based on any legal ruling (the communists were also good at leaving many subjects vague and indefinable), it was left to the local official or cadre, who usually did not even have a high school education or legal experience, to define it any way he desired. Any government official could come and requisition anyone's house or belonging. If the owner did not give in, he could be labeled as "anti-revolutionary" or an enemy of the society, and therefore, could be shot or sent to the NEZ. Application of the law was very arbitrary and flawed since there was no standard legal ruling and no clearly defined laws.

Lastly, the penalty was usually harsh especially for trivial accusations compared to international laws. The accused were usually starved, beaten and tortured first in order to extract forced confessions that would simplify and legitimize the process. They bore violent scars, were worn out, malnourished, and dressed in torn and bloody outfits. Many of the accused were half dead when time came for the execution that was swift and irrevocable.

On one occasion, in front of the temple at Phuoc Hung, 18 of 25 people accused for unspecified charges were condemned to death. The communists "knifed them in the neck, cut the windpipe and jerked the head of the victim back in a very professional manner."[53]

Higher levels of government had not only condoned but also approved this type of execution. Le Duc Tho on May 15, 1975, stated, "We must quickly stabilize the people's lives, maintain public order and security, and resolutely punish counterrevolutionary elements."[54] The biggest problem was that without a good legal system and due process, anyone who worked for the Saigon regime or simply made a disparaging remark about the Hanoi regime could be labeled as counterrevolutionary.

Desbarats found that "two thirds of the executions occurred in 1975 and 1976" (after the takeover of Saigon) happened mostly in Saigon and in the Mekong Delta, and involved high ranking officials. A Berkeley group of human rights researchers had estimated the number of political killings to be "65,000 after Hanoi took over Saigon."[55] This was based on statistical analyses and computations of one million people going through reeducation camps. But since Nguyen Co Thach in 1985 made the statement that close to "two and a half million people" went to concentration camps, the number of extra judicial executions had been revised to about 100,000 people.[56] Metzner put the number at 250,000.[57]

Since many of these executions were done illegally, attempts to cover up these acts explained why many prisoners still remained unaccounted for. Their bodies and belongings were never returned to their families. In Vietnam, a place where people believed in proper burial ceremonies to allow the deceased's souls to peacefully leave this world and move onto the "other-world" (*the gioi ben kia*), many families were still wondering where the remains of their loved ones were located and whether they had a proper burial ceremony. If not, their spirits might be wandering hopelessly and aimlessly somewhere between this world and the other-world without hope for final deliverance. As some American families were still looking for their MIA's (Missing in Action), many South Vietnamese families were anxiously awaiting news of their loved ones who had vanished without a trace after being transported to the camps. They were tortured by the fact that their husbands, fathers, or brothers were still unaccounted for almost three decades following their incarceration.

XI

Thought Reform

This was the harrowing picture of these bamboo gulags that were located throughout this war-battered land from the north to the south. The vanquished were trucked off to these remote, malaria-infested camps like a "consignment of pigs to the market."[1] They were neither charged nor sentenced. They were never allowed to defend themselves or speak on their behalf. They were separated from their families, thrown into camps, and subjected to daily brainwash.

They were not regular criminals, but political detainees or more accurately "prisoners of conscience"[2] whose goals and dreams were to defend their free country and to live under a democracy where human rights were respected. They were dumped into concentration camps similar to the Mathausen Nazi camps of the years 1933–40[3] where they suffered from overwork, underfeeding, lack of medical treatment, and severe punishment.

Their rights as prisoners of war were not respected. They fared worse than American POWs for unlike the latter, there was no government or institution that would take up their cause. Reeducation camps thus became "experimental models for unethical psychological abuses." Its characteristic was detainment without sentence or indication of parole.[4] "Thought reform" was used to alter the inmates' reactions and feelings during this incarceration period. And they were kept in jails until the Hanoi government made the ultimate decision to release them.

Cai Tao Tu Tuong (Thought Reform)

This *cai tao* (to be made over) program had the following goals: 1) eliminating individual and capitalist thoughts 2) learning the Marxist-Leninist theory 3) becoming a new socialist man through self-criticism, and 4) acknowledging of own faults and repayment of debt.

First, *cai tao* for the communists did not have the poetic significance the word implied. It was a frightening experience: it meant a radical thought change, especially for the South Vietnamese who were used to a capitalist (free) way of thinking. Before 1975, they each thought the way they liked. Being a South Vietnamese was almost synonymous with being a free thinker. This was exemplified by the fact that under the Thieu regime, there were at one time more than 30 different political parties vying for positions in the South Vietnamese Congress.

Cai tao was designed to force the individual to give up his freethinking process, to unlearn everything he had learned since childhood, and to "reform his thoughts" along Marxist-Leninist lines. He was forced to follow and think the party's way, for no longer was he allowed to think for himself. From that moment onward, the party did all the thinking for him, as he just became a mere automaton: the free individual had ceased to exist. And this change was forced on him and it had to be assimilated on the spot. Before April 30, 1975, he could think whatever he wanted, but after that date, there was only the communist way. The process not only killed the individual's imagination, initiative, spontaneity, and progress, but also rendered him uniform, dull, and submissive.

Second, the inmates were indoctrinated daily with the following topics[5] over a ten-week period:

1. Glorious history of the Labor Party (communist).
2. Labor is GLORIOUS.
3. South Vietnamese are lackeys of the imperialist U.S. government and the CIA.
4. American defeat.
5. South Vietnamese were guilty of betrayal, and therefore, owed a blood debt.
6. Socialism and communism.
7. New economic zones (NEZ).

Before and after each meeting, inmates were taught to sing revolutionary songs and clap their hands in time to the music to reinforce their new thoughts. Inmates then sat in rows on the ground or on self-made benches and were forced to listen to presentations given by political cadres. Since the latter were not literate, they had to learn their speeches by heart. They then talked nonstop for two hours with revolutionary fervor and unabashed conviction. They recited their lessons without even thinking about what they were saying. Some cadres, however, knowing they faced an educated audience appeared timid and hesitant. As for the inmates, they soon became bored and tired of the propaganda, but had to sit there and listen.

After each session, inmates were divided into small groups of four to seven to discuss the topic of the day. An evaluation was held during which they had to answer questions from the lecturer. Those who could not were placed in isolation and given half-ration meals. Topics were taught over and over and soon the prisoners became brainwashed. Sitting in the dark, away from their families, feeling abandoned by their generals and their government, isolated from their friends, surrounded by antennas, threatened with a cut in their daily food ration if they did not listen, and stripped of their dignity, these poor souls had no choice but to force themselves to learn. They were taught everything in the socialist world was the best, that the Soviet Union was first in everything[6] and that Soviet cosmonauts had landed in the moon before the Americans. Lecturers insisted, "Oxen and cows in the rich and powerful Cuba weighed 50 tons each," to which an inmate whispered to another, "its genitalia must be heavier than one ton."[7]

The fact they were forced to listen to this nonsense irritated many of them. They could not comprehend how this army of unschooled soldiers and cadres could have defeated them. But no one dared argue with or laugh at the cadres or even express his personal thoughts or disagreements. They had to suppress their feelings, and those who could not balance their own beliefs with communist teachings either became cynical or crazy over a period of time. It was particularly difficult for an ARVN soldier who firmly believed in freedom and had fought for it for ten to twenty years to suddenly switch camp and start praising the communist world. A rare few, who could not resolve this dilemma, stood up and openly contradicted the lecturer. They were rapidly overpowered, beaten in front of the crowd then sent to high security camps. No one ever heard from them again.

Others simply bent their heads and pretended to change heart. But as soon as they were released from the camps, the first thing they did was to plan for an escape out of the country either legally or illegally. They simply felt they could not live under such an oppressive regime. The diaspora of the South Vietnamese in the late seventies and eighties bore witness to their distrust and disagreement with the communist regime. Many more would have escaped if they just would have had the means to do it.

The only remark that made sense was that before 1968 the Viet Cong had better weaponry than the ARVN. The enemy had automatic AK-47s when the ARVN soldiers were still using single-shot M1 rifles, and the Viet Cong used AK50s when the latter started switching to automatic M-16s. The enemy's T-54 tanks and their improved versions were in use before the US M-48 tanks saw action.[8]

Third, inmates had to reassess in writing their former actions against the new teachings of the revolution. If killing a Viet Cong during the war was justified from Saigon's perspective, it was a crime when viewed from the revolution side. They had to criticize themselves for all their past errors (i.e., serving in the puppet army, making war against the communists, etc.) in writing and then in front of the other inmates. After they had criticized themselves, other inmates took turns to criticize them. And the sessions went on and on, and many new "crimes" were found and debated. Not to be outdone by another inmate, each individual would accuse himself of many more crimes in order to be regarded as "progressive" or a new socialist man who deserved the forgiveness of the party. But as he tried hard to become a "progressive" man, he realized that being progressive was apparently not good enough because his sentence was neither commuted nor his workload cut back. As he noticed that the communists did not use a rational approach to anything, he became discouraged. Mental torture was too hard to bear. Depression soon set in. He became aware that he might never get out of the camps alive. This explains why many inmates committed suicide — two or three a day in one camp.[9]

Confined to the camps, dispirited, disillusioned, starved and overworked, many slowly imbibed the lessons, acknowledging that they in fact had "betrayed the revolution" and were guilty of charges drummed up by the cadres.[10] A few in the end "believed" in the revolution and asked the party for forgiveness. They in turn became staunch communist supporters and some went on to even denounce their own parents.

Fourth, having acknowledged their errors, they had to pay for them. Reeducation meant "years of hard manual labor on starvation rations" with constant punishment. It was a painful experience to be insulted and repeatedly beaten for no valid reason especially by someone younger and less schooled than you. Worse, most inmates remembered "an all consuming and degrading hunger, maneuvering for a chance to drink the water their food had been cooked in, trying to catch birds and rats, scrambling to sneak a mouthful of wild berries ... to supplement their meager rations."[11] It was a shameful and humiliating experience to feel hungry all the time and to behave like non-humans trying to hunt for food at every moment of the day.[12]

Cai tao worked not only on the mind, but also on the body. If the instruction was designed to change the mind of the inmates, the physical labor, the bodily punishments, and the starvation rations weakened the body so much that the inmate offered minimal resistance to the Marxist-Leninist instruction.

Short-term Effects on the Prisoners

By its ruthlessness, *cai tao* broke many prisoners physically and mentally. "The power of their masters was total and totally arbitrary."[13] Hundreds of thousands of people died as a consequence of mistreatment, malnutrition, starvation and diseases,[14] and hundreds of thousands more bore permanent physical and psychological scars that would hound them the rest of their lives. These scars forever widened the chasm between oppressors and oppressed, between northerners and southerners, and left minimal room for reconciliation. Whatever faint admiration a few might have for the steeliness of the socialist army, which had defeated them, soon evaporated and was replaced by a loathsome disdain or even hatred for the communists.

Under a combination of pressure, hardship, hunger, torture, or simple inhumanity, many inmates simply broke down. In the A-30 camp, one detainee, a former teacher, ate his own excrement[15] while Lieutenant Colonel Hoa, a former base commander at the Da Nang Air Base, hanged himself in an open hut in July 1978.[16] Depression,[17] infectious diseases, and starvation were the most common killers in the camps. Prisoners became psychologically disturbed during their long, senseless, and rough stay in the camps.[18] The more free time they got, the more depressed they became. "Idleness encouraged depressing thoughts as well as reminded us of our imprisonment, humiliation, and hopelessness."[19]

The world as they knew it had tumbled down before their eyes. They did not know what and whom to believe anymore. They could not understand how their country could collapse under North Vietnamese attacks. They could not figure out why the United States with all its might had not done anything to save them. They could not envision how they landed in jails in their own land. South Vietnam was their country and they had fought hard for twenty-one years to protect their land. Their own leaders had betrayed them and left the country long before the fall of Saigon. They were then forced to pay for "commitments" made to their former country with blood, tears and own lives. They were enslaved in their own land forced to do hard labor and to study communism.

The majority, however, did not want to have anything to do with communism. They just listened, silently waiting for the time they would be free of this oppressive environment. They would not accept defeat lying down.[20] They knew very well that the lessons were just propaganda that contradicted the realities they were facing daily. They saw right before their eyes the behavior of the teenaged *bo doi* who mistreated young as well as old inmates daily, while Asian culture had always stressed respect for elderly people. The prisoners were thus caught between the virtuous teachings of Confucius and the lies of the communist teachings. If they went along with their conscience, they surely would be punished and starved to death. If they did away with their conscience in order to survive, they would be remorseful for the rest of their lives.

Some bravely challenged their wardens, stuck with their beliefs and met their fate. ARVN Lieutenant Commander Than, then a detainee, "overly criticized the arbitrary policy of the camp, the misuse of the prisoners' manpower, and the mistreatment from the cadres and guards, as well as the different forms of corruption." He challenged the camp commander to shoot him in front of the central hall on many occasions. He finally went before the firing squad after his failed attempt to escape from the camp.[21] Others simply decided to cooperate with their wardens and became their most infamous informers.

For many, the more they studied, the more they felt "discriminated against by the new regime and discarded by the new society"[22] with which they had nothing in common. To accept communist teachings would be to renege on the concept of freedom they had fought for for so long. Since they had tasted some form of freedom under the Thieu-Diem regimes, they definitely wanted more freedom and not less, which the new society obviously would not allow. They then realized that it would be difficult for them to fit smoothly back into the new autocratic society. They concluded that after their release from the camps, they and their families would most likely be discarded or relegated to new economic zones.[23] And that thought intensified their worries and deepened their depression.

Communism for the prisoners was a foreign theory imported into Vietnam by Uncle Ho. It went against all the basic Confucian concepts the South Vietnamese had been taught all their life. While Confucius taught them about virtue, co-existence, truthfulness and respect of life. The *bo doi*, on the other hand, during the long reeducation sessions, emphasized lying and spying on each other for the "good of the socialist society." Communism as an ideology is "inconsistent with being Vietnamese. While communism is collective, the Vietnamese are highly individualistic" in nature.[24] They also believed in private property and ownership and civil rights while communists strongly favored state communes, restriction of freedom, and a centralized party-led power. Therefore, there was "a fatal inconsistency between communist beliefs and Vietnamese culture."

Long Term Effects

The reeducation treatment was so arbitrary, unjust, and irresponsible that it rendered the captives "utterly cynical, concerned only with getting out of Vietnam or with the survival of themselves and their families in a society from which they were completely alienated."[25]

Instead of bringing freedom, justice, equality, or economic riches to Vietnam, the goals of the new socialist society were to tear down a democratic society and to further impoverish the people in order to establish a socialist state. Communism created an new class of arrogant leaders who used their positions to enrich themselves at the expense of the people and to secure their stronghold.

Indeed Ho Chi Minh had never envisioned a true democracy for Vietnam. His aim was "the advance of communism throughout the world.... His understanding of the need for democracy and legality were limited, not to say greatly defective."[26]

It was thus not surprising to see the establishment of reeducation camps after the fall of Saigon. After touring many camps at Thu Duc, Long Thanh, Quang Trung, Baria in the south, and Tuyen Quang in the north, Bui Tin, a colonel and party member, realized the "harshness" of the reeducation policy. The whole program was "hopeless." In the south, he saw "numerous young women who had served in the Saigon army having to sleep on a cement floor covered only with a thin sheet of plastic without any mat or mosquito net." In the north, "many detainees were in their seventies ... the food was unsubstantial and lacked nutrients, and this caused blindness and weakness." He shivered when he thought "about the hundred of camps set up along Stalinist lines after 1975."[27]

In other camps, this harsh treatment did not break the inmates will to survive and their yearning to live in freedom; it made them thrive. In the darkness of their jails, north and south, they had ample time to compare the difference between a socialist world where human rights were trampled and a free southern society where freedom, despite its drawbacks, was the norm. They certainly could not live in a socialist society where labor was forced on people, where food and medicine were not available, where education was denied to all its citizens, where leaders were despotic and backward, and where revenge was engrained in the minds of the leaders. Instead of a government looking for peace, reconciliation, and healing, they faced a close-minded, harsh regime bent on revenge. This attitude alienated the majority of the prisoners to the point that they could not expect to find acceptance in their own land after release from concentration camps. They were marked for life. Their only goal after the ordeal was to escape.

This led to an exodus of more than a million people who would rather brave violent storms on un-seaworthy vessels, cruel pirates, thirst, starvation and death at sea than suffer under a socialist regime. On the other hand, under the Orderly Departure Program, in 1980 "over 130,000 Vietnamese had legally emigrated while 670,000 applications for departure had been submitted."[28] Nguyen Chi Thien,[29] a dissident who was jailed by the communists on and off for more than twenty years wrote:

> If Uncle and the Party, let's suppose,
> allowed free movement in and out,
> Grandfather's Marx paradise
> Would soon become the wilds where monkeys roam.

XII

Hard Labor and Poor Medical Care

Besides starving, torturing, executing, confining, and attempting to reform the inmates' thoughts, the communists neither cared about their safety nor their physical health. They overworked them and fed them meals with minimal nutritious values. They then sent them to a certain death by ordering them to defuse the mines left over from the war without giving them any training or protection. They did not even provide adequate medical coverage in case they became injured or got sick. Physicians, X-ray machines and even simple medications like anti-diarrhea pills and antibiotics were not available in any camp.

Hard Labor

Inmates worked nine hours a day followed by three hours of political lecture or thought reform at night and one hour of self-criticism, at least during the first three years of incarceration (1975–78). A ten hour day was the norm at the A-30 camp.[1] The routine camp schedule was as follows:

530 hours: Communist National Anthem
700–1200 hours: Work
1200–1300 hours: Lunch
1300–1700 hours: Work
1700–1800 hours: Dinner

1800–2100 hours: Political indoctrination
2100–2200 hours: Self-criticism
2200 hours: Sleep

Work consisted of completing any task they were assigned: tearing down a runway, clearing landmines, cutting down trees, plough and cultivating land, digging irrigation canals, and so on. In one camp on Phu Quoc island in January 1976, inmates were ordered to cut thatch to make huts for the cadres. After cutting and bundling the thatch, they had to carry the bundles on their shoulders back to the camps. The lack of padding between the bundles and their bare shoulders caused their shoulders to become red and sore. The other task was to pick up firewood in a forest three miles away and carry it back to the camp. After a while, not only their shoulders hurt, but their legs also ached. Sometimes, they were led around and around and the three-mile trip became an agonizing five-mile walk under a torrid sun. Later, they were sent to hoe furrows on the farms until their hands blistered or later became callused.[2] In another camp in July 1975, inmates were forced to tear down an American-built runway with their bare hands and wooden sticks. They were of course unsuccessful no matter how hard they labored; they, however, were constantly criticized for being lazy.

If they did not work hard enough, they were either yelled at or beaten right in front of the cadres or camp commander who just stood there and watched.[3] Under such an intense pressure to perform, inmates forced themselves to work harder. As they worked harder, they realized they were in for a long run and had to perform hard labor for an untold number of years. At that simple thought, many became frightened and depressed.

At the KaTum camp, they were ordered to cut down trees around the camps to prevent any escape. The work was exhausting, not only because of the humidity and the heat, but also because their only tools were worn out bayonets. The other mindless job was to move rocks from one place to another or to break them in smaller units. Each team was given a quota: to cut down a number of trees or to move so many rocks a week. Those who did not meet their quotas had to work on Sunday to complete their assignment and many ended up working seven days a week for a long time. Those who failed again were placed on half-ration or assigned to dump waste containers.

At the Song Mao camp, built by the Australians during the war, inmates were ordered to dig a canal to divert the water from the local river to the camp. The canal was designed to go through a virgin forest and had to be dug out of hard rock. They were given dynamite to blast the rock but no remote control, just a fuse. The job was particularly dangerous. If they could

XII. HARD LABOR AND POOR MEDICAL CARE

not get away in time, the explosion of rocks killed or injured many people at a time. And while digging the canal, many in the camp contracted malaria.[4] At night, they slept on a mat with a plastic sheet under it on the sandy ground. The wet and cold weather exacerbated their backache and rheumatism.

At the Da Ban camp, they had to move big trunks of precious wood from the forest to the camp after cutting them down. Each was about two to three feet in diameter and fifteen feet long. It had to be carried from the work site to the river and then singly rafted back to the camp. The work was so dangerous that inmates had nightmares when they were assigned to the job. The mountain river could be sixty feet wide and the current very swift and dangerous in certain areas. The water was cold and full of leeches and green-striped bloodsuckers. If they were not careful enough, they could easily be crushed by the trunks, stabbed by its branches, or drifted by the current against big stones lining the course of the river.[5]

In many camps, their first task was to build housing for themselves and the cadres from scratch with their bare hands, as tools were not widely available. The worst working areas turned out to be the malaria-infested forests of the highlands (Bu Gia Map, Buu Loi, Da Ban) and the western provinces of South Vietnam (KaTum) where most inmates contracted the disease. In building their dwellings, they dug their own graves. If they did not die from work exhaustion or malnutrition, they eventually died of malaria. Under these working conditions, tuberculosis, which was endemic in Vietnam, spread like wild fire and many inmates died of advanced TB, as no drugs were available at the dispensary.

Their next task was to cut down trees and prepare the land for cultivation. At camp D1 in the southern highlands, 660 inmates were transported to the middle of a forest and ordered to clear 250 acres of forests over one month period while building their lodging at the same time. Each was only given a hoe and a bush knife for this type of work.[6] Since the highland soil was poor and rocky, all they could do was to plant cassava to supplement their rations. The work was hard and intensive. They had to till the soil by pulling the plough all day long either in the sweltering southern or the frigid northern weather. There were no buffaloes to pull the plough. Winter months in the north were the hardest ones to bear as inmates were not accustomed to cold temperatures. They had to plough in the icy and muddy ground.

They labored six days a week. Sunday was a day of rest for many, but it was a catch-up day for others who did not meet their quotas. In other camps, everyone had to perform "socialist labor" every other Sunday. Although this extra work was designed to extol the virtues of physical labor, for the already overworked and tired inmates, it represented the ultimate punishment. They were ordered to work in the fields shoeless to prevent them from escaping, but for many it was simply a form of humiliation.[7] The act made the inmates feel less worthy or humane than their masters.

Although physical labor was hard, the combination of beating, torture, indoctrination, humiliation, and hunger made life in the camps much harder to tolerate. The real purpose of reeducation according to one inmate was: *amoindir, avilir, affamer, aneantir*, to diminish, to debase, to starve, and to annihilate the individual.[8] The goal was simply to destroy the capitalist and individualistic mind of the South Vietnamese and to replace it with a new socialist mind.

Nguyen Chi Thien who had been jailed by the Ho Chi Minh's regime for writing anticommunist poems had some of his works, written in northern reeducation camps, smuggled out of the country. He personally experienced the terror and oppression in the camps. In the poem reproduced below, he tried to convey the true picture of Ho's regime:

> From ape to man, millions of years gone by,
> From man to ape, how many years?
> Mankind, please come and visit
> The concentration camps in the hearts of the thickest jungles!
> Naked prisoners, taking baths together in herds,
> Living in ill-smelling darkness with lice and mosquitoes,
> Fighting each other for a piece of manioc or sweet potato,
> Chained, shot, dragged, slit up at will by their captors,
> Beaten up and thrown away for the rats to gnaw at their breath!
> This kind of ape is not fast but very slow in action, indeed
> Quite different from that of remote prehistory.
> They are hungry, they are thin as toothpicks,
> And yet they produce resources for the nation all year long
> Mankind, please come and visit!
> Nguyen Chi Thien[9]

Mine Clearing

The *bo doi* simply did not care about the inmates' well being or rights. No job was deemed off limits for these inmates. They were sent to the camps to work and expected to do anything they were ordered to do. The most dangerous job was cleaning up mines left over from the war. "Mine clearing is a practice expressly forbidden by the Geneva Convention, the universally accepted standard of humane treatment of POW."[10] But the communist government skirted this regulation by stating that the prisoners were "volunteers" not POWs and that they themselves had planted the mines, and therefore, had to remove them. And without any special instructions or training, the prisoners, whether they were military personnel (but not exactly specialists in the field of defusing mines) or lay people such as teachers, students, bureaucrats and so on, were herded to minefields surrounding the camps.[11]

In some camps, they were given rudimentary instructions about handling the mines while in others they were left to themselves to figure out the details of the procedure. They did not even have mine detectors to help them in their search. The guards took them to the designated area and retreated to a remote corner to watch them work. The procedures were far from being uniform and differed greatly among the various camps. At the Minh Luong camp, prisoners cleared two separate parallel paths fifteen yards apart in a minefield. Ropes were tied to opposite ends of a log. A team of three men on each side pulled on the ropes while walking on the cleared paths. They detonated the mines by dragging the log on the ground between them.[12] This crude way of uncovering mines led to many injuries. One inmate blew off his hand while another suffered a wound to the leg. The wardens replaced the log and the two prisoners, and work went on as if nothing had happened.[13]

In other places like at Trang Lon, Hiep Tam and Phu Quoc camps,[14] inmates were down on their knees, huffing, puffing, and sweating heavily due to a combination of anxiety and fear, uncovering and defusing the mines one by one. Captain Ben Cai, who had some knowledge about working with mines, tried to advise the other prisoners about disarming these sensitive mines. His techniques proved helpful. But at the self-criticism session that same evening, he was criticized in front of everyone for being "individualistic" instead of following the cadre's instructions to lift off the mine and carry it to the jungle. He had to plead guilty and agreed to have his food ration cut in half.[15] The next day, inmates followed the cadre's technique and one of them was blown up and a few others got injured.

The thought of dealing with mines not only paralyzed the prisoners, but also rendered them nervous and irritable. For them, handling a mine was like signing their death warrant. Being fearful, they easily lost concentration and, in the process, blew themselves up by stepping in the wrong place or by not being fast enough. Explosions ripped the thin air; dirt, powder, debris and even human flesh blew up into the sky. Nearby prisoners were stunned by the explosion as well as by their injuries. Injured prisoners were brought back to the camps that had neither medications nor medical facility to treat them. They lay on the ground in agonizing pain[16] with no bandages to cover their wounds and no medications to soothe the pain. Nature soon took its course as the injured died rapidly from massive bleeding[17] while their friends watched in despair.

The disfigured bodies were brought to a corner of the camp for burial. Since there were no shovels, the other prisoners had to dig the ground with the "sharp ends of the wood and [scoop] the loose dirt with their hands."[18] Most graves were thus very shallow: about two to three feet deep. The bodies were rapidly covered with a heap of dirt. The families, of course, were never notified of prisoners' deaths and were never told the whole truth. Nguyen Ngoc Thuan, one of the survivors of the re-education camps, cried out for his unlucky friend in the following verses:

> A mountain's pebbly soil is hard to dig:
> Please settle for this shallow grave...
> Your coffin is a ragged mat,
> Your winding sheet a towel that smells...
> A stick of firewood is your tombstone, friend-
> I've carved your name with this dull knife...
> You had your moment in the sun-
> The hero of a hundred battlegrounds.
> But now you've died a prisoner's death
> Unworthy of some birds or beasts.[19]

Lack of Medical Care

The medical needs of the 2.5 millions inmates was completely ignored. There was not even a first-aid kit in most camps. Bandages and antiseptics were nowhere to be found and manpower almost non-existent. Without diagnostic procedures and X-ray, the diagnosis of any illness was mostly guesswork. The only medications available were aspirin and quinine in the southern camps and *xuyen tam lien* in the northern camps. Everything including heart disease, hypertension, headache, flu, and so on, was treated with these medications or with herbs. The treatment of colic was "young buds of guavas," for toothaches kitchen salt, and for colds "crushed garlic to be injected in the nostrils."[20]

The result was predictably tragic: inmates died like flies mostly of curable diseases like malaria, TB, and dysentery. Since there were no medications for dysentery, patients would end up having 20 or 30 bowel movements a day only to die after a few days from dehydration. The picture of the inmate getting in and out of his bed every hour was mind-numbing. "When he could no longer walk, he crawled; when he could no longer crawl, he dirtied his own bed-platform."[21]

Nurses with minimal medical knowledge provided care to inmates. In rare cases when doctors were present, no operating room or medicines were available. Inmates who worked in the forests often sustained cuts, which rapidly became infected. Without antibiotics, infections got worse. Inmates' legs rapidly turned gangrenous, requiring an amputation. The patient was brought inside a mosquito net where the "nurse-surgeon" performed the operation without anesthesia and with a handsaw sterilized only in hot water. Three or four other inmates held the patient down. He cried loudly as no anesthetic was used to numb his pain. He usually fainted early on and the procedure continued as nothing had happened. Often the stumps became infected a few days later, and because of lack of antibiotics, the patient eventually died. Six men in one battalion in a camp died in a similar fashion.[22]

A camp commander was shot in his leg when Khmer soldiers crossing the border into South Vietnam attacked a reeducation camp. This was the beginning of the border wars between the two communist countries: Vietnam and Cambodia. After the attack was repulsed, one inmate was ordered to accompany him to a regional hospital some eighty miles away not in an ambulance or military truck but on a local bus. The commander was later taken to surgery for what was supposed to be a wound debridement. Upon recovering from anesthesia, he was horrified to find his leg was amputated. He could only cry as he realized his military career was over. Even the inmate, who did not know much about surgery, did not think the wound was serious enough to warrant an amputation. At that time, communist nurses staffed all hospitals, replacing the physicians from the Saigon regime who were sent to the reeducation camps. The "nurse-surgeons" had learned this kind of medicine in the jungle by watching someone perform it and then apply it indiscriminately to everyone.[23] If a camp commander had to suffer from marginal medical care, it seems obvious the fate of the inmates was not any better.

In the Long Khanh camp, a university professor was injured during an explosion and underwent a similar amputation without anesthesia and under non-sterile conditions. Even when the wound became infected, the inmate was not transferred to the local hospital, which was located two miles from the camp. The nurse continued to treat him despite the lack of manpower, appropriate facilities, and medications and offered him a second amputation. The frightened inmate committed suicide rather than going through the agonizing procedure once more.[24]

In the South, inmates in the beginning could ask the *bo doi* to buy for them common western medicines (antibiotics, anti-diarrhea agents, vitamins, antiseptics, bandages and so on), which were readily available from pharmacies outside the camp. The *bo doi* made a killing just by providing this service. As rules changed, the families themselves had to buy the medicines and ship them to the inmates, provided they had money. In the north, however, western medicines were not available. In addition, the distance between north and south as well as secrecy and strict regulations prevented rapid communication between inmates and their families. By the time contacts were made, the sick inmate was already dead or had recovered from the disease. As a result, inmates in northern camps suffered and died unnecessarily from common diseases, which could have been easily treated if they had been in the South.

XIII

Defense Mechanisms

What characterizes humans is the mind that houses the intellectual, emotional and spiritual essences of mankind. Thanks to this inner capability, prisoners could devise different defense mechanisms to deal with the oppressive environment. This ability to cope with adversity depended upon the degree of sophistication of the mind of each individual inmate: the higher their emotional or spiritual levels, the stronger their defense mechanisms were.

Defense Mechanisms

For the sake of simplifying the discussion, response to internment can be divided into three categories of low, moderate and high levels of sophistication with the fourth one representing the failure or the inability to cope with adversity.

A. low level
1. collaborate with the *bo doi* and spy on the other prisoners
2. bribe the camp commander or other higher authorities
3. pretend to be stupid

B. moderate level
4. actively resist: escape
5. bear down and do what the jailers said without arguing
6. passively resist
7. share thoughts and try to be helpful

C. high level

8. identify the reality of the situation
9. challenge the situation
10. cope using higher spiritual functions: religion or poetry

D. *failure*
11. have a nervous breakdown
12. commit suicide

At the lowest level, some prisoners simply opted to collaborate and report the other inmates.[1] They became the "antennas" of the *bo doi* and cadres who showered them with various perks and called them "progressives." Some even thought they could get released earlier as a result, but this was not always the case. Final decision about the release rested in the hands of the Hanoi politicians.[2] They were the ones who ordered the incarcerations, executed the programs, and decided who would be freed or remain incarcerated.

No one could assess the damage caused by the antennas, but there was no question many lives were adversely affected by false accusations and reports. As a result of these reports, many inmates were sent to high security camps or to discipline cells, beaten, denied family visits, starved, or kept in camps longer than expected. One colonel who had been very ill for a certain time was placed on the amnesty list for early release. Since an informer denounced him as a CIA agent, he was taken off the list and transferred instead to the Nghe An camp[3] where he was jailed for a few more years.

The "antennas" were not always identified since they worked in utmost secrecy. In some camps, those who were suspected of dealing with the *bo doi* were "beaten up and their (sleeping) places fouled with excrement."[4] For beating an informer and group leader, all the inmates in one company were punished with seven days a week work. They then had to collect human wastes with their bare hands and were not allowed to wash their hands afterwards.[5]

A few inmates bribed the camp commander for a light duty assignment[6] or an early release. This had been reported mostly in southern camps where the commanders had almost total control of the camps. Captain Ben Cai was "allowed" to escape from the Suoi Mau camp because his parents had bribed higher authorities.[7] At the scheduled date and time, the *bo doi* happened to fall asleep while watching prisoners do work outside the camp. Ben Cai got away without any problem. The plot must have involved a lot of people: the commander, the major who "worked out" the deal with the family, and the *bo doi*. The bribe, therefore, must have been big. Since everything was staged as an escape, if Ben Cai had been caught afterwards, he would have been severely beaten or killed.

Those who could not afford to bribe could pretend to be stupid. The *bo doi* usually left these people alone because they did not feel threatened by them:

XIII. Defense Mechanisms 161

> I meet with people who are stupid, so stupid that
> their lives are quiet
> As the lives of the priests, and I am one among the
> stupid.
> I have become half priest, half prisoner.
> Anonymous

At the moderate level, one form of active resistance was an escape attempt. There were multiple solo attempted escapes from every camp around the country, but most of the escapees were recaptured either immediately or a few days later. Despite the fact that most who were caught escaping were shot to death or severely punished, inmates continued to try their luck out of desperation. Escapes seemed to be more successful in the south than in the north because they either knew the southern countryside well or were helped and sheltered by the local population. The fact that northerners were given rewards to help catch the escapees explained the lack of successful escape attempts in the north. There was only one reported case of successful group escape by 11 inmates who overpowered the guards and escaped to the forest. They were all recaptured a week later. The leader was sentenced to life in prison, the second-in-command to twenty years in jail and two others were killed.

There was also one major revolt in the history of the camps reported involving the takeover of the Ham Tan camp by inmates in 1980 for three or four days. The government rapidly recaptured the camp with the help of tanks and the army. The leaders of the uprising were sent to the infamous Chi Hoa jail and the remaining inmates to a disciplinary camp.[8] To be successful, resistance had to be organized and the inmates were too dispirited and too frightened by the prospect of communist revenge to mount an effective uprising. Even if they had been successful, there would have been no place for them to hide outside the camp. The fact that there even was an uprising in a communist jail was astounding. It not only suggested the brutality of the camps, but also the bravery of these inmates who risked everything to have their voices heard.

The majority of inmates, however, accepted their fate in silence and did their best to conform to regulations. They knew who the masters were and felt no need to antagonize them. These were people who played "it safe." They did not like the communists but had to go along with them in order to escape corporal punishment and win back their freedom. When asked if he had committed any faults towards the revolution, one detainee simply answered:

> If what you have said is true, then I am guilty.
> My fault is as the leaves in the forest.
> They are so many you cannot count them.[9]

Another inmate's strategy was, "Do not talk, do not hear, do not see, do not read. What they said went in one ear and out the other."[10]

Other inmates got involved in passive resistance. Too weak to confront their wardens face to face, they expressed their dissatisfaction by disobeying orders or by sabotaging their own work. There were, however, no overt leaders because they were skeptical and distrustful of one another.[11] They did not know who among them was the antenna who would turn them over to the camp authorities.

They tried to work as little as possible. In one camp, they took turns taking as many bathroom breaks as they could. When told to collect forty kilos of sweet potatoes a day, they brought in half that amount in sweet potatoes and the other half in dirt or rocks. The *bo doi* soon found out about the trick and ordered them to dump the contents of the bags on the ground before weighing them. Inmates also damaged the teeth of saws by hitting them against steel or stone. Sometimes they threw away a pick or agricultural tool. When they were ordered to cut a 4 by 0.25 meter tree, they would cut a crooked one so it could not be used. To build a meetinghouse, inmates had to fit bamboo dowels into beams made of logs since nails were not available. They sabotaged their work by using broken or weak bamboo for the dowels. As a result, the house collapsed after a big wind blew over it, killing a cadre and a *bo doi*.[12]

Communist songs and slogans had been changed and circulated widely in South Vietnam as a form of passive resistance. The motto, "The more we work, the more we are rewarded," was changed to, "They give us less to eat, so we must work less; no reward, no work."[13] The following song was also changed:[14]

> Last night I dreamed of meeting Uncle Ho
> His beard was long, his hair was gray.
> I kissed him tenderly on both cheeks...
> The song was changed to:
> Last night I dreamed of meeting a lost wallet
> In the wallet I found 4400 dong.
> I was so happy I ran and showed it to Uncle Ho
> He smiled at me. "Let's split," he said.

"The Great Victory" song:
It's just as if Uncle Ho were present
On the joyful day of the Great Victory

> His words are now a glorious victory
> After thirty years of struggle for independence and freedom...
> The song was changed to:
> It's just as if Uncle Ho were being kept
> In the Cho Quan Mental Hospital
> His words, after thirty years of Struggle,
> Have made the whole country crazy....

A few prisoners were lucky to find friends with whom they could share their travails and pains, thus, decreasing their stress level and loneliness. This was a difficult task because they were moved frequently from camp to camp and even from building to building as part of the *bo doi*'s plan to disrupt potential associations or escapes and minimize rebellions. From 1978 onward, with some relaxation of the regulations, prisoners were able to gather and discuss a little more freely than before,[15] although they still remained under the watchful eyes of the antennas.

A few inmates, selected as camp assistants, were resourceful as well as helpful to others. They not only increased their self worth, but they were also excused from heavy work. For his knowledge of music, Nguyen Ngan was able to gather a few prisoners, form a band, and give performances during the Tet festival. Out of wood, tin, telephone wires and empty AK-47 or M-16 cartridges, they were able to make a guitar, the pegs of which were made of cartridges. The musical performances were widely appreciated by all the inmates, who felt lonely and lost in the camps.

At the highest level, a few carried on with their routine braving insults, punishments, despair, hopelessness, and hunger. The whole process required a lot of courage, determination, and pure will. To survive in the camps, these prisoners must have a strong inner force and belief that sooner or later they would be released. It is not that they did not have their moments of doubt, weakness, or fear. On the contrary, they lived in constant tension and conflict under an oppressive regime. The torture environment hovered over their heads as long as they remained in the camps. But, they bravely accepted their ordeal (from three to twenty-two years of jail) and made the best of it. Badaracco called these people the realists or quiet leaders. They had the moral conviction that they were right and would sooner or later be vindicated. They, however, did not see the fight for survival as an epic struggle for human rights. Their approach was more personal and subtle, although it could "sound calculating and narrow. It lacked grandeur and wouldn't even register on an inspiration meter."[16]

Others continued to brave and challenge the *bo doi*. These inmates acted alone according to their conscience and bravely accepted the consequences of their behavior. They were relentlessly beaten,[17] dumped into a conex for a prolonged period of time or even shot. A former Tank Corps Lieutenant continued to read his self-criticism essay in front of everyone even after suffering from ten brainwashing sessions. Proud of his past military experience, he enumerated all the medals he had earned and the number of Vietcong he had killed during the war.[18] He finally exhausted the *bo doi*'s patience and was taken away. He was never heard from again. Another inmate would starve for 55 days in a row to prove he could challenge the communists.[19] He succeeded but at a heavy price: he became markedly dehydrated, physically wasted and almost died in the end. There was also the case of the sculptor Nguyen Thanh Thu who simply accepted the consequences of having designed the *Tiet Thuong* sculpture. He ended up spending 22 months in a conex and barely made it out alive (chapter 18). Another inmate got upset when he saw a *bo doi* use a South Vietnamese flag as a dust rag. He took the flag away from him and ended up fist-fighting him. Brought to trial before the camp commander, he argued the flag stood for South Vietnamese national honor and that many people had died for it. He also insisted the flag was there when the South Vietnamese chased the French out of the country in 1956. The inmate was found guilty and shot to death.[20] In the A-30 camp, ARVN Lieutenant Commander Than overtly criticized the arbitrary policy of the camp, the misuse of the prisoners' manpower, and the mistreatment from the cadres and the guards. He challenged the camp commander to shoot him in public. He finally faced the firing squad in a nearby rice field.[21]

Many in this group were the true believers in freedom. They refused until the end to bow under communist oppression. They were the modern examples of Nguyen Hue, an 18th century Vietnamese general who not only refused to surrender to the Chinese who had invaded Vietnam, but also booted them out of the country. Their actions not only uplifted the spirit of the rest of the inmates, but also defined the true value of a man and a soldier. They can be viewed as heroes who sacrificed themselves for the cause of freedom. There was no doubt that life in the camps would have been meaningless and dull without their presence. They deserve our admiration.

The inmates not only needed heroes to uplift their spirit, but also realists to guide them during their lengthy incarceration and fight for freedom. Alas there were not too many of them because of the successfully repressive strategy of the *bo doi*. The latter not only controlled the inmates with the help of the antennas, they also moved them around systematically from one company to another and from one camp to the next one, preventing them congregating or planning anything.

A few resorted to yoga or religion to make peace with themselves, although this was rarely reported in the literature. But there was no question

XIII. Defense Mechanisms

many inmates did some soul searching during their lengthy and agonizing incarceration in the camp. Some Catholics were even able to celebrate clandestine masses[22] since priests and nuns were jailed in the same camps.

On the other end of the spectrum, there were cases of people who were unable to adapt to incarceration. Some, unable to resolve their moral conflicts with the communist ideology, either had nervous breakdowns or killed themselves. The most vivid example was that of Tran Van Tuyen, who as a South Vietnamese senator and a member of the third force used his political immunity to challenge President Thieu in the early seventies. This brash lawyer thought he could do the same thing with the communists. However, while the Thieu regime at least cared about legality and world opinion, the communists did not bother about anything. They simply ignored and berated him in a southern camp before sending him to the Ha Tay camp for reeducation. Unable to challenge the communist system, Tuyen broke down, paced alone in the camp yard and finally committed suicide in a northern camp (chapter 8).

Time spent in the concentration camps could be compared to that spent in a boiler room. Inmates were stressed to the maximum while trying to survive the senseless incarceration, starvation, hard work, and oppressive environment. Depression was a common occurrence in the camps. The *bo doi* treated the detainees in a most inhumane manner one week then pumped up their hopes the following week by promising a relaxation of the camp rules or an early release. And the cycle would repeat over and over again.

This emotional roller coaster and the erratic and senseless treatment by the *bo doi* severely affected the morale of the inmates. Nothing in the end really made any sense to them. They became confused and could not understand why rule-obeying and hard-working inmates were detained in the camps longer than less deserving inmates who were released earlier. They also could not understand why they were singled out for a certain punishment. Some tried to escape the harsh reality of the camps by running away only to be caught and shot to death. Others had a nervous breakdown. One inmate ate his own excrement at the A-30 camp, a second challenged the guards to shoot him and was shot to death as a consequence, while another built a pyre and burned himself to death. One colonel attempted suicide twice by overdosing of anti-malarial medications.[23]

Reactions to the incarceration and the repressive system in the camps thus varied depending on the maturity and judgment of the inmates. Although many were despondent and scared at the thought of never getting out of the camps alive, those who took a mature and philosophical approach to the incarceration fared better than those who did not. Although the latter were not released any sooner than the others, they were physically and psychologically better positioned to handle the stress of the camps as well as the post-reeducation ordeal.

The best examples were the colonels or generals who were incarcerated in northern camps without any hope of being released. They just hung on until one day out of the blues, some twelve or twenty years after they were first incarcerated, they too were given their exit papers. It is not hard to imagine their joy when they were finally allowed to leave the camps for good, which they had thought all along would be their last resting places. That joy, however, was short lived and tempered by the fact that they had aged a lot, were physically malnourished and morally battered during their long years in the camps. They were just shadows from the past and were thought to be harmless even by Hanoi's paranoid standards.

XIV

Well-Known Prisoners

No one, not even priests, teachers, military personnel, politicians, engineers, and so on, was immune from poor treatment. Any detainee was a priori guilty and had to be reformed.

Disinformation

When released inmates brought to the outside world the news of the reeducation camps, international opinions raised questions with Hanoi about the mistreatment of prisoners. The CPV members rapidly proceeded to deflect worldwide opinion and churned up the propaganda machine with the intent to misinform the world. In some areas, inmates were forced to build a nice camp adjacent to an established one. The new camp was well designed and planted with trees along with a "meeting hall for the cinema or theater, tennis court, a volleyball court. Afterward the communists brought many units of their soldiers to live in." To fool international opinion, they brought western journalists in to visit the "ideal" camp and not the shacks the real prisoners lived in.[1]

A few selected western journalists were given a guide tour of a showcase camp in the north (Ha Tay). Tiziano Terzani wrote:

> The detention cells are clean; flowers bloom in the garden; the food is excellent; the guards smile.... In a classroom, a prisoner's orchestra plays a waltz. Twenty-four former generals, colonels, and judges of the Supreme Court under the Thieu regime rise up and applaud when the camp commander examines them in turn and explains that one or the other man

has made great progress but that, alas, there are still inmates who have not yet written a full and frank report on their misdeeds.[2]

If the Nazis were a model of efficiency that killed with method and efficiency (gas chambers), the communists on the other hand killed with a calculated indifference. Human beings were just numbers and did not mean much for them. By design and careful planning, they just let starvation, diseases, and nature take care of prisoners. "That way the stain of bloodbath was faded, and attrition was attributed to natural hardships.... Life was hard for all — so no one should be surprised if soft imperialist lackeys succumbed to Spartan conditions."[3]

The handful of visitors from communist countries had not been able to observe what actually occurred behind these bamboo gulags. According to Col. Chinh, the Ha Tay camp was kept in good condition because it was used as a model camp for foreign visitors. Prior to a French delegation's visit in 1979, the place was spruced up. Half of the prisoners were sent away to make it appear less crowded than it was. The kitchen was cleaned and better food was prepared. In the clinics, two milk containers were displayed, but prisoners were not allowed to drink it.[4] Any infraction was severely punished. Sick inmates were taken elsewhere, libraries were filled with books and magazines, sewers were made functional, and only the cadres were allowed to answer the visitors' questions.[5]

In 1980, a delegation from Amnesty International came to visit the camp. Visitors became skeptical at the sight of inmates playing music, volleyball, and reading books. They did not fail to notice the presence of 75 sleeping mats and towels in rooms that supposedly held only 40 prisoners and enquired about the discrepancy. After the visit was over, a reporter came back to the camp claiming to have forgotten his camera. He noticed a group of inmates returning from work after being sent away during the delegation visit.[6]

Nguyen Cong Hoan, a one-time communist legislator, wrote after he fled the country in 1977:

> Taking advantage of my position as a congressman and also of my acquaintance with lieutenant Colonel Xuan, a camp commander, I asked permission to visit his camp. However, I was allowed to come and observe only some showcase areas and to make contact with just a few prisoners who, I know for sure, were not stupid as to tell me the truth about their prison — that is, if they did not want to die.
>
> The party leaders themselves have told me they are very proud of their talent for deceiving world opinion. "We have been worse than Pol Pot," they joke, "but the outside world knows nothing."[7]

Well-Known Prisoners

The SRV never revealed the true number of detainees despite many requests from various organizations and countries. Their answers changed from, "We don't know," or, "A few detainees," to, "They all have been released and returned to their families." Terzani, an Italian reporter who remained in Saigon until June 1975 suggested that more than 250,000 had been sent to the camps.

A former ARVN field officer put the number of detainees at 343,000 by the end of 1975.[8] They included 13,000 elected officials and civil servants, 20,000 nationalist party members, 60,000 members of Rural Corps, 70,000 ARVN and police officers, 150,000 NCOs from political warfare, intelligence, police field forces, and 30,000 others (anticommunist leaders, students, writers, etc.). This did not include those who were taken prisoners in the central highlands and on highway 7B.

By 1978, an official mentioned 50,000 people who had committed "major crimes," mostly high-level officials or military personnel in the Saigon government, were still interned in the camps while the rest had been released. The number of detainees was then estimated at more than one million[9] until Nguyen Co Thach, a Hanoi official, mentioned in 1985 the whopping number of two-and-a-half million people having to go through the camps.[10] This process turned out to be the most systematic repression known in the world. It also meant all males above age eighteen had suffered incarceration and almost no one had escaped Hanoi's justice.

We should include to this list the 250,000 *chieu hoi* (Viet Cong who had defected to the Saigon government under the Open Arms program during the war). After the war, they were tracked down, confined at local jails and sent back to their former units. There, they had to confess their crimes, recount all their services to the enemy and listen to the stories of those who had died or suffered on their account.[11] Their fates are not known although few were ever seen again.

Many high-ranking officers were detained up to eighteen or nineteen years without trial or charges. They were just left to rot in jails. The proximity of the northern camps to Hanoi suggested the seriousness of their "crimes" in the view of the northerners. The most important prisoners were held in Hoa Lo prison in Hanoi itself. General Bui Van Nhu of the police and Colonel Tran Van Thang, former director of ARVN military security, were among this group.[12]

Generals Le Minh Dao, commander of the 18th division, and Ly Tong Ba, commander of the 25th division who fought the North Vietnamese until the last minute, were jailed in northern camps for 17 and 13 years respectively.[13] General Dao almost lost his eyesight during this period.

Many former South Vietnamese notables were also jailed in northern camps. Premier Nguyen Van Loc, Minister Cao Van Tuong, Senator Nguyen Thon Do, and Ambassador Nguyen Xuan Phong, head of the South Vietnamese delegation at the Paris Peace Conference, were interned at Nam Ha camp, 45 miles south of Hanoi.[14]

Hoang Xuan Tuu, senator (1967–1973) and vice president of South Vietnamese Senate, died at Nam Ha camp in 1980, after five years of incarceration. Senator Tran The Minh (1967–1973) died at Nam Ha camp in 1977 of poisoning. His relatives had to bribe the officials to have his body exhumed and brought back to Saigon for evaluation and burial.[15] The cemetery of the Nam Ha camp contained the graves of thousands of "puppet soldiers and civil servants."

Tran Van Tuyen, attorney and former president of the Saigon Bar Association, was interned at various camps in the north. He was a former Saigon congressman and leader of one of the opposition groups. He could not stand being jailed in the camps and committed suicide in 1976 by slashing his wrists.[16]

Father Hoang Quynh, former leader of the Catholic anti-communist forces at the Bui Chu-Phat Diem dioceses in the North before 1954, was tortured to death at Chi Hoa prison in Saigon in early 1977.[17] Dr Phan Huy Quat, a physician and former South Vietnamese prime minister, was left to die in the Chi Hoa prison.[18]

Mai Van An, justice of the GVN Supreme Court, was detained at Nam Ha, where his health was deteriorating rapidly as of 1982.[19] Many others had died in the camps during this period from wear and tear, mistreatment, malnutrition, and diseases.

South Vietnamese Supreme Court Justice Tran Khuong Trinh spent eight years in reeducation camp[20] and a lady justice spent a similar period of incarceration before being allowed to emigrate to France.

Venerable Thich Thien Minh, Buddhist monk of the An Quang Church, was one of the Buddhist leaders calling for immediate cessation of U.S. bombing in the north during the war. He died in Ham Tan Z-30D reeducation camp most likely after a long period of torture and mistreatment by the communist government.[21]

Archbishop Francois X. Nguyen Van Thuan, the nephew of President Ngo Dinh Diem, was appointed to the post of deputy archbishop of Saigon six days before the fall of the city. The Hanoi government refused to accept the nomination and placed Thuan under house arrest. He was transferred to the north where he spent almost 13 years in reeducation camp.[22] He was then allowed out of the country to become president of the Pontifical Council for Justice and Peace. On Feb 21, 2001, he was elevated to cardinal, the first and only one in Vietnam.[23]

Father Nguyen Cong Doan was sentenced to 12 years in 1983 on a charge of conspiracy to overthrow the government. Father Tran Dinh Thu and an aide were condemned to life in prison on the charge of "undermining the revolution and public security."[24]

The noted journalist Nguyen Tu was incarcerated in various camps for 13 years. He now lives in France. The poet Thanh Tam Tuyen spent five years in reeducation camps and now lives in Minnesota. The poet Tran Da Tu was jailed for 12 years until international protest led to his release. His wife, poet Nha Ca, had to spend many years in a reeducation camp.[25] Thao Truong, the "gentle writer who had begged the ideologues on both sides not to teach the children to hate was jailed for 15 years." He was arrested, released, and rearrested several times. As of 1990, he was back in prison.

Dr. Nguyen Dan Que, a Saigon endocrinologist, spent ten years in jail without trial from 1978 to 1988 during which he endured torture, beatings, and was chained in solitary confinement. An intensive international campaign by Amnesty International led to his release from jail. He became the first person in Vietnam to join the human rights organization Amnesty International in 1990.

In 1991, he was tried for "subversive activities" (appeal for political pluralism and respect for human rights) and given a twenty-year sentence on the new charges,[26] which he served at Xuan Loc labor camp. In 1994, he received the Congressional Human Rights Foundation's Raoul Wallenberg award in absentia. For four consecutive years, he was nominated for the Nobel Peace Prize by the bipartisan board of U.S. Members of Congress. Since his release in 1998, he remained under house arrest and was unable to work because his license had been revoked.

It is also interesting to note that quite a few prisoners died unexpectedly in the prison camps: whether this was premeditated or coincidental is still unknown. Col. Chung Van Bong, province chief of Vinh Binh and Dinh Tuong provinces, died in a reeducation camp.[27] Between 1978 and 1983, a few colonels died suddenly in northern camps. Col. Phan Duy Quan of the 9th infantry division died in his sleep. Col. Nguyen Van Hoc of military insurgency died while eating dinner, as did Col. Nguyen Van Ton and Col. Ton That Dinh. Col. Phan Khac Tuan of the Bureau of Military Training died from eating spoiled food.[28]

According to one source, although the majority of inmates were released between 1978 and 1987, the Hanoi government kept 127 inmates they considered the most dangerous because they were suspected of being CIA agents. They were finally released in 1993, eighteen years after their incarceration. Besides, there were forty to fifty former officers sentenced as political prisoners who were still being held. One intelligence officer was sentenced to twenty-one years in the camps for having escaped from the camps for a few days. He ended up spending a total of twenty-one years in the camps, one of the longest terms endured by any former political prisoner.[29]

XV

Post-Reeducation Ordeal

Release

The duration of the incarceration was arbitrary as the rules of law were not only non-existent, but also applied in an erratic manner. A private who had joined the ARVN in 1973 was, for unknown reasons, detained in various camps for five years. An old civilian, who had been employed as a guard at a U.S. depot, was considered to be a CIA agent and as a result had to spend five years in the camps.[1] These political prisoners were detained as long as Hanoi desired, so there was no set limit on the length of the incarceration. Detention without due process and sentencing was a violation of human rights.

Inmates were also released from the camps in an unpredictable manner. The process was shrouded as much in secrecy as well as mystery to prevent them from plotting their escape or communicating with their families. Many factors seemed to have affected early releases, including bribes, connections with the government, severe illnesses, and intervention of foreign governments.

Reports of bribe-induced releases appeared to be more common in southern than northern camps: southern camp commanders could either give mitigating explanations about these releases or mask and report them as escapes from camps. The danger in the latter case rested on the "escapee": if he were caught, he had to pay with his own life. The typical example was that of Captain Ben Cai. At the scheduled date, right after lunch time the guard who was watching him work outside the camp dozed off and Ben Cai just walked away from the camp. But he was so afraid of being caught afterwards that he had to live "underground" until he successfully managed to escape Vietnam a few years later. Two teachers at the A-30 camp were released after offering one ounce of gold each in bribes. Another was let go for half an ounce of gold.[2]

A few detainees who had relatives in the Hanoi government were also let go early. As the Vietnam War was a civil war, family members were separated after the 1954 armistice. Some might have remained in the North to work for the Hanoi government while their brothers or nephews went south and fought for the Saigon government. Severe illnesses made some of them eligible for an early release, sparring the government the expense of their burial and deflecting the criticism that the internment in the camps actually caused their deaths.[3] However, this was not always the case as exemplified by the fact that many inmates died unnecessarily in the camps away from their loved ones not only of malnutrition, but also of their untreated medical conditions: heart diseases, cancer, stroke, diabetes, and so on.

The majority of inmates were released following intervention of foreign governments. Many physicians were released in the late seventies as a precondition for French medical aid to Vietnam. A number of high-level ARVN officers were let go in the late eighties as the result of General John Vessey's presence as the president' special emissary in Vietnam between 1987 and 1990 and the subsequent thawing of the relationship between Washington and Hanoi.[4] Others were simply released for economic as well as political reasons to demonstrate the magnanimity of the Hanoi government. While some inmates were released one at a time, others were let go in batches on the occasion of major national communist holidays.

Overall, the release process appeared to be arbitrary and the Hanoi Ministry of Interior, which decided which "puppets" should be released and which ones should be kept in jail, most likely made the ultimate decisions. As a result of the French intervention, although the majority of physicians were released two and a half to three years after their incarceration, many were sent to northern camps and remained there for more than four years.

In some southern camps, hints about an imminent release were spread through the system of antennas prior to major holidays, although no specific names were mentioned in advance. The main purpose was to raise hope in a psychologically depressed population. The inmates after hearing the planted news were all thrilled about the prospect of freedom and behaved extremely well in order not to jeopardize their chance for release. As time went by, they became skeptical about these rumors, as many previous ones had turned out to be false. A few wardens in the southern camps, who were aware in advance of the release list, contacted well-off families of certain prisoners. They told the anxious families that they would put in some good words for the prisoners in exchange for money. A few days after the prisoner's release, they went and collected their bounty.

Prisoners were not notified in advance of their release. When they got in line in the morning to go to work, a few were told to report to the office with their meager belongings. Expecting the worst, they tried to remember what they had done wrong the day before. They also wondered which antenna had reported them the night before, which new sanctions they would receive and where they would be shipped to this time.

To their surprise, they were advised about their release, ordered to fill out a few forms, and told to forget about their "bad experience" otherwise they would be returned to the camps. From that time on, they were allowed no further contact with the rest of the prisoners. They were all stunned and did not know what to say. On one hand, they were genuinely happy to hear about the news, but on the other hand, they just wondered how the memory of all the bad treatment they had endured for years could simply be erased. They wore the stigmata of the camps on their clothing, on their skin and bones as well as in their minds.

They passed through the gates as fast as they could, hoping the *bo doi* would not change their minds at the last minute. A released inmate turned around about 100 yards from the front gates, "knelt down facing the camp and bowed down three times as a sign of getting rid of that hell. He was immediately seized and had to spend six more months in camp."[5]

Released inmates walked or were trucked to the nearest bus or train station if their camps were located in a remote area and given a few *dong* for the trip home. Many had experienced the communists' double talk during their incarceration and would still not believe in their newly found freedom until they were separated from their wardens or when they finally reached home. Only at that time would they let a smile light up their bony faces. They would like to yell and scream for joy but held themselves back in order not to attract undo attention. No one summarized that feeling of freedom better than Kim:

> The worlds inside and outside the camp were separated only by a gate and a fence. They shared the same plants and sun. However the life inside and outside of the camp were as different as the sun and the moon. When I got outside of the camp's gate I felt a great sense of relief. From inside I could see the trees and plants outside, but once I got outside they looked different. Everything seemed more alive and hopeful.[6]

An Apartheid System

On their way home, especially if they came back from the northern camps, they tried to savor their newly found freedom by stopping at any local eatery to taste a bowl of *pho* (Vietnamese beef soup) or their first meal outside the camp. The meal was without a doubt "out of the ordinary" and much better than any meal served in the camps.

But as soon as they reached home, they found a "world turned upside down"[7]: the *bo doi* were the new masters and they, the old ones, became the servants in their own land. The country was impoverished; the overall mood was somber and police were everywhere. Their houses, if they were still theirs, looked old and dilapidated: the paint had faded away from the walls a long time ago and the windows or doors were broken as no one had taken care of them since they left home many years ago. Inside the empty house, a few chairs and a table were the only furniture left. Their wives had sold everything else in order to survive. They felt sad at the sight of poverty they were facing. This was new to them. Their wives who met them in the camps had not told them how things had changed outside the camps. Or they might have hidden the truth in order not to cause unnecessary worry. The hideous face of poverty was saddening and depressing.

The ordeal, however, did not stop when the physically wasted, emotionally broken, and nutritionally malnourished prisoners were released from the camps. As matter of fact, it was just beginning for they would face new, endless, and sometimes insurmountable hurdles: lack of jobs, loss of citizenship and homes, and strict control by the police. They found that, instead of being accepted as "reeducated" members of the society, the new government continued to wage a brutal policy against them. The uniformity of the process throughout the country could only be traced to orders from a centralized office: Hanoi.

Former inmates were confined to an area close to their dwellings and watched closely by local authorities to which they had to report weekly. They could not move freely like other citizens as the police monitored their every move and could inquire about their whereabouts at any time. The local security agent just dropped by unannounced at any time of the day. He used the occasion to ask the former detainee for a pack of cigarettes, a bottle of cough medicine, or a new tire for his motorcycle.[8] The former detainee had to fulfill to these requests for fear of jeopardizing their freedom.

Their voting rights had been revoked a long time ago. But being penniless, they cared less about voting rights than about putting food on the table. In short, they just lived at the margins of a society that not only did not like them, but also watched them like hawks. They felt that tension every day as well as the intrusive and omnipresent watch of the secret police. They soon realized this land where they and their forefathers had lived for many centuries had been systematically "conquered" by greedy northerners. They had become the victims of Ho's revolution. Nowhere had they seen

XV. POST-REEDUCATION ORDEAL

the prospect of freedom and justice. All they had known was servitude and their own decrepit existence bore witness to Ho's farce: the revolution was just another form of colonialism. Having endured the Chinese and the French, they now had to suffer from the communist invasion. Of course, they could not express these feelings freely for they would be immediately sent back to the camps.

Many prisoners had probably lost their home to northerners who simply took over their house and evicted their families. They had to live with their parents or friends, or simply on the streets. They could volunteer to go to a NEZ if they had lost their homes. But the prospect of living in a NEZ was probably worse than living with a relative in the city. They were lucky if they still had a place to go, a roof under which to hide or a family to return to. They were lucky if they did not have to look for their families who were sent somewhere to a far away NEZ or if they could find a job, usually as a farmer or a low-key technician. Others were tricked into signing up for the NEZ. Many signed up, hoping to prove their loyalty to the new regime.

A former ARVN lieutenant, after spending five years in various camps, was sent to live as a "confined man" in a communist hamlet in Kien Giang. Land was confiscated "in the public interest" from its original owners and redistributed equally to each family. The government then provided fertilizer, gas, oil, and insecticides at inflated rates. The new owner's job was to farm and harvest. At the end of the season, he had to pay the government back for oil, gas, and fertilizers in addition to the land taxes. As he could not repay his debt, security agents took and sold his belongings and applied the proceeds towards the family's debts. In the end, everyone worked hard but no one could make a living within this system. One by one, each family found ways to escape from the hamlet.[9] In central Vietnam, the former detainees along with civilians were coerced into volunteering to dig a canal and build a dam under the threat of being sent to the NEZ if they refused.[10]

With their former jobs lost to northerners, many took on menial jobs. They usually subsisted by working as farmers, fishermen, handymen, or factory workers if the jobs were available or as pedicab-drivers using their leg muscles to pedal tourists or civilians around in their tricycles. A former major worked in such a lowly position. During the French filming of *Indochine*, he had been the pedicab-driver for the actress Catherine Deneuve.[11] Many physicians had to work as orderlies in their former hospitals that were now staffed by nurses who had been promoted to physicians due to their long time service to the party. If they were lucky or had some connections, they were allowed to work under the direct supervision of these nurses: government positions were assigned based on allegiance to the party not on merit or qualifications. The returnees not only had to work harder to earn a living, but also to show the authorities that they were "awakened" and contributing to the "new society."

For many, the change from a middle class status to that of a prisoner and then an unwanted or discarded person was painful and traumatic. The loss of self-esteem and "face" was so great that many lived dispirited and disheartened as if "they were snails inside their shells and did not dare go anywhere to meet anyone."[12] They recoiled into themselves, living in a world that they knew well, cherished deeply, and had vanished a long time ago. Many became depressed: their energy and fighting spirit, already low when they left the camps, rapidly withered with time. They did not want to do anything else but *cho ngay chet* (wait for the time to die).

Close observation, weekly reporting to the local authority, loss of citizenship and voting rights, loss of job, and inability to obtain food or medical support from the government further aggravated the disillusion and despair of the former inmates. They felt they were not only discriminated against, but also continually "oppressed" by the communist government. "Those who were involved with the former regime were shunned like lepers."[13] They were the new "untouchables" of the new regime.

The threat of a "forced return to the camps" loomed large in the background if they did not behave according to communist regulations. Again, "regulations" was a misnomer in the SRV; local officials could make any decision they wished, thus subjecting the reeducation returnees to their whims and pleasures. Many inmates were sent back to the camps for trivial reasons: anti-revolutionary stance, refusal to follow orders, etc. This situation had forced many of them to attempt to escape the country in any way possible despite all the potential risks and dangers.

Families

Prisoners' wives during all these long and difficult years of incarceration had to hold menial jobs to support their children. Cash strapped, they had bartered away whatever belongings they had left, including rings, bracelets, furniture, clothing, and other objects of value. Everything had been sold, "including the marble and tile from the floor"[14]; the house stripped of all its furniture and decorum appeared ghostly with an oddly old fashioned table, a few broken chairs, pots and pans. Soon they might have to sell their houses to northerners who came in and scooped up all the good deals. They then had to depart to the NEZ or move in with their friends or relatives.

One could not say enough about the detainees' wives, these brave women who for five, ten or twenty years faithfully waited for their husbands'

XV. Post-Reeducation Ordeal

return, took care of their children, and at the same time became the breadwinners of the families. Many who had never worked outside their homes before were suddenly thrust into a new and hostile society and had to find a way to make money in order to feed their children. They took on whatever jobs were available as seamstresses, teachers, factory workers but they usually earned their living by peddling common things at the markets. A colonel's wife had to return to her former job as a schoolteacher to earn a living. At school, she had to work under the former maintenance lady, who because of her affiliation with the revolution and despite her lack of education had been elevated to the job of headmistress. The colonel's wife also had to attend one-week course of reeducation before being allowed to teach again. As it was a low paying job, she had to work as a seamstress at night to earn extra money.

Some were wise and resourceful while others were not, but all tried their best to survive and care for her children. They then had to save money for the trips to the camps to visit their husbands, to buy them food, and later to nurse them back to health, physically and emotionally. They were the living examples of these Confucian virtues Vietnamese had always cherished and extolled.

As for the few who had strayed, one could trace their errors to the difficulties of the times or the lack of news during this war period. Many inmates, who were not allowed to contact their relatives until years after their incarceration in the northern camps, had probably led some wives to assume their husbands had died either at war or in the camps. Many officers were captured by the communists from January to April 1975, jailed and sent directly to the reeducation camps without ever having the chance to notify home. Unable to wait any longer, a few wives simply forged ahead with their own lives. They either remarried or escaped abroad.

Their children did not recognize the inmates on their return, having grown up away from them for many years. The children made them feel like strangers in their own home. During this period of separation, the children had also been mistreated by the SVR and in turn blamed them for their low social status. Since they were denied education, they could do nothing else but spend their time foraging through garbage dumps to get something to eat while their mothers worked somewhere else. As no one was taking care of them, they had dirty, unkempt hair and ragged clothing. Not only were they uneducated, they also learned bad habits from other street kids like cursing, doping, and stealing. Even if they had had the chance to go to school, they did not learn much because education had become political in orientation. Questions in arithmetic were worded as follows: "If a revolutionary soldier shoots three soldiers from the old regime and five Americans, how many people has he killed?"[15] A whole generation of southern children was thus lost as a result of Hanoi's vindictive policy.

Children were also harassed. If a policeman did not like one of them, he might "make up a reason and take you to jail.... They beat one of my friends even though she was pregnant, and she lost her child,"[16] said Ha Nguyen, a fifteen-year-old girl. The government, which shunned them, classified them according to their parents' past employment history. They were ranked from 1 to 14. Children of deceased communist soldiers (*liet si*) were ranked first. Children of traitors were ranked fourteen and those of southern military officers who had gone to reeducation camps were ranked thirteen.[17] Students from the last two classes could not attend any college, except that of agriculture.

If they were lucky enough to be raised by their grandparents or relatives, they could continue to go to school while their mothers worked hard trying to make ends meet. But many were usually thrown into mainstream society even before finishing school for they had to help their single mothers earn a living. For those who attended school, enrollment became expensive. In this socialist country, parents had to pay tuition in order to put their children in school. Teachers were so poorly paid at that time they had to make money on the side: selling candy and snacks to the students or tutoring them at home.[18] Children whose parents could not pay for the tutoring did not receive enough adequate instruction to move to the upper classes.

Children of civil servants of the former regime were blacklisted and could not enroll in universities even though they had graduated at the top of their classes. If they enrolled at a university under aliases, or forgot to mention that their parents were former ARVN officers, they were immediately expelled from the university once their real identities were discovered. On the other hand, children of *liet si* could apply to any university of their choice and were immediately accepted, even though their grades could be lower than those of other children.[19]

One student, Lien, who was a *liet si*'s daughter, was admitted to medical school with a mark of 8/30 (equivalent to an "F") with 30 being the highest mark for the admission test. Another student, Thu, who was the daughter of an army officer of the former regime scored 25 out of 30 (equivalent to an "A") but was not accepted into medical school. This was after the 1988 *doi moi* (renovation) policy was enforced. The following year, she took the test again, scored 29 out of 30, and was finally accepted for admission. After many years of schooling, Thu, despite being a straight A student, was not allowed to study obstetrics-gynecology, her primary choice. She was forced to specialize in herbal medicine. Lien, the failing *liet si*'s daughter, was allowed to graduate and even study gynecology.[20] It was no wonder students graduating from Vietnamese medical schools during the 1975–1985 period, especially *liet si*'s children, did not perform well when they opened their practices. Word got around the community about the low-scoring graduates, and people who fell ill did not want to go to these physicians for care, but only to those graduating from medical school before 1975.

Discrimination against the southerners still persists today. One former high school teacher of the old regime was able to immigrate to the United States recently. His two children, still living in Vietnam, advised him that one of them was demoted when news of his departure reached the authorities and the other was blacklisted and had no chance to move up the ladder.

Planning to Escape

Stripped of their wealth, belongings, jobs, citizenship, and dignity many former inmates bore resentment against the communists. Since they could not get even with them, they just tried to get out of their ways and looked for ways to escape. After spending two years in reeducation camps and three years working under the communist system, Son Ha realized:

> The communists are snakes of the most venomous kind.... They hide their power like a cat hiding its sharp claws.... They talk softly, but they are in fact experienced ferrets. They are hungry for status, so they try every means to down their opponents. They lust for women, so they force their female subordinates to surrender to them. They are greedy for money, so they look for every means to extract bribes. But their breath is always scented with the perfume of the revolution....[21]

If these former inmates had a choice, they would rather remain in Vietnam and die in the land of their forefathers. They were attached to this land that had been theirs for many decades and the prospect of abandoning it weighted heavily on them. Besides, they were all in their mid-forties to sixties when they got out of the camps. Trying to rebuild their lives anew in a foreign country at that age and with their little education was a challenging if not daunting task. But they certainly could not live forever under this oppressive communist regime where they were shunned and discarded.

They had thought on many occasions, in as well as outside the camps, they had wasted the best years of their lives fighting the communists then being jailed by them. Having lost to their enemies, they now saw no future in their own land. What they hoped to do with the rest of their lives was to give their children a future better than theirs. And the only place they could accomplish this goal was in a foreign land: one that respected their human rights. They felt sad each time they thought about Ho and his followers who had basically denied them the rights to live happily in their own country. It was ironic for them to think that Ho supposedly had stated, "There is nothing more precious than freedom." Yet he denied them the basic freedom he had eagerly sought.

The disenchantment with the communist regime soon led people to organize to a massive escape by boat out of Vietnam, which rapidly saturated the absorption and processing capacities of Southeast Asian countries. As of November 18, 1997, a total of 839,228 Vietnamese asylum seekers were registered by UNHCR in Southeast Asian camps,[22] not including more than 150,000 people who were spirited away to the United States and other countries right after the fall of Saigon. All these refugees came in waves, with two peaks: the first one around April 30, 1975, and the second one in 1979. The latter wave corresponded to a large number of prisoners released in 1978–79 period.

In the beginning, surrounding Asian countries reluctantly accepted the refugees, dumping them in fairly decent camps. But soon they became overwhelmed by the rapid arrival of large numbers of boat people. They closed their borders and their hearts by turning away the boat people, and even towing their boats back to the high seas. They returned refugees back to Vietnam by land through Cambodia or by sea,[23] causing many to be killed by the Khmers and the Vietnamese government. A Comprehensive Plan of Action for Indo-Chinese refugees (CPA) was adopted in June 1989, combined with expanded legal departures from Vietnam, stemmed the tide of clandestine departures. The United States also negotiated an Orderly Departure Program (ODP) whereby those who had spent more than three years in reeducation camps were eligible to apply for residence in the United States. There were, however, more applicants that spots available. Since most physicians were released after two and a half years of incarceration, they were not eligible for the ODP and had to escape by boat.

Former prisoners had to have both the means to escape, and also the will and courage to plot their escape. They had to work to put money aside to buy their way out of the country at a time when work was scare for former inmates. They then had to negotiate the "escape fee" with boat owners. They had to evade the scrutiny of the police, make dangerous trips to the countryside to get on the boats, and risk their lives on rough seas and in crowded refugee camps. All this entailed not only luck, but also a lot of planning and hard work. Since many escapees did not succeed the first time around, they were forced to try and try again if they wanted to get out of the country. A failed attempt not only cost money, but also carried the risk of jail sentence if they were caught. And many former detainees were so physically and mentally "disabled" by the harsh treatment in the reeducation camps that they simply lost the will to fight and resigned to stay back in their native land.

Others who were eligible could not take advantage of the American offer for lack of money or because of family problems: they had to obtain, complete, and submit forms to the Vietnamese government (each step necessitated a bribe) before being considered by the American side. Many thus had to remain in Vietnam, and as a consequence held stored-up anger. A former lieutenant was kept behind because his wife's depression had degenerated into mental illness. Another former political figure who was jailed 14 years in 22 camps was compelled to stay back to care for his ailing mother.[24] There were thus many reasons that could prevent the former detainees from escaping from Vietnam, although the foremost factor was luck. Without it, many had ended up in communists' jails or drowned in the depths of the ocean. It could be said that those who had reached foreign soils were among the luckiest or bravest people in the world. At least that's what they felt at the time.

Post-Reeducation Dysfunction

Many former inmates had "remade" themselves anew or bounced back thanks not only to their own will, but also to their supportive families. They did not want to dwell on the past and on things they could not change. They gathered their strength and went back to work to deflect the close monitoring of communist authorities and to gather necessary skills in order to escape and rebuild a new life somewhere else in the world.

No one, however, could really envision the long-term physical and psychological effects this brutal reeducation system had on the prisoners. After incarceration in the camps came the constant reminder of an oppressive system: "behave or you will go back to the camps." The experience was simply too barbaric and traumatic for a regular person to bear. In many instances, prisoners simply broke down. A few began to behave irrationally in the camps. They started running around, yelling obscenities or muttering incomprehensible words. Many had bouts of depression.[25] Some just withdrew into themselves and died of inanition and starvation. Others became real automatons, losing all interest in life itself: they just tagged along only to disappear later in total obscurity, physically and mentally. Some simply lost their humanity and became a non-entity to be supported by their families. They just starred into the horizon unable to function as a person.

Even after they got out of the camps and successfully landed in western countries, they were still watched by overseas communist agents. With the threat of reprisal against them, they wondered whether to speak out about their camp experiences. While Al Santoli was interviewing a former Vietnamese reeducation camp prisoner somewhere in France, the phone rang. A voice at the other end of the line threatened, "*Ils seront juges et condamnes.*" They would be judged and condemned. This simply meant reprisals would be taken against their families still living in Vietnam.[26] This relentless attack on the prisoners and their families could only come from a well-orchestrated and Machiavellian institution designed to silence opposition and people's aspirations for freedom.

Many prisoners had been observed to be dysfunctional and the degree of dysfunction could be lessened by family support. Some appeared to be bitter and unhappy while others became stressed to the point that they simply crashed no matter how much support they received from their family. Many in this group ended up filing for divorces. As a result the former inmate was unable to care for himself, became homeless, and simply faded away. This condition was simply another form of PTSD (post traumatic stress syndrome). The only difference was that in a repressive third world country, these people were simply ignored and died unknown and unattended.

The majority of former reeducation camp detainees in general suffered from a milder form of dysfunction that was sometimes difficult to diagnose: they either became easily irritable or withdrew into themselves refusing to acknowledge even close friends. Some had bursts of anger, self-doubt or depression and were unable to get over their incarceration and the mistreatment. They were "startled from sleep by a scratch at the door or the singing of the bird. They had nightmares about hearing the reeducation camps' bell summoning them to work," being caught and beaten by the *bo doi* or being held back and not allowed to emigrate.[27] They were especially scared about being sent back to the camps and about the communist secret police in general.

An unpublished report found that among former Vietnamese political prisoners, "51 percent reported to have been beaten, 39 percent reported having been placed in a sack, box, or container, 86 percent had witnessed others being tortured, and 10 percent had experienced mocked executions."[28] A recent study of Vietnamese ex-political detainees revealed they had suffered more torture events (12 vs. 2.6) and higher rates of PTSD (90 percent vs. 79 percent) and depression (49 percent vs. 15 percent) than the comparison group. Individuals in the first group were better educated (12 vs. 8 years) and spent longer time in the military (12.7 vs. 7.5 years) and in reeducation camps (7.8 vs. 0.1 years) than the control group. Although the control group also exhibited some evidence of psychological dysfunction, it is concluded that torture was highly associated with psychiatric morbidity in Vietnamese refugees.[29] PTSD symptoms were most intensely observed during the years following their release from the camps and slowly disappeared although never completely with time.

Others faced different problems. After five to fifteen years of confinement, they returned to an empty nest. Although the majority of the spouses were faithfully waiting for their husbands, the length of the confinement had disastrous effects on some marriages. On his return from the camp, Captain Ben Cai found his wife had eloped with his former driver and even had a child by him.[30] A colonel's wife, unbeknownst to him, divorced him while he was still in the camp, married another person and dumped her daughter to the care of a neighbor. Others realized for the first time their wives and children had been sent to the NEZ and had died there. But the worst nightmare for the former officer was to see his own wife marry a cadre or *bo doi*. Not only had he lost a war, his home, and his freedom, but also his wife to a former enemy. War history was replete with these tragic cases. The experience was extremely traumatic for the person involved.

A few inmates were told their wives had escaped to foreign countries with or without their children. The single mothers had become independent and assertive during these long years: they became employed, raised the children by themselves, and later even sponsored their husbands to the new countries. The husbands who were used to submissive wives in Vietnam became frightened at the sight of a domineering partner and began to experience an inferiority complex. The loss of social and employment status had morally decimated the husbands and the couples eventually split.[31]

The mistreatments, tortures, and hardships in the camps and post-camp period left long lasting, and sometimes permanent scars, on these former inmates. In all cases, the experience forever changed their lives. In spite of all these sufferings, these Vietnamese soldiers and officers were too proud to open up and talk about their personal experiences. "They had been taught to bear their feelings stoically and alone."[32] Therefore, no one knows the extent and the depth of their despair for many had taken their feelings with them to the graves in order not to inconvenience or burden their families. They would slip away, but with panache.

Looking from a different point of view (i.e. the effect of camp hardships on their ability to fight against communism), Dr. Tran Xuan Ninh, a former pediatric surgeon at the Saigon's Children Hospital who spent three years in a reeducation camps, was able to group these former inmates into four categories.[33]

Some prisoners who were neither heroic nor cowardly in the camps, once released behaved differently and "worked diligently and actively to replace the communist regime." They seemed to be transformed by their ordeals and were determined to bring justice and freedom back to Vietnam. They were toughened by the mistreatments and hardships and were now more convinced than ever before about their quest for freedom. For them only freedom could cure all the injustices and bring down communism. They also realized that before 1975, they had lived in a fairly free society compared to the autocratic communist society, but did not value freedom until they lost it.

On the other hand, prisoners who had behaved heroically in the camps had not done anything "remarkably anti-communist" since leaving Vietnam. They were the "heroes of the moment" who could galvanize people on a short notice. They stood up to the challenge and danger. But once these factors had disappeared, they suddenly lost interest in the "cause" itself. Some of them might have become fatigued or wiser under the ordeal, and decided not to waste or risk losing the rest of their lives in future confrontations.

A large number of former reeducation detainees became "withdrawn and unable to cope with their new lives. Many families had been broken up under the strain of PTSD." Yet others were "ambiguous in their stance against communism. Although professing their hatred and fear, they nonetheless returned to travel leisurely in Vietnam." Dr Ninh also noted, "Some who were controlled and converted by communists, were now carrying out their duties as directed by Hanoi."

Overall, it is sad to say the communists had been in some ways successful in their attempts to discredit, discourage and wear down the fighting spirit of half of the population, the southerners, for more than a decade (1975–1985). This, however, came at a price: a total destruction of the economy, an overall impoverishment of the nation, and a deep bitterness and resentment against the communist regime. After finding that the economic situation was getting worse with time, the communists backtracked and began embracing the *doi moi* philosophy (1988), championed by party secretary Nguyen Van Linh. The South Vietnamese, on the other hand, had shown their resilience by immediately embracing the market economy. With the timid opening of the free market, they went back to their business with a vengeance: they marketed, bought, sold, and traded. As a result of their hard work, Saigon again became a vibrant and strong economic center of Vietnam in the late eighties.

The North Vietnamese, however, were also unhappy with their government. After winning the war, the Hanoi government bungled the peace by actively pushing ahead with their socialist agenda and trying to emasculate South Vietnam. Northern veterans coming home from the war did not receive any welcome: "no trumpets, no drums, no music." They felt ignored and discarded not only by the government but also by the people.[34] The war and its "brutality that warps soul and personality"[35] had landed them into depression and induced them to forget the past through drinking. Common people were poorer than before and had to face famine in the late seventies. Rations were cut, and people were fed with imported eastern European cattle feed. The end result was an economic fiasco and nightmare that brought Vietnam to the brink of failure and poverty.

Bao Ninh, a novelist and former North Vietnamese war soldier, astutely noted:

> The victory of the north ... was an attack by the north on the south ... after fifteen years, what we achieved was the poverty of the whole nation. We feel sorry for the southerners who had to become boat people, and for the soldiers of the south who could find no work. We feel sorry for those who spent years in reeducation camps. That is why there is bitterness in the hearts of both sides....[36]

XVI

New Economic Zones

Not content with sending southern military personnel to reeducation camps, Hanoi also decided to relocate civilians to new economic zones, or NEZ. The transfer represented a case of forceful civilian relocation and isolation. It had three main goals: 1) to decrease the overcrowding in major cities, 2) to empty out large sections of towns and cities to make room for North Vietnamese, and 3) to consolidate power and to impose socialism. In many cases, the NEZs were just the civilian equivalent of a reeducation camp.

Goals

The first goal was to decrease overcrowding in large cities. In the 1960s and 1970s, a large number of farmers or villagers were displaced by the war. They suffered at the hands of the Viet Cong (VC) who came to their villages to levy taxes, collect rice and farm products, or take their children away as unwilling recruits for the communist army. The VC, dressed in black pajamas, walked silently and appeared like ghosts in the middle of the night. They operated with speed, brutality, ruthlessness, and in a cold-blooded manner. They forbade villagers to raise dogs so that they could come to the village undetected at any time. Those who disobeyed these orders were dealt with harshly. If villagers did not meet the demands for taxes and recruits, they also suffered innumerable hardships. When the VC randomly shot to death one family member or killed the village representative as a warning, every villager would toe the line.

During the daytime, villagers who were found to pay off or bribe the VC would be dragged to the police station and interrogated on charges of collaborating with the enemy. Caught in this tangled web of instability, fear and mistrust, villagers simply left their houses and fields behind and migrated to bigger cities to place themselves under the protection of the government. As the war went on, the number of villagers who moved to larger cities increased. Having lost their roots, they became unwilling war refugees who tried to make new lives in rapidly growing slums around the cities. They swelled the number of the cities' unemployed and bankrupted South Vietnam's limited assets.

The first thing the communists did after the fall of Saigon was send these former villagers and the unemployed either back to their villages or to the NEZs. In the process, they carted away any groups of citizens who were not to their liking such as teachers, civil servants, and small merchants.

The second goal was to make room for new immigrants from the North. Following the fall of Saigon, the Hanoi government decided to absorb and conquer the South overnight by completely replacing the southern system. They reformed education, policed and administered the government as well as opened new reeducation camps. This required a massive infusion of more than one million northern administrators, policemen, politicians, teachers and so on. The latter in turn required permanent housings or temporary places that were not available on short notice. The simplest way to create vacancies was to move people out of huge sections of towns and cities.[1]

The main goal was to send all experienced, knowledgeable, or educated people of the former South Vietnamese government to the NEZs and replace them with communist supporters. This process consolidated the military invasion by a political and administrative takeover. It stabilized the communist power and gave credibility to the annexation of South Vietnam, while getting rid of potentially dangerous "antirevolutionary" elements. Instead of overtly mass executing "former enemies," the CPV let nature slowly wither its opponents with famine, starvation, hard labor, and disease. The end result was a slow, agonizing but sure death somewhere in the jungles away from the prying eyes of the world. It also created a new uniform socialist society where all citizens were brought down to the lowest denominator: a manual worker without any future or rights. It provided for a communal life where hard labor was the norm and where workers were ruthlessly exploited. It was an environment in which the inhabitants were subjected to the rule of a communist leader who had the power to make or break the worker. This oppressive bureaucratic environment simply represented a civilian form of the reeducation camp.

The economic goal of this transfer appeared to be minimal for a few reasons: 1) the transfer plan was drafted in such a haste that no planning was possible, 2) the relocation sites had minimal or low agricultural value, 3) the displaced people were not seasoned farmers but city dwellers.

Besides this city to countryside relocation in South Vietnam, there was a simultaneous North-to-South program designed to transfer people from the northern Red Delta to the southern central highlands. The Montagnards, living in the hills of the highlands, were in turn transferred to the lowlands.[2]

Inducement and Coercion

In order to move as many city dwellers out of town as possible, women's organizations fanned out through the entire precinct to draw up a list of families qualified for resettlement. Families with a father or son working for the old government or a relative in the "puppet" army were prime targets. They were subjected to a "persuasion" in three stages. During the first stage, a cadre came to each family and encouraged it to volunteer for resettlement. During the second stage, in case of refusal, the family was formally notified it had to leave for the NEZ. Finally, if the family refused to budge, it was forcibly put aboard a truck bound to the wilds but was not allowed to bring along any possessions whatsoever.[3]

At the farewell ceremony, Hoang could only see faces showing "bewilderment, anxiety, grief, despair. They looked like a gang of convicts who would soon be transported to their penal colony for life."(4) Tha, a widow, and her four children were sent to the NEZ. It was not hard to figure out that a widow with four young children could not do a man's work (build a house, plough a field) and take care of her children. She would have been eligible for welfare in the States. Three months later, she had "died leaving four children in the lurch."[4]

To avoid being drafted for the zones, people resorted to various ploys. One woman whose husband was an former army colonel being detained at a reeducation camp, built a pigsty "smack inside her house" and proceeded to raise pigs. She thus became a citizen engaged in "production, not a bourgeois parasite,"[5] thereby avoiding banishment to an NEZ. Another woman allowed her daughter to "lavish her favors on the People Revolutionary Committee, the Party's local branch, the secret police. But they don't have to pay: they are 'family.'"[6] After the takeover of Saigon, communist authorities never ceased to proclaim, "The new society has no room for prostitution and the human dignity of women must be restored in full." But prostitution not only survived, it also thrived thanks to its most faithful customers who turned out to be those "supposed paragons of socialism," political cadres and officers of the People's Army, who had either come back from the jungle to civilized life or left the "great rear of the North" for the South.[7]

In other areas, the communists tricked city dwellers into signing up for the NEZ program. Each volunteer was promised about ten acres of land. A family of five was supposed to get fifty acres. But when they arrived at the NEZ, instead of land, they were told they would be given five or ten points for each working day. The points could then be traded for rice or vegetables. If the government did not have enough rice for trade, the people not only starved, they were also stuck with worthless points. Families having relatives confined in the reeducation camps were also tricked into signing up for the NEZ. They were told their relatives would be sent home earlier if they signed the agreement. Prisoners were urged to sign up for the NEZ with a promise of earlier release.

In certain areas, the communists just cordoned off sections of towns usually at night, and went knocking on doors to tell the tenants to move out.[8] The owners could not do anything but cry. Overnight they lost everything, from their houses to belongings, from the comfort and stability of a home to their jobs, from the security of a large city to the amenities of modern life. Owners were warned not to sell, transfer, or destroy their properties; household necessities and furniture were to be left in place for the benefit of incoming northerners.

Those who refused to move out were threatened with jail sentences or trips to reeducation camps. The *Quan Doi Nhan Dan* (People's Army) reprinted article 13 of the law promulgated by the Hanoi regime on November 10, 1967, which was reactivated in 1976: "Anyone who opposes or sabotages or hinders the plans to serve national defense or creates serious obstacles to the implementation of state policies, laws and plans, will be sentenced life in prison or will be executed."

New Economic Zones (NEZ)

People were then trucked and dropped off at a NEZ that was usually a wooded, malaria infested area to make a new life. The area was a virgin place in the middle of a jungle that had been so far left untouched by civilization. Tall forests thick with underbrush formed the roaming range of wild animals. Ferocious tigers coexisted with elephants, wild buffaloes, snakes, and monkeys. Vicious ants, which could devour an animal carcass within a few days, lurked in the bushes. Malaria-carrying mosquitoes were omnipresent and buzzing around the unprotected new settlers day and night. In one night people were thrown from the coziness and comfort of their houses in a large city into the middle of nowhere, from civilization to a prehistoric time. The reality was overwhelmingly depressing. Their first job was to rapidly set up a few huts to protect themselves from nature as well as from wild animals and insects.

Workers who were disenfranchised of their city homes, belongings, and ways of life were forced to do labor to make a living. It did not matter how much education they had. Teachers or white-collar workers had to do the same manual work as laborers. The slogan of the day was, "Labor is glory."[9] They were assigned to cut down trees, clear the land of bushes, level the ground, plant rice or vegetables, and build their own straw huts. They had to work from dawn to dusk to make a living, which was extremely difficult for many reasons: they were not seasoned farmers, the land was not farmland, and good seeds, insecticides and fertilizers were not readily available. Even water that was needed for irrigation purposes had to be brought in from far away through tiny canals that had to be dug up in rough soil. No heavy equipment or farm machinery was available for use. Everything had to be done by hand. The deportees were so busy looking for food that they did not have time to think about politics or to organize opposition to the new government. Communists had simply turned them into nothing more than agricultural slaves.[10]

If the head of the family had to labor all day long in the fields, his wife had to help him, for without help one man's work would not suffice to make this arid land a fertile one. No matter how much work he put in, he always fell behind. The end result was that he and his family had nothing to eat despite hard work. At night, many settlers were hit with severe hunger pains that made them "crawl on the floor and curl up like they were going to die."[11]

Children were left unattended. In one camp, they had to cut wood to make charcoal. But the local government prevented them from selling it.[12] In another camp, a widower was able to bring with him to the NEZ only two tools and a couple of pans. When his twelve-year-old son saw trees everywhere, he was frightened by the wilderness and cried all the time. It took them three months to build a house. Although the father worked from dawn to sunset, there was nothing to eat. Children had to clean the yard, cut down bamboo trees, and plant tomatoes and corn, but "we still did not have enough food ... we would cut the bamboo and boil the inside to eat." They finally had to gather wood to sell in the market to get something to eat while their father worked in the fields. Nothing was more painful than watching a twelve-year-old brother learn to cook rice and hunt for food to feed three younger brothers. Having spoken against the coercive system of management of the camp, the father was beaten by the group leader and jailed. The fatherless children were left to fend for themselves. They could not escape and had nowhere to go: the main street of the camp was closely guarded and anyone who tried to get out would be shot.[13] The eldest son resorted to collecting wood to sell for a living. The family eventually escaped from the camp.

Education was virtually non existent, since children had to spend time looking for food and fighting their gnawing hunger instead of going to school. The majority of the NEZ children thus became illiterate. Their emotional stability and learning skills were severely challenged by these recurrent hunger episodes and by the fact that they had to fend for themselves. Had they gone to school, they would not have learned much. Time dedicated to academics was slashed in favor of "compulsory labor, political education and learning revolutionary songs. Labor consisted of planting cassava in schoolyard, sweeping public roads" and so on.[14] Children were taught about socialism and had to participate in government-organized demonstrations or painting slogans.

A System of Oppression

Those who were able to survive the hardships struggled on with their work. At harvest time, all the collected rice was given to the communist leader and workers got only a fraction of it. They were so upset about the system that they had devised their own slogan to mock the system: "From each person, 100 percent work, to each person 30 percent crop." The government usually would take 40 percent of the harvest, and the NEZ leader would keep another 30 percent, and the rest went to the workers. The NEZ leader who did not do any hard labor sold his share on the market at high price and kept all the money. One settler who spoke up against this form of management was beaten by the NEZ leader, and then sent to jail.[15]

In another camp, people were given points for their work instead of the land they were promised. At the end of the month, families were given food rations according to the number of points earned. Basically, they had to slave for the government, but in the end did not own anything. Under this communist system, they were bound to remain perpetual workers for the regime. And since there were no clear written rules and regulations, they were forced to remain under the communists' whimsical control, and ended up being forced to trade their points for nothing. For example, one point could in the beginning be traded for three kilos of rice and the following month for only two kilos. Since points were not hard currency, they could become worthless, and their hard work would not lead them anywhere. This situation led people to become upset and to lose trust in the communist system. "The communists were all liars." To escape this corrupt system, the deported slowly escaped from the NEZ and returned to their hometown.

Despite this overall bleak outlook some families were even less fortunate, especially when they were forced to go to the NEZ in the highlands. First, they were relocated deep in the forests or to deserted areas[16] with no access to civilization. Second, some camps, being more militarized and secure than others, limited the number of escapes. Third, having lost their houses and possessions to the communist government and having their original residence permit confiscated, they could not reestablish themselves as city dwellers.

On the Phu Van collective farm, youngsters had to do "compulsory labor" instead going to school. They were forced to hoe the earth like adults. After they refused, their food rations were withdrawn. Others were thrown in a ten-foot deep dry well for punishment. The wells were then "covered with heavy planks and weighted with logs" to muffle the cries.[17] Not being allowed to get out, they relieved themselves in the well, which stunk badly in the hot humid weather. In the same camp, one group leader of the relocatees was a pretty woman. The *bo doi* called her almost every night to the command center to "receive order." On many occasions she had to remain at the center the whole night. This went on for some time until one morning her body was "discovered hanging from a rope in the latrines.... She had decided she had enough" of the night calls.[18]

Even the progressive Voluntary Youths from Thai Binh in the North who volunteered to settle close the reeducation camps of Bu Gia Map and Buu Loi could not make it in the remote and unhealthy central highlands. They then turned to robbery to survive. On a deserted stretch of Highway 14, they robbed passengers who were on their way to visit relatives interned in a nearby camp.[19] They took anything they could get their hands on. They even stole trees that were cut down by the camp inmates.[20] They stole a brand new bicycle from a *bo doi* who had just received it as a gift from his relatives in Saigon. A bicycle was worth more than a year's salary of a *bo doi*. The latter had to walk back to the camp and he was lucky to be given a truck to help with his search. The *bo doi* and his friends tracked down the thieves who turned out to be the Youths from Thai Binh.[21]

Economic and Social Disasters

According to Vietnamese officials, between 1975–1976, half a million people left Saigon to move to the NEZ, 20 percent of which (or 100,000) did so under coercion.[22] This percentage however might be higher according to refugees who had been able to escape from the camps. However, if the number of people who were deceived into signing for the NEZ was also counted, it was easy to understand the majority of the transplants had left against their will. Under the second five-year plan (1976–80), 1.3 million people were sent to the NEZ. Many were northerners who were sent to the South as part of the redistribution plan. There were 700,000 people relocated from southern cities. Under the third five-year plan (1981–85), about one million, mostly Northerners, had been relocated to the NEZ. Overall, an estimated 1.2 million southerners were sent to the NEZ to make place for three quarters of a million Northerners who moved to Saigon. The master blueprint called for the relocation of ten million people during a twenty-year period.

One Viet Cong sympathizer, a schoolteacher, mentioned that the Hanoi government had the power, and absolute power had corrupted it. It had slowly displaced him and later replaced him with a northerner who did not need to be watched. He and scores of others were just shipped to the NEZ whether they agreed or not. The idea of systematically "developing the unproductive areas of the country would not have been opposed by anyone if it would have done fairly. It is all too frequently a way to punish former upper- and middle-class people whose property has been already confiscated."[23] The plan was to forcibly move them to "the isolated and desolate NEZ where it was nearly impossible to eke out a living." And all these acts were carried out according to the "sound and scientific" teachings of Lenin. It was "terrifying to think that millions of people, from children to the aged, were being systematically subjected to discrimination, harassment, and deprivation of citizens' rights because of a dogma called Marxism-Leninism."[24]

The totalitarian character of the Hanoi regime was evidenced in three major features. First, the striving for absolute political control dominated the goals of the population transfer program. Northern communists took over the running of the southern government, pushing and confining the southerners to the bottom of the society. Second, the policy of relocation underscored the territorial expansion of the regime. It moved millions of northerners to the south and southerners to desolate and unhealthy areas. The southerners were basically disenfranchised of their government, society, wealth, and belongings. Third, the persuasive use made of deceit to implement various policies was obvious in official text.[25] People were told to move to the NEZ because they would receive lands, be reunited faster with their incarcerated husbands, or be pardoned of their past errors.

Since the goals behind the relocation were purely political, no attempt was made to assess the feasibility, usefulness, and potential for success of the project. The Hanoi-based party made the decision to relocate millions of people and administrators and *bo doi* saw to it that the plan was implemented and executed. Under a communist regime, no one dared to raise any question for questioning was equivalent to being anti-revolutionary, thus liable for disciplinary action. But no one in the party knew what agriculture entailed and no one cared whether the lands were arable, whether the equipment, tools, and seeds were available, or whether the people were trained and motivated or not. The SRV just looked at the person as a number devoid of personality, skills, and potential. This approach could have been successful in a war, but not in the running of a society. By reducing a person to an automaton, it killed initiative, ingenuity, motivation, and diversity, which forms the basis of a prosperous and free nation.

This lack of attention to technical details and to human factors led to disastrous results. Failure to perform careful evaluation of the soil prior to the resettlement resulted in the failure of many NEZ. At the Le Minh Xuan NEZ, the high acidity of the soil was discovered only after planting had started. It poisoned the entire planting area, forcing the people to abandon the NEZ. In another area the cultivated land, being too close to the sea, was inundated with salt water, rendering agriculture impossible.[26] Some areas did not even have roads, utilities, or canals, safety and people lacked equipment, buffaloes, tools and seeds to perform adequate work. Some areas were not even safe. A few farmers blew themselves up when they stepped on mines left over from the war.

The SRV did not care much about the human factor although it was dealing with family units, not with automatons. If both parents were forced to do manual labor someone needed to take care of their children, which was not the case in many NEZ. Not having relatives close by forced them to leave their children home by themselves with tragic results: they starved, did not receive an education, got injured or depressed, or were exploited. And if the parents labored to the point they could not feed their children, their chance of staying in the NEZ would be minimal. Besides, not everyone was good at farming. Forcing a white-collar person to farm while he could be useful as a teacher or a scientist was a waste of national resources.

Montagnards or tribal villagers used to live freely in the highlands within their century-long environment. They derived their existence from the forests, from deer, wild pigs, coffee, "slash and burn" type agriculture. The government somehow uprooted and shipped them to low land areas in the hope of "civilizing" them.[27] In the new environment they, however, continued to use their low yield slash and burn culture that caused rapid soil erosion and environmental disasters. Lowlanders who were used to a high yield fixed culture of the land were on the other hand transferred to the highlands where the land was not suitable for their techniques. They had to turn to the slash and burn technique to survive. As a result, the population shift had created "maximum disjuncture between people's culture, production techniques, and their environment."[28] The end result was both an economic and environmental disaster.

People also had basic needs such as food and health care. Ignoring them could only lead to social disasters. Many people, especially children and elderly people, were totally unprepared for the hardships of the relocation and as a result died of malaria, hunger, malnutrition, and oppressive work.[29] More than 50 percent of the displaced people escaped back home.[30] The rate was higher for those who were forcibly moved to the NEZ. Two thirds of the NEZ were later deserted and abandoned. The lives of the relocatees were forever dislocated. Unable to survive in the NEZ, they either had to return to their hometowns[31] or go to the seaside to escape by boat.[32] If they went back to their hometowns, many had no choice but to live on the margins of the society at their friends or families' houses since their houses had been confiscated and their residence permits revoked. They also incurred the risk of being deported back to the NEZ at any time if they were caught. If they had money, however, they could buy themselves a new residence permit. But not too many people could afford to get back on their feet right away after losing everything overnight, including their bank accounts.

The communists were never willing to learn that free enterprise drove the economy, not forced labor. But they just didn't care. They only wanted to further oppress their people. The system of relocation and forced rural labor not only did not make sense, it was simply criminal: the fact they dumped people into the wilds and expected them to survive was by itself an inhumane act. The whole policy suggested "class punishment and ethnic repression."[33]

Had the people, North and South, been aware of the type of revolution and leadership they would be facing, they would have resisted and revolted a long time ago.

XVII

Disillusion

To enforce their hold on the whole country, not only did the Hanoi government send military personnel to the reeducation camps and civilians to the NEZ, they slowly silenced the Viet Cong and their southern sympathizers. These southern communists who had greatly assisted Hanoi in their fight during the war had expected to govern the South and deal with the North on equal basis after 1975. The end result turned out to be completely different.

Viet Cong and Sympathizers

Back in the sixties, many students who sympathized with the communist revolution promoted walkouts and revolts with the purpose of bringing about the downfall of the South Vietnamese government. They created havoc not only in the universities, but also at social and economic levels. These were unstable times for the South Vietnamese government. The Saigon police had to intervene: melees ensued and fights broke out. Rebellious students threw tables, chairs, and Molotov cocktails at the policemen who in turn retaliated by spraying tear gas at the students. Universities were temporarily shut down until the situation stabilized.

A few days later, demonstrations led by Buddhists broke out in another part of the city and new confrontations with the police ensued resulting in further disruption in the stability of the city. The majority of the students, however, did not condone the demonstrations and only wanted to finish their schooling. School years were shortened to five or six months and the quality

XVII. DISILLUSION   199

of education plummeted. As a result of the political instability, markets and businesses were also closed. Food delivery and distribution were affected, hoarding became common and prices increased.

On the political front, the frequent demonstrations undermined the elected Diem and Thieu governments. The activists' main goal was to bring down the government by "weakening the Saigon government and isolating it from domestic and international support."[1] They did not care about the silent majority who strongly disavowed their actions and wished the government had acted more aggressively and taken care of these leftists. However, had the Saigon government handled the situation too harshly, students and demonstrators would have called for the resignation of the officials or complained about "religious persecutions." This would have set off another round of demonstrations, confrontations with police and finally "self immolation by monks," which eventually led to the downfall of the Diem regime.

Communist agents, whose goals were to topple the Saigon government, heavily infiltrated these activist groups. These former "activists" now claimed that they "had no first hand experience of socialism or [communist] revolution" and were not informed about "the state of human rights in North Vietnam, the iron ideology of the Northern leaders...." These statements were not only confusing, but also misleading.

After the fall of Saigon, some of these leftist students and demonstrators became important leaders in the new communist government. However, they were not trusted by the Northern communists and were slowly discarded by the wayside. Other people who had "sympathized with the revolution were now sickened by the society they have helped bring about."[2] In an ironic twist, those who had conspired to bring down the legally elected South Vietnamese government were in turn sent to jails and attempted to escape from the country later. This was the price they paid for supporting the Ho Chi Minh regime.

Doan Van Toai, a communist sympathizer, spent 863 days in two different jails in Saigon[3] under the communist government for what turned out to be a mistaken identity. The police were looking for another person with a similar name. Once he was in custody, he was guilty until proven otherwise, subjected to questioning, isolation, solitary confinement, shackling, and placed on a starvation diet. The whole process took more than two years before he was released without being charged. Scared of the communist regime, he bought his way out of the country a few months later.[4]

Buddhist Thich Tri Quang, the radical monk who helped topple the Diem government, was jailed in an underground dungeon—a poorly ventilated hole just large enough for one person—in Chi Hoa Prison for sixteen months before being released. In comparison with such holes, the much publicized tiger cages appeared large and well appointed. He was reduced almost to a skeleton and his legs atrophied as a result of the treatment.[5] He was ruthlessly silenced and remained under house arrest until 1990. In 1994, he was found "swabbing the latrine floor at the Xa Loi pagoda, reduced, like anyone else outside party circles, to a subsistence standard living."[6]

Buddhists Thich Huyen Quang, Thich Thuyen An, and Thich Quang Do were also arrested and banished from Saigon. Thich Quang Do was sent to exile to Hanoi from 1982 to 1992. In 1994, he sent a scathing letter to party secretary Do Muoi documenting government abuses of Buddhists.[7] He was jailed in 1994 for participating in the Buddhist rescue mission of flood victims in the Mekong Delta. Other monks were also sent to reeducation camps or NEZs. Overall, the communist treatment of the religious leaders was much worse than under the Diem and Thieu regimes.

After the fall of Saigon, Truong Nhu Tang, one of the founders of the National Liberation Front (NLF), became Minister of Justice in the Provisional Revolutionary Government (PRG). His father, however, had warned him not to follow the communists: "My son ... you have abandoned everything—to follow the communists. They will never return to you a particle of the things you have left. You will see. They will betray you, and you will suffer your entire life."[8]

Two weeks after the fall of South Vietnam, the communists had their first victory parade in the middle of downtown Saigon. On this occasion, North Vietnamese President Ton Duc Thang said, "From this time on, the whole Vietnamese people will share a new happiness in a new era." A representative of the communist Worker's Party declared, "Only the American imperialists have been defeated.... Anyone with Vietnamese blood should take pride in this common victory of the whole nation. You, the people of Saigon, are now the masters of your own city."[9]

While the communists were talking and gloating, the round up of former South Vietnamese officials and military personnel began. These words ironically marked the beginning of many years of torture, starvation, and forced imprisonment of millions of southerners in remote re-education camps. They also marked the beginning of the most ruthless imposition of socialism in South Vietnam. Millions of Saigonese, who were supposed to be "the masters of their own city," were forced out of the city to live under substandard conditions in the NEZ.

During the 1975 victory parade, the northern communist forces marched first in their brightest outfits followed by tanks and artillery guns. The Vietcong units on the other hand came last, "Several straggling companies, looking unkempt and ragtag" under the flag of the North Vietnamese communist flag instead of their own. The northern communists overnight had wiped out the contribution of the Vietcong to the war effort.

As the minister of justice of the PRG in Saigon, Tang witnessed more than three hundred thousand South Vietnamese being detained without rhyme or reason and without due process.[10] These people were sent to the camps and no one had been released one year later. The communist police forces followed only the northern Politburo orders, not those of the PRG.

Disillusioned and frustrated, Tang resigned from the ministry position and set out to look for ways to get out of the country. At the end of 1976, like millions of other South Vietnamese who fled the communist regime, Tang escaped by boat from Long Xuyen, landed on an Indonesian oilrig, and transferred to the United Nations refugee camp on Galang Island. He later relocated to Paris, France.

Nguyen Cong Hoan, the Buddhist opposition assemblyman of the years 1971–1975, who participated in the students' demonstrations in Saigon in the sixties, worked hard "to oust the Thieu regime." In 1976 because of his anti–Thieu stance, he was chosen to be a member of the National Assembly of the Socialist Republic. In 1977, he noted that close to three hundred thousand people were arrested for openly expressing their disillusionment toward the Hanoi regime.[11] In the North in 1977, the Hanoi regime "enforced collective labor on Sundays and Christian holy days to dig ditches or patch roads, to prevent people from going to church." The communists controlled and repressed religions by "appointing priests and monks who obeyed the Party blindly" to lead these associations. He also noted that the authorities "ruled by force and terror…. The An Ninh secret police is feared worse than any previous regime."[12]

He soon became "sickened" by the Hanoi's regime where he could only rubber-stamp decisions made by the party. He fondly remembered the Saigon Assembly where "at least he could speak his mind and represent his people."[13] He escaped by boat in 1977 and came to the United States in 1978. After his escape, he was sentenced to death in absentia. His wife and four children were evicted from their home and the children expelled from school. They too escaped by boat in 1979.[14]

It is interesting to note many former communists who had fought against the United States in turn had to escape the communist regime. They "look back with consuming bitterness on lives they now see as having been sacrificed for what turned out to be ignoble purposes…. Their ideals were betrayed by their leaders." One Southerner, formerly a party official now living in Paris, whispered, "I wasted 25 years of my life with them [communists]. My wife still won't forgive me." By 2000, "all the rank and file of the NLF had been quietly either jailed or executed."[15] Col. Summers commented: The "great loser of the war was the Viet Cong. Those poor bastards lost to everyone. They lost to the Americans, they lost to the South Vietnamese. And most conclusively of all, they lost to the North Vietnamese."[16]

Disillusioned Comrades

> This (Hanoi) regime obliges people to live in lies and shame. The lie is that we are made to say that this regime is a thousand times more democratic than the 'bourgeois' regimes. I can bear deprivation and pain, but not shame. The lie debases the human being. It is an affront to human dignity, and it is rooted in the ideology of this regime.— Duong Thu Huong [17]

She is a North Vietnamese who spent seven years in the military system during the war entertaining troops at the front as part of the Communist Youth Brigade. Her first brush with reality came in 1969 when she faced prisoners of war who had black hair and yellow skin like hers. They were Vietnamese like her instead of foreign invaders as suggested by the Hanoi's propaganda. She then awoke to the fact that the party, "tolerating no rivals became a club of the privileged, of the sole holders of power over others."[18]

After 1975, she traveled south to reunite with her brothers and sisters who moved down there in 1954. She was surprised at the sight of

> so many books being sold everywhere on the sidewalks ... and the availability of media and books from around the world. I started to realize that a regime that forces people to listen to just one radio station, that blocks all sources of information and keeps its people in a dark corner must be an inhuman regime. This was the first shock I got about the society I was living in.[19]

She then wrote *Paradise of the Blind*, which is the story of a young woman whose Communist uncle led a land reform committee in the fifties. He drove her father out of the village and dispossessed her mother. Despite his misdeeds, he rose up through the ranks of the party. Her main themes were the dishonesty of the party and the hypocrisy of its members.

She became more outspoken as her works gained in popularity. She was expelled from the party in 1990 and was arrested on smuggling charges. She remained in jail for seven months without trial until released as a result of the efforts of Amnesty International. She continued to write and speak scathingly about the corruption and selfishness of officials who never learned the most basic morals. "They study their Marxism-Leninism, and then come and pillage our vegetable gardens and rice fields with Marx's blessing."

Bao Ninh joined the North Vietnamese army in 1968 and fought the

American invaders. He saw war in the Central Highlands of South Vietnam and learned to "cause the blood of others to flow in torrents." He then realized, like Duong Thu Huong, he was fighting a fratricidal war, which turned out not to be that heroic at all.

He noticed, "Soldiers waited in fear, hoping they would not be ordered in as support forces, to hurl themselves into the arena to almost certain death."[20] Then he witnessed one of the battle-hardened soldiers of his company call it quits. The soldier had had enough of the war and decided to return north to visit with his mother he had not seen for three years. He went AWOL, was hunted down by the military police, and found dead in the jungle a few days later very far from his goal.

In their spare time, northern soldiers gambled and smoked rosa canina, a common weed in the highlands, which the political commissar declared a banned substance. At other times, they suffered from food shortage and medical treatment:

> Hungry, suffering successive bouts of malaria, they became anemic and their bodies broke out in ulcers, showing through worn and torn clothing. They looked like lepers, not heroic forward scouts. Their faces looked moss-grown, hatched and sorrowful, without hope. It was a stinking life.[21]

Above all, they were depressed and tormented by the violence:

> I'm not afraid of dying, but this killing and shooting just goes on forever. I'm dying inside bit by bit. Every night I have the same dream, of me being dead.[22]

After the war ended, he returned home only to find the peace "painful, bitter, and sad." Neither the government nor the people cared about them:

> There had been no trumpets for the victorious soldiers, no drums, no music. That might have been tolerated, but not the disrespect shown to them. The general population just didn't care about them. Nor did their own authorities.[23]

As the memories of the war came back, he became obsessed by its cruelty, death, and inhumane violence. Postwar life was riddled with the "demons of war," hallucinations, painful memories, and broken relationships. Most of the soldiers in his company were dead. "Those who survived continue to live. But that will has gone, that burning will which was once Vietnam's salvation."[24]

After drifting around a while, he wrote *The Sorrow of War*, "a complex dream-like novel ... filled with shocking scenes of violence and depravity."[25] His realistic depiction of the war contrasted sharply with socialist ideals and caused an immediate uproar. It was denounced as a falsification of history. He was shunned by his colleagues, closely monitored by the police and forced to flee Hanoi to the countryside. The government refused to publish his next novel. His works are not readily available in Vietnam today although they sold very well overseas.

Bui Tin joined the communist forces in 1945 and witnessed Ho's declaration at the Ba Dinh Square on September 2, 1945. In his memoirs, he suggested that Ho Chi Minh wrote two autobiographies using pseudonyms, and that he had two wives and was not as celibate as the communists pretended. One was Marie Briere, a French Socialist Party member in the early twenties. The other one was Tan Tuyet Minh, a midwife whom he married in Canton on October 18, 1926.[26] Stories about "uncle Ho's nocturnal wanderings were much more troubling." He apparently had a mistress Nong Thi Xuan, with whom he had a child in 1956. She was found dead a few months later near West Lake, a victim of a car accident.[27]

The communist leadership worshipped Mao. "But to lose the identity of a nation, of oneself and of one's power of thought is a colossal mistake."[28] The spread of Maoism in North Vietnam in 1951 did a lot of damage to the country, especially when Ho spearheaded the bloody land reform campaign, which killed tens of thousands of people.

He became disillusioned with the emergence to power of the "red capitalists": Le Duan and Le Duc Tho. Party General Secretary Le Duan in 1985, on his return trip from Moscow, took with him "six tons of accompanying luggage," instead of the usual 60 kilos per person allowed to prominent passengers.[29] Airport officials decided to teach him a lesson and refused to let the plane take off for safety reasons. They knew he "had engaged in a shopping spree, buying water pumps, sewing machines, pressure cookers, medicines ... etc. to take back home duty free to sell on the open market."

Bui Tin's son and daughter-in-law left North Vietnam in 1989 as boat people and spent 28 days at sea before reaching Hong Kong. They were held in Whitehead Detention camp for a year and a half before relocating to Canada.[30]

In 1990, on a trip to Paris, he decided to remain in exile in that city, citing "a regime which has no sense for personal responsibility before the law ... and where individuals no longer matter." The Cong An (secret police) also reigned supreme, branding people right and left as "anti Party, anti leadership, revisionist, paid agents of colonialists or imperialist spies" in order to detain them without trying them in "a whole network of prisons, sometimes for decades. There they exist in unsanitary conditions and have been ill treated, oppressed and dishonored."[31]

Once party members had spoken against the Hanoi regime, they were

XVII. Disillusion

immediately silenced. Nguyen Trung Thanh was head of the security and protection department of the Central Committee from 1955 to 1988. His role was to maintain a tight grip on all party members. He was asked to review the files of the Revisionists who spoke out against the excess of the Hanoi regime. He then found that the accusations were based on "forced confessions and distorted reports."[32] His report, however, was disregarded and the revisionists, four members of the Central Committee, a foreign minister, a deputy minister, four department heads, a general and four colonels were purged. The trials and purges caused irreparable damage to the victims. Furious at the lack of a response, Thanh released his letter to many party members. He was reprimanded and later expelled from the party.[33]

Nguyen Ho, one of the party members, founded the Club of former Resistance Fighters in 1987. But the government denied his group permission to form an official association. Nguyen Ho then published a petition in which he urged "elderly and incompetent cadres to resign."[34] The government cracked down and closed the club, following which he went into self-imposed exile on a farm outside Saigon. The party then excommunicated him and subjected him to arrest and harassment. In 1993, after spending three years under house arrest, he released an autobiography detailing his incarceration.

Nguyen Ho argued he was not issued warrants for his arrest and that the constitution and laws were not respected in Vietnam. He stated, "We experienced the iron manacles of the Vietnam Communist Party, which are no different from the iron manacles of imperialism. We were imprisoned and isolated and became completely captive and separated from the world."[35] He languished under house arrest for years and was even denied access to medical care for his heart condition. Human Rights Watch honored Nguyen Ho with a Hammett-Hellman Award granted to jailed writers.

Cao Giao was once a Newsweek's political reporter.[36] He had been imprisoned 21 times[37] by various regimes, north as well as south. He could have left in 1975 with his friends at Newsweek, but thought communists would not imprison a former collaborator of the communists. He had collaborated with them back in 1945 and worked for Pham Van Dong, future communist prime minister. A few months later, the communists jailed him for having cooperated with the Japanese in 1941 and the French did the same thing to him at the end of 1946. After his flight to South Vietnam, Diem put him in prison in 1958. After Diem's death, he went to work for the South Vietnamese government until 1975.

After the revolution, the communists tracked him down and in 1978, this sixty-one-year-old man vegetated in a dark cell in the headquarters of the state security police for 13 months and was repeatedly interrogated on charges of being a CIA agent. He was then placed in solitary confinement by the Chi Hoa police for three and a half more years before he was finally released. He remained under police surveillance and was allowed to emigrate to Germany in 1985 where he later died.

Nguyen Chi Thien, a poet, had been jailed behind these bamboo fences for more than twenty years. He was released from jail once only to be returned to jail a short time later. He is a remarkable poet was able to cope with adversity by writing poems. At least 400 of them were smuggled abroad. It could be said he represented the "conscience of humanity": his cries for freedom and fair treatment of prisoners bore such a sad and tragic tone that it earned him the International Poetry Prize. His collection of poems published as *Hoa Dia Nguc* (Flowers from Hell) detailed the horrors of the reeducation camps and the hells of Ho Chi Minh.

The SRV had intended since 1975 to rule supreme over Vietnam and tolerated no opposition from either nationalists or non-nationalists. Many communists and communist sympathizers had found to their dismay that, despite their years of service to the party, they could be silenced like any enemy if they dared to waver from Hanoi's teaching.

XVIII

Of Cemeteries

Blinded by their rage and desire to wipe out all the vestiges of the South Vietnamese nation, the communists went to the extreme of leaving no stone unturned. Not happy with sending its citizens to concentration camps or banishing them to the NEZ, they unleashed their furor on the dead. Right after 1975, they started bulldozing dozens of South Vietnamese "military cemeteries, obliterating the grave markers that bore the names of the dead or, often, the single word "Unknown."[1] In the province of Vinh Binh after 1975, villagers were led and forced to go to cemeteries to witness bulldozers raze all the southern soldiers' graves. "The smell of decay thickened the air. Coffins broke as bulldozers ripped through them, and worms crawled out."[2]

Bui Tin, a North Vietnamese colonel, summed up the philosophy behind this brutal and insensitive behavior: "Enemy puppet, whether alive or dead, was always a puppet — a second-class citizen or somebody who had no citizen's rights at all."[3] And the second-class citizen had to make way for the northern communists or be wiped off the face of the earth. The thought of committing a sacrilege by seeking revenge on the dead did not even cross their mind, and if it did they did not even care about it.

Mac Dinh Chi Cemetery

It was by far the largest, cleanest, and best-kept cemetery in Saigon. It was located right in the middle of the city, with a gated entrance on Hai Ba Trung Street. Eight-foot, bone white concrete walls enclosed it all around and gave it an air of isolation and solemnity in the middle of the noisy neighborhood. It was one of these, if not holy, but sacred areas reserved for former war heroes, high-level officials, and prominent members of the South Vietnamese society (i.e., President Diem, Prime Minister and one time Head of State Phan Khac Suu) who had contributed their efforts and talents to the building of the country. It was the last resting place of these esteemed people who had been important to their friends, families and community. In this solemn place were also laid to rest a few French nationals who had contributed to the building of the South Vietnamese nation and who had decided to remain in this second fatherland instead of being repatriated to France.

There were magnificent mausoleums, eight to ten feet high and six to eight feet wide, erected by their families as a sign of respect to the memory of the deceased. Others were simple tombstones, but no less impressive, with a block of stone marking the gallant deeds of the beloved person. The cemetery was built by the French and breathed a European style confined within a quiet environment. Small winding roads, lined with eucalyptus trees interspersed with straight roads, gave access to all corners of the cemetery. Within its confines, the visitor felt submerged in an air of simplicity, eeriness, and majesty.

On one of these tombstones were engraved the last words of a young widow who had lost her husband to the war. He had served as a colonel in the South Vietnamese army. The tombstone read:

> Mai mai nho chang,
> Nguoi da hy sinh vi To Quoc.
> Forever remembering you,
> A hero laid down for his country.

Touching many visitors' hearts with tears in their eyes, these simple words rang throughout the cemeteries of South Vietnam.

Two unmarked tombs of the late President Ngo Dinh Diem (1954–1963) and his brother and adviser Nhu, both assassinated during a military coup in 1963, were located in the Mac Dinh Chi cemetery. A stern Catholic in a land of Buddhists and Confucians, Diem first served as prime minister to the last Vietnamese Emperor Bao Dai and worked hard to reorganize South Vietnam following the partition of the country in 1954. He was then elected as first president of the Republic of South Vietnam in 1955. He had brought this young nation from the backwardness of a French colony to a more civilized country. In the late fifties he wrestled the besieged South Vietnam from a few religious sects: Hoa Hao, Cao Dai as well as from the Tran Van Giau-led communists. Single handedly, President Diem successfully disarmed the

Hoa Hao and Cao Dai sects and unified the country under his leadership. He, however, antagonized the Buddhists who later helped topple his government. The event marked the tragic end of the first president of South Vietnam who was shot to death in an armored vehicle during a military coup in 1963, then placed in an unmarked tomb in the military headquarters. His remains were transferred to Mac Dinh Chi cemetery in 1965.

What the communists did after the takeover of South Vietnam was erase its past. Orders were given to family members of those who were interred at Mac Dinh Chi cemetery to remove the remains within a two-month period and transfer them somewhere else. Then the memory-laden tombstones and mausoleums in the cemetery were bulldozed to the ground. The remains of President Ngo Dinh Diem and his brother Nhu were removed and transferred to a small cemetery in the province of Lai Thieu. The communists had cordoned off the cemetery that day to prevent any potential uprising of the former president's ardent followers.

Tiet Thuong Sculpture

On the road leading to and just right in front of the National Cemetery of Bien Hoa once stood a ten-ton, six-meter *Tiet Thuong* Sculpture of a grieving soldier in uniform, sitting on a short stool with his gun on his lap, remembering his deceased friend. The sculpture drew rave reviews from everyone who saw it, including the mourning family members. The sculpture not only blended well in the austere and solemn atmosphere of the cemetery, but also evoked a long lasting bond between soldiers: the departed and the living.

The man behind the sculpture was ARVN captain Nguyen Thanh Thu. In August 1966, then Head of State Nguyen Van Thieu commissioned the sculptor to design a statue to be dedicated right in front of the National Cemetery with the goal of commemorating and remembering the war dead. Having only one week to draft the design, he visited the military Hanh Thong Tay cemetery (Go Vap province), which was almost full at that time, to learn about its ambience. The place turned out to be sad and eerie. Due to lack of space, hundreds of caskets were spread out right in front of the reception area, waiting to be interred. Hundreds of women, children, and family members openly mourned, wept, and prostrated themselves in front of the caskets while helicopters brought in new dead bodies in sealed bags against the background of bombing, shelling, and exploding mines in the distance. Every day and for six long days, he came and sat in this environment to try to come up with an idea for the sculpture.

On his way home on the sixth day, he fell thirsty as the weather was steamy hot and stopped by a roadside café to get a drink. In the small room, he noticed a sad looking soldier sitting alone on a low table immersed in deep thought. The silence was occasionally broken by the soldier's monologue. On the table in front of him, sat two glasses, one for him and the other for his ghost friend along with many empty beer bottles. He apparently had returned from the cemetery after mourning his lost friend. While drowning his sadness in beer, he chastised his friend for having died and leaving him alone. He poured his soul out, talked and talked to his ghost friend. The sculptor tried to step in but was waved away as if the grieving soldier did not want to be bothered. The soldier, however, gave him his wallet and the sculptor took note of his name and address.

Back home the sculptor spent the whole night working on six drafts dealing mostly with war sceneries. The next morning while waiting to be introduced to President Thieu, he drew the seventh sketch, picturing the mourning soldier. Of the seven drafts, only the last one entitled *Tiet Thuong* was chosen. After he was commissioned to work on the statue, he hunted down the soldier and asked him to pose for the ultimate drawing from which the sculpture was to be derived. For many years, the statue adorned the entrance of the National Cemetery and became the symbol of Saigon remembering its war dead.

After 1975, Nguyen Thanh Thu was sent to a reeducation camp for being a captain in the puppet army. He first refused to answer the *bo doi*'s usual questions and was severely beaten for three days. As he was found to have conceived of the *Tiet Thuong* sculpture for the puppet government, he was thrown into a conex from which he was only removed for interrogation. As he continued to admit having created the statue, he was thrown back into the conex on half ration a day. During the eighth month of his incarceration, a political commissar from Hanoi came by to interview him and suggested that by acknowledging he was only the assistant sculptor but not the real culprit, who had since escaped abroad, his sentence could be commuted and he thus could be sent back to the camp. Thu refused, stating he was the sculptor and, therefore, would bear all the responsibility for having created it. The commissar went wild, accused him of being anti-revolutionary, then hit him, perforating his eardrums and rendering him deaf in the process. Thu was sent back to his metallic jail. He was dragged out of his conex at 4 A.M. on the 22nd month of his internment. He was feeble and barely able to walk for what he thought was his final execution. Instead, he was spared and thrown back into the reeducation camp where he continued to be interned for a few more years.[4]

The sculpture was destroyed in 1975 and Thu came to the United States later through the Orderly Departure Program.

Bien Hoa National Cemetery

Situated in the outskirts of Saigon, built in 1960, modeled after Arlington National Cemetery and dedicated in 1966, it was designed to be the final resting place of thousands of soldiers who had served their country. At the height of the war, 30,000 to 40,000 South Vietnamese died each year and the Bien Hoa National Cemetery was designed to absorb the load of smaller cemeteries around the country. Generals as well as simple soldiers were buried in the cemetery in full honor in what supposed to be a glorious final resting place for those who had sacrificed themselves to defend the freedom of the country.

In front of the cemetery stood the *Tiet Thuong* sculpture. The huge main entrance was flanked by two tall brick walls adorned with a curved tile roof. Two smaller side entrances adjoined the main gate. Dragon motifs were carved on its walls. In the early seventies, through this grandiose entrance passed many solemn funeral corteges of those unsung heroes. "From the high ground in the middle of the cemetery where the towering concrete skeleton of the unfinished central monument stood, one could ... see the pagoda on a hill at the other end."[5] In the pagoda was a symbolic grave of the Unknown Soldier and a tablet remembering the war dead. The main avenue was lined with eucalyptus trees, graves were arranged in parallel rows, and the cemetery was carefully tended. Although the main building was still unfinished by 1975, the lots filled up pretty fast.

Alas, things changed drastically with the communist takeover. Not even cemeteries could escape the wrath and vengeance of the northern communists. No one was allowed to tend the cemetery anymore. Graffiti were written on many of the tombstones, which were knocked down, left "astray on the ground," while grazing buffaloes, cows, and goats roamed around this supposedly solemn place. "Graves were violated and headstones served as shooting targets."[6] A look at this place would bring any visitor to tears. The cemetery had become the "no man's land" for the families of the buried who had become the pariah of the communist regime. No one was supposed to be associated with the losers and no one dared challenge the winners.

The communists desecrated the area[7] by tearing down the mausoleums, leveling the headstones, or simply preventing family members from taking care of the graves. Grass grew everywhere obliterating the paths leading to the graves as well as whole sections of the cemetery. Being neglected, the place fell into disrepair.

Villagers from a nearby hamlet dug up "the roads through the cemetery to sell the stones in the roadbeds for house foundations."[8] Soon all the paved roads became dirt roads, which were later invaded by weeds. The trees withered with time and the memorial became a wasteland occasionally populated by a few cows and their herders. Like an aging lady, the cemetery rapidly lost its charms and pride for lack of care. The pagoda did not fare any better.

> The six sets of stairs leading up to the pagoda, were crumbling. Inside the pagoda was a large memorial tablet, shaped like the stone memorials to feudal mandarins in the ancient Temple of Literature in Hanoi. In front of the tablet was a symbolic grave. The Land of Your Ancestors Will Always Be Grateful (*To Quoc Ghi On*), the words on the tablet read. The tablet had been defaced. The glazed ceremonial tiles that once covered the symbolic grave had been stripped away by scavengers. There was nothing left but brick and mortar. The decorative tiles were also gone from the walls and ceiling of the pagoda and replaced by obscene graffiti....[9]

The tombstones, although leveled or knocked down proudly, continued to display their bright past as well as the faces and names of the unsung heroes.

> When these boy-soldiers died, bereaved mothers encased their photographs and attached them to the stone markers. Surprisingly, many of these pictures had not faded.... These were the faces of the vanquished ... and for answering their (Saigon) government's call to duty-as nobly as Northern soldiers had answered Hanoi's — they had been dishonored by victors who desecrated their headstones. In a country whose pride and dignity and sense of nationalism I had come to greatly admire, the cemetery stood as a symbol of national shame.[10]

The past, especially for the "puppet soldiers" slowly faded away. There is no sign directing the visitor to the National Cemetery today and many locals did not even know its exact location. Other South Vietnamese cemeteries were also desecrated without even minimal respect for the dead: "an offense of particular gravity in a civilization that considers family graves as places of worship.... The vendetta against soldiers' graves was indecent."[11]

De Behaine, the bishop of Adran, who in the late 18th century helped Nguyen Anh conquer and reunify Vietnam, died in 1802. He was buried in Saigon in a pagoda-type mausoleum designed by Barthelemy Sang, a Vietnamese architect. The mausoleum, which was kept in excellent shape during the last two centuries, reminded the communists of colonialism. Even the mausoleum of Monsignor Pigneau de Behaine was taken down in the presence of the French consul in late February 1983.

The huge 6 by 3 meter sarcophagus was opened. "A two-century old smell filled the air and the coffin revealed its intact beauty of precious wood lacquered with gold and red.... It was opened. The bishop of Adran appeared in his mandarin robe with golden buttons, the last gift of the king [Gia Long] ... a well-preserved skeleton; the head still coiffed by a bonnet adorned with laces."[12]

On March 2, 1983, the Saigon department of health presented to the consul five urns containing the remains of bishop of Adran, of two other French bishops along with those of Francis Garnier and another sailor. Garnier was the one who conquered present-day North Vietnam, formerly Tonkin in 1873.

An Inhumane Act

The losers lost everything. They lost their lives defending their country against the invading enemies. Without the war, which was instigated and carried out by communists, they might still be alive, well, and enjoying the beauties and natural riches, which doted the Vietnamese countryside. What the South Vietnamese government did was give them a last salute and a last resting place in a respectable setting as a reward for their gallant deeds.

But when the communists came in, they did the worst thing possible: they tore down the cemeteries and bulldozed people's last resting places. Even Bui Tin,[13] a communist, wrote in his memoir that all these actions "stemmed from a lack of moral values, the inhumanity and blindness of a communist leadership which had become arrogant and lost touch with the people."

While South Vietnamese cemeteries were razed, new cemeteries with tall spires adorned with a red or gold star at their apex were built almost every day for the northern dead. The latter were frequently remembered and commemorated sometimes with extravagance while those who died for the Saigon regime had disappeared "from official discourse."[14] Such a mistreatment should never have happened to a human being.

Based on thousand-year-old Confucian beliefs, once a person died his or her soul was thought to wander around the corpse for a few days. The goal of funeral rites was to facilitate the passage of the deceased's soul to the "other-world." With a smooth and proper send-off, the soul would tend to become a benevolent family ancestor who would care for the family it left behind. These rites were repeated yearly at the anniversary of the deceased and formed the basis for "ancestor worship." However, if a person died of a violent death, if his body became severely mutilated, and if rites were not appropriately performed, the soul could become a "malevolent, wandering, hungry ghost that is doomed to eternally roam the earth."[15] The angry spirit would be inclined to take its anger out on the living.

Therefore, the process of razing cemeteries and not allowing remembrance of southern dead could be seen as an "inhumane act" from the Hanoi regime. This apartheid mentality tore up the conscience of the southerners and remained a dividing issue between northerners and southerners. "Condemned to the shadows, southern dead refuse, however, to remain unmourned. Their demand to be recognized, however, threatens the peace of the community at the level of family, community, and nation."[16]

History will not forget this sacrilege for these acts belittled not the dead — for they were gone — but those who had committed this grave offense. The Hanoi government no doubt had followed the uncivilized ways of Gia Long who in turn had copied the appalling cruelty of the rulers of the Chinese Qing dynasty. During the civil war that divided Vietnam in the late eighteenth century, Nguyen Hue defeated the southern Gia Long and the northern Trinh to unify the country in 1788. His reign was shortened as a result of his early death in 1792. Gia Long used this occasion to conquer the whole country and proclaim himself emperor in 1802. He settled the score with Nguyen Hue by having his remains exhumed and urinated on by his soldiers in the presence of the late emperor's son Quang Toan. Then Prince Quang Toan was "drawn and quartered by elephants to which his limbs were bound."[17]

XIX

Epilogue

In retrospect, revolution and nationalism were just words behind which the North Vietnamese communists hid to justify their invasion and conquest of South Vietnam. They provided convenient smokescreens for communists who were expert in the art of double talking and concealing their goals. They talked about nationalism, but their true goal was the invasion of South Vietnam by force, which they succeeded in doing in 1975 after 21 years of brutal aggression.

The South Vietnamese had long ago tried to publicize this fact, but because of poor public relations, because of their mellow and benevolent attitude, or because they simply thought the world could sort things out, make its own decisions and see the truth as it was, they did not aggressively use propaganda efforts for their own benefits. Even if when they did use propaganda, many people in the media and academia did not listen to them. The latter had already made up their minds. They loved the revolution and had sided with the communists.

The American Side of the War

The U.S. State Department had issued the White Papers on "Aggression from the North," confirming northern belligerence back in the sixties. These statements were somehow ridiculed by many US "experts," some from major universities, who thought that the war was just an "indigenous local rebellion."[1] Since South Vietnam was invaded and overrun by 20 northern divisions,[2] which crossed the demilitarized zone in full violation of the 1973 Paris Accords, no one heard from these experts again.

On the other hand, being the unequal "ally" of the powerful United States did not help matters either. First, when the Americans decided to expand the war, they sent half a million of their troops to Vietnam, and when they felt that the war was not worth fighting anymore, they just packed up and left a war torn country with a job undone. Second, the conflicting U.S. views and policies about the war only signaled the disarray in Washington. General Taylor once told the Senate, "We were not trying to defeat North Vietnam, only trying to cause them to mend their ways."[3] This was a strange assertion coming from a top U.S. official who had sent half a million of his men into harm's way in a faraway land to defend against an "invasion from the North."

Third, after the 1961–62 Geneva Conference on Laos, the United States "tacitly agreed not to invade the Southern Laotian panhandle so long as the North Vietnamese did not overrun eastern Laos."[4] That Laotian panhandle through which passed the Ho Chi Minh Trail turned out to be the bloodline of the communists for without that trail no northern soldiers or military supplies could have infiltrated into the South, and the war would have remained under control. And last but not least, despite the fact that Secretary of Defense McNamara had admitted that as far back as 1965 he did "not think that the war could be won,"[5] he did not have the dignity and courage to resign and let someone else take over his position. This lack of leadership was certainly bound to affect the conduct of the war.

The antiwar movement and the Watergate scandal, despite being internal American problems, were indirectly anti–South Vietnam since the United States was its main supporter. The South Vietnamese watched painfully as the war resisters flew to Hanoi to publicize the communist cause in spite of the fact that the North Vietnamese were the invaders and the perpetrators of the war. This could only suggest how well the communist propaganda was working.

With the conclusion of the war, the communists pursued their hegemonic aspirations over Southeast Asia. The Vietnam War was thus neither a war against imperialists and the United States nor about nationalism, but about domination and control of all Southeast Asia. Failing to understand this point would be failing to understand Ho Chi Minh's long-term strategic goals. Ho, far from being a saint or a patriot, was simply a modern reincarnation of Genghis Khan. However, bloodied by a 21-year war against South Vietnam, a ten-year war in Cambodia, and a skirmish with China, Hanoi's hegemonic aspirations collapsed due to lack of resources.

South Vietnam as a Bastion of Freedom

South Vietnam had its share of the blame. Established in 1954, no one had expected South Vietnam to survive more than five years. However,

President Ngo Dinh Diem performed miracles by steering the country out of the ashes of colonialism. But to expect a young country to become a full-fledged democracy within a few years of its birth proved to be an illusionary expectation for many Americans. Then Diem was killed during an uprising. Without proper leadership, with its politicians and parties squabbling for power and its generals using their positions for their own gains, South Vietnam could not put up an organized agenda to fight the war. The cacophony of voices proved to be too disruptive for the society to mount a united defense. The Hoa Hao and Cao Dai sects, the Buddhists, the students, the politicians and finally the Catholics, all wanted to take power and bring down the Thieu government. Unfortunately, none of them wanted to fight the war and no one had a plan to defeat the communists. They simply proclaimed themselves pacifists or "third force," ready to surrender to the enemy.

At least there was freedom under the republic. When the communists took over the country, they ruthlessly wiped out the opposition: nationalists, Buddhists and third force, and kept the power for themselves. First, they sent politicians (Truong Dinh Du, Tran Van Tuyen, etc.) to northern reeducation camps where they later died.[6] Others were silenced. Although Nguyen Cong Hoan, an anti–Thieu assemblyman, could say whatever he wanted without impunity before 1975, all he could do after 1976 was to rubberstamp the decisions of the party. Unable to stand the communists any longer, he too had to escape from communist Vietnam. Second, they put all the monks and priests in jails or camps where they were shut out. Third, students were also jailed. Doan Van Toai spent two and a half years in jail and finally bribed his way out with thirty taels of gold.[7] Fourth, elements of the NLF who thought they were fighting for a free South Vietnam were simply discarded. Truong Nhu Tang had to fight for his life by escaping by boat. Then came the silence of the Gulag.

For 21 years, the South Vietnamese battled against the North Vietnamese communists only to lose the war in the end. April 30, 1975, thus marked the end of freedom not only for the 25 million South Vietnamese but also for the people of Cambodia and Laos. It marked the takeover of a relatively democratic country by the communist forces against civilized rules of laws. Although the short-lived democratic South Vietnam had ceased to exist, the fighting spirit of these people still lived on. The sad and tragic images of the thousands of frightened people fighting on the rooftop of the U.S. Embassy, trying to board the last chopper out of Saigon, of the tank that broke through the gate of the South Vietnamese Presidential Palace, of the millions of people laboring and starving in the communist concentration camps, and of the thousands of boat people who braved the violent seas in search of freedom elsewhere in the world forever lingered in the hearts of the South Vietnamese. They only knew they had freedom after they had lost it.

During the post–1975 years, they found themselves in the abyss from which no one was expected to survive. The infamy of the defeat and the despair over the loss of their homeland, however, brought them unexpected energy. Cornered against the walls, they sprung up and attempted to escape from these depths to start a new life. They found a new will to survive and a quarter of a century later they became the fastest and most successful group of immigrants in many western countries.

According to Singapore's Lee Kwan Yew who was quoted in the *Wall Street Journal*, the resistance of the South Vietnamese and the "American effort in Vietnam bought time for the rest of the region" to prosper and become strong. This containment effort did work and the dreaded domino effect never materialized. The unsung 300,000 South Vietnamese soldiers and 58,000 American GIs had given their lives to contain the communist expansion.

South Vietnam was, thus, a sacrificial lamb in the Cold War. It had served its purpose and was discarded like a used item. The *Wall Street Journal* mentioned in an editorial in April 2000 on the 25th anniversary of the fall of Saigon, "With Vietnam, America blundered badly and abandoned an ally to a fate it didn't deserve. But surely America's willingness to fight, somewhere, sometime, was instrumental in bringing about the better world we see today."

Looking back at history, Tung Tri Thien left us these thoughtful verses:

Life's Beautiful

"Prisoner 1001!"
Woke me up from lethargy,
[Exhaustion, and shaken up from apathy,
My feet barely following the mind,
Searching for the voice coming from behind.
"Prisoner 1001!"
I could hear, but could not see,
Anyone there? Or my eyesight, could it be?
A dream, just a dream, I consoled, may be,
But persistent, demanding, my mind ready to flee.
For decades, imbued in Darkness,
Blinded by bright light, can't see Openness.
For decades, they tortured and killed my parents,

XIX. Epilogue

At thirteen, I watched their blood flow in torrents.
They took away my Innocence,
And planted seeds of Anger and Violence.
"An eye for an eye," I vowed, "No repentance,"
Like a furious child thinking in happenstance.
I was poor, uneducated,
Yet they stripped away my long heritage,
Then taught me their science and historical adage,
Tools I had used as my journey's baggage.
Overflowing with rage, I found Big Brother,
Arming me with guns, he promised instant power.
"Kill ye oppressors, reduce him to powder!"
With evil schemes, I stood tall like a tower,
While the red plague metastasized like a cancer.
Downing enemy's blood, I became more thirsty,
Eyes wide open, yet I could not see,
Hearts as rocks, no room for Mercy.
Men, women, children alike, deserved no Pity.
The Gang men were all so powerful,
Drunk with victory, we were oh so pitiful!
No excuse, we became the World's fools,
Sowing Fear, Hate, Poverty in basketfuls.
Patting on our backs, we drowned in congratulations,
On mountain-top only miles of Destruction.
From South to North, all men to re-education,
Leaving our children and grandchildren lost in oblivion.
[Poor, un-educated, I lived with no tomorrow,
Massive killings, destruction, greed, my life's hollow.
Still poor, un-educated, now only in Sorrow;
No one to blame but me, and what I sowed.
Certainly I have no one to blame but myself,
When abdicating all my rights to someone else,
Whether conscious or not, results are still the same;
That is: hitching my wagon to hell.
Refusing to stand on my own two feet,
Led by Anger, Hatred, I embraced Defeat.
[In Despair, I yelled and leaned on someone else's fists;
With no inner strength and clarity of mind, like walking on sleet.
Ignorant of the "Ripple" effect,
Casting stones onto the Lake,
Just like children playing with their toys defect.
In perpetual Infancy, oblivious of high stakes.
"Prisoner 1001! First name?"
"Sir, my name is NAM."
"Prisoner 1001, last name?"

"Sir, my name is VIET-NAM."
Courage, where art Thou? Help me break the Mold,
Understanding assist me in asking questions ever bold.
Faith in values that can't be bought or sold,
Believing in Human Dignity since times untold.
Pitch-black, I cannot see! But ... I can hear.
Then total silence, the sound so eerie.
A bright shining reflection striking near;
A tiny object my jailer left behind, but why a key?
No walls or iron bars, but this is my prison;
Hopelessness, Despair, Ignorance: fruits of my Persecution.
A slow Death brought on my people's Eradication,
Then, God, show me ... my Redemption?
                              Tung Tri Thien

Ho's Revolution

It ended on April 30, 1975, with the fall of Saigon. The war claimed two million lives, one each from the North and South while 12 other million people had been displaced.[8] This was followed by a diaspora of more than a million South Vietnamese who piled up on leaky boats to escape the new repressive regime. Tens of thousands of people lost their lives at sea from dehydration, starvation, rough weather, or at the hands of pirates. If the whole war were not tragic enough, Ho's followers turned South Vietnam upside down by sending millions of people to the gulags and letting them die slowly of starvation, hunger, hard labor, and natural diseases. Millions of other civilians were banished to the NEZ that were just the civilian version of the military gulags.

South Vietnam became part of a police state where neighbors were ordered to snoop on neighbors, children on parents, cousins on uncles and aunts. Mistrust and suspicion were prevalent. Private property and industries were nationalized. What was a conquest for some became oppression for others. An atmosphere of dejection and resignation fell over the land, but peace was nowhere to be found. People were just "consigned to live in oppressed silence."[9]

Behind Ho Chi Minh's bamboo fences life was hard, degrading, and hopeless. Not only had Ho destroyed North as well as South Vietnam, but he also had brought terror to Laos and Cambodia. The Hanoi regime revealed itself to be ruthless and is known to be one of the worst human rights offenders in modern times. On the seven-point scale measuring political rights, the Comparative Survey of Freedom gave the SVR the "lowest possible rating, in category seven." In the nations in category seven, "the political despots at the top appear by their actions to feel little constraint from either public opinion or popular tradition."[10] In 1987, SVR ranked 80th out of 89 countries as far as human rights were concerned.[11]

> The period (1975–1985) is seen in retrospect as a time of tyranny and waste, a heedless attempt to create a visionary socialist state in defiance of reality, a folly that compounded the troubles inherited from the war and drove Vietnam into bankruptcy. [12]

After three decades, the communist experimentation turned out to be a miserable failure from the economic, social and political point of view, leading the Vietnamese nation to an economic abyss with a debt of 22.4 billions of dollars (or 87 percent of GNP) to the World Bank alone. Politically, socialist Vietnam was not a free or democratic country. Corruption was rampant: the anti-corruption chief was sacked for corruption and the deputy head of the national drug squad was caught smuggling heroin.[13] The Political and Economic Risk Consultancy honored Vietnam with the "Imelda Marcos Golden Shoes Award for grand larceny." This caused major investors to pull out of the country. "US investment had dropped more than 80 percent since 1996 to $127 millions last year."[14]

In the end, it was still a revolution. Its purpose is now clear: take over the power and wealth of the southerners and spread the red gospel. The North had both economic and political reasons. With its crowded population and lack of natural resources, it could not survive without the wealth of the South. Back in the 17th century, the Le-Trinh dynasty in Hanoi was keeping itself in power thanks to southern subsidies. In 1945 and 1955, with the famine ravaging the north, it knew it could not survive without the South. Therefore, it had decided to conquer the South.

It was not a people's revolution, but that of the communist party. It was not an uprising of peasants, but a well-organized military intervention by Hanoi. Therefore, "as a people's war, the Vietnamese revolution was a fraud."[15] What Ho's government did was induce and force people to fight for them. It was an exploitation of the people's manpower. But in the end, average people derived no benefit from the revolution: they were poorer now than before, despite losing 21 of their prime years. The revolution had never planned to give the proletariat material wealth or education, but only to use its power to work for its ultimate goal. It is a regime known for its "mendicity and mendacity."[16]

It was not even a true proletarian revolution for there has never been social equality or a classless society. It set up a corrupt regime, in which the new wealthy people were the party members and the cadres. It redistributed the wealth by taking the riches of the Southerners and giving it to the party members, not to the workers. This was basically a case of stolen wealth, an act of banditry. Communist regimes are "criminal enterprises in their very essence: on principle, they all ruled lawlessly, by violence, and without regard for human life."[17]

A socialist revolution does not have any humanistic tendency: it is narrow-minded and geared toward acquisition of power and self-interest. It has no moral values and could not offer the wealth and freedom of the capitalist society.

It then sheds its socialist image and tries to metamorphose into a free enterprise society only for the purpose of hanging on to power. It is neither communist nor capitalist. It maintains a single party dictatorship and uses nationalism to rally the masses. It tries to embrace Confucianism to provide legitimacy to the regime. It is an autocracy, a form of fascism. Like communist China, it "is no longer a system based on charisma, but on political repression, cynical not idealistic, endlessly summoned to emulate the greatness of its ancestors."[18]

Socialist Vietnam, like communist China, sadly may be with us quite a while unless its people are willing to do something about it. For without true freedom, Vietnam is bound to remain a crowded, stagnant, and poor third world country.

Glossary

AK 47 Standard automatic rifle used by the Vietcong and the NVA.

Antenna Informer.

ARVN Armed Forces Republic of Vietnam.

Bo bo Grain used to feed horses.

Bo doi Communist soldier.

Can bo Cadre or officer.

Cao Dai Religious and political sect combining Buddhism, Confucianism, and Christianity with the worship of Vietnamese and Western heroes.

Comintern Communist international.

Cong An Internal security service.

Dai Viet Greater Vietnam Party.

Dong Or piaster; Vietnamese money.

DRG Democratic Revolutionary Government of Hanoi.

CPV Communist Party of Vietnam.

SRV Socialist Republic of Vietnam.

GSV Government of the Republic of Vietnam (Saigon).

Hoa Hao Buddhist sect in western Mekong Delta.

Ho Chi Minh Also called Uncle Ho. Leader of the North Vietnamese communists. Died on September 3, 1969.

Hoi chanh Former Viet Cong who had rallied in support of the South Vietnamese cause during the war.

jicama Roots of a tropical plant the size of a large, round potato with a sweet and crunchy taste.

Khmer Cambodian.

Khmer Rouge Cambodian communist.

M-1 World War II vintage American (single shot) rifle.

M-16 Standard American (automatic) rifle used in Vietnam after 1966.

Montagnards Aboriginal tribespeople of the central highlands of Vietnam.

Nam tien Southern expansion of the Vietnamese.

NLF National liberation front or Vietcong liberation movement.

Ngo Dinh Diem First President of South Vietnam 1955–63.

Nguyen Van Thieu Last elected president of South Vietnam 1965–74.

NVA North Vietnamese Army.

Pho Vietnamese noodle soup.

PRG People Revolutionary Government (Viet Cong).

Pol Pot Khmer Rouge leader who took over Cambodia in 1975.

SRV Socialist Republic of Vietnam. Unified communist Vietnam as of 1976.

Trat tu vien Detainee appointed to maintain order in the camp.

Vietcong Local South Vietnamese communist.

Vietminh Northern Vietnamese communist.

VNQDD Vietnam Quoc Dan Dan (Vietnamese Nationalist Party).

Notes

Preface

1. Desbarats J., "Human Rights: Two Steps Forward, One Step Backward?" in Thai Quang Trung, p. 61; Metzner p. xiii.
2. Bui Van Cao, "Living Under Communism," in Hawthorne, p. 168.
3. Sheehan, p. 79.
4. *Ibid.*, p. 121.
5. Mydans, 2000.
6. Wiesner, pp. 346–47.

I. North and South

1. Le Thanh Khoi, p. 245.
2. Li Tana, p. 85.
3. Le Thanh Khoi, p. 300.
4. *Ibid.*, p. 307.
5. *Ibid.*, p. 312.
6. *Ibid.*, p. 323.
7. Li Tana, p. 153.
8. *Ibid.*, p. 156.
9. N.M. Vo, *The Duality of the Vietnamese Mind*, p. 51.
10. Li Tana, p. 102.
11. Graetz, pp. 18–19.
12. Turner, pp. 9–11.
13. *Ibid.*, pp. 52–53.
14. Dooley, pp. 184–85.
15. Kamm, p. 218.

II. The Last Heroes

1. Lomperis, p. 173.
2. Summers, p. 182.
3. *Ibid.*, p. 190.
4. Dawson, p. 24.
5. *Ibid.*, p. 47.
6. *Ibid.*, p. 19.
7. Bui Tin, pp. 82–83.
8. Smith, H.D., "Setting the Record Straight," in J.E. Lee, pp. 42–44.
9. Hosmer, p. 62.
10. Summers, p. 196.
11. Dawson, p. 38.
12. *Ibid.*, p. 58.
13. Summers, p. 196.
14. Dawson, p. 22.
15. Summers, p. 196.
16. Dawson, p. 72.
17. Summers, p. 196.
18. Dawson, p. 285.
19. Summers, p. 200.
20. Dawson, p. 302.
21. Summers, p. 176.
22. Sheehan, p. 112; Engelmann, p. 242.
23. Engelmann, p. 244.
24. Dawson, p. 8.
25. Dommen, p. 922.
26. Pham Phong Dinh, QLVNCH (Stories of Heroes of ARVN) in Dac San

Vo Khoa Thu Duc Bulletin, Houston, Texas, Summer 2000; Dommen, p. 923.
  27. Dac San, p. 102.
  28. Metzner, pp. 52–53; Dawson, p. 2; Dommen, p. 924.
  29. Dawson, p. 7.

III. Prelude to a Tragedy

1. Turner, p. 6.
2. Duiker, p. 97.
3. Turner, p. 44.
4. Marr, p. 519.
5. Duiker, p. 320.
6. *Ibid.*, p. 376, 384.
7. *Ibid.*, p. 383, 386.
8. Truong Chinh quoted in Turner, p. 44.
9. Turner, p. 52.
10. *Ibid.*, p. 58.
11. *Ibid.*, p. 137.
12. Nguyen Ngoc Thuan, p. 64.
13. Bui Tin, p. 24.
14. Turner, p. 138.
15. Bui Tin, p. 29.
16. Ho Chi Minh quoted in Turner, pp. 140–141.
17. Turner, pp. 141–142.
18. *Ibid.*, p. 143.
19. *Ibid.*, p. 166.
20. Phan Quynh Giao, "What Happened to My Village," in Hawthorne, pp. 43–44.
21. *Ibid.*, pp. 45–46.
22. Nguyen Ngoc Thuan, p. 52.
23. Mallin, p. 59.
24. *Ibid.*, p. 69.
25. *Ibid.*, p. 80.
26. Hosmer, p. 16.
27. *Ibid.*, p. 42.
28. Wiesner, p. 162.
29. Taylor, p. 141.
30. *Ibid.*, p. 142.
31. Hosmer, p. 49.
32. Taylor, p. 143.
33. Turner, p. 251.
34. *Ibid.*, p. 250.
35. Wiesner, p. 163.

IV. Bamboo Fences

1. Dommen, p. 2, 878.
2. Lomperis, p. 162.
3. Desbarats, "Human Rights" in Thai Quang Trung, p. 61.
4. *Ibid.*, p. 63; Metzner, p. xiii.
5. Bui Diem, p. 343.
6. Chanda, 1975.
7. Pham Lan, p. 156.
8. Huynh Jade, pp. 47–49.
9. Desbarats in Thai Quang Trung, p. 63.
10. Nguyen Ngoc Thuan, pp. 79–81.
11. Metzner, p. xiv.
12. *Ibid.*, pp. 62–65.
13. Pham Anh Dung, "Souvenirs de Vu Duc Giang," in Tran Xuan Dung, p. 524.
14. Nguyen Van Canh, p. 124.
15. Nguyen Cong Hoan, "Promises," in Santoli, p. 286.
16. Phan Quynh Giao, "Living with Communism," in Hawthorne, p. 188.
17. Nguyen Van Canh, pp. 126–127.
18. Nguyen Tuong Lai, "New Socialist Man," in Santoli, p. 293.
19. Desbarats in Thai Quan Trung, p. 62.
20. Ngoc Dien, "Life as a Schoolteacher," in Hawthorne, p. 200.
21. Nguyen Ngoc Thuan, p. 301.
22. Huynh Jade, p. 49.
23. Nguyen Ngoc Thuan, p. 306.
24. Son Ha, "After the Communist Takeover," in Hawthorne, p. 140.
25. Cargill, p. 10.
26. Nguyen Van Canh, pp. 45–47.
27. Nhu Van Lo 1978.
28. Cargill, p. 9.
29. Pham Lan, p. 170.
30. *Ibid.*, p. 167.
31. Nguyen Van Canh, p. 37.
32. Templer, pp. 57–58.
33. Nhat Tien, "In the Footsteps of a Water Buffalo," in Huynh Sanh Thong, pp. 3–13.
34. Vo Ky Dien, "The Old Man who Believed Only What He Saw," in Huynh Sanh Thong, pp. 19–25.
35. Desbarats in Thai Quan Trung, p. 49.

36. Nguyen Van Canh, p. 181.
37. Dommen, p. 628.
38. Desbarats in Thai Quan Trung, p. 50.
39. Huynh Jade, p. 191.
40. Thanh Dung, "To Serve the Cause of Women's Liberation," in Huynh Sanh Thong, p. 45.
41. *Ibid.*, p. 44.
42. *Ibid.*, pp. 70–72.
43. McKelvey, p. 3.
44. *Ibid.*, p. 29.
45. Nguyen Kien, p. 279.
46. Truong Nhu Tang, p. 289.
47. Bui Tin, p. 89.
48. *Ibid.*, pp. 100–101.
49. Pham Lan, pp. 166–169.

V. A Police State

1. Pham Lan, p. 183.
2. Nguyen Mong Giac, "Suicides," in Huynh Sanh Thong, p. 199.
3. Truong Nhu Tang, pp. 279–282.
4. Doan Van Toai, p. 278.
5. Tran Tri Vu, p. 297.
6. *Ibid.*, p. 302.
7. *Ibid.*, p. 323.
8. *Ibid.*, pp. 364–366.
9. Freeman, p. 89, 341.
10. Doan Van Toai, p. 23.
11. *Ibid.*, pp. 66–69.
12. *Ibid.*, pp. 95–100.
13. *Ibid.*, pp. 210–215.
14. *Ibid.*, p. 228.
15. *Ibid.*, pp. 242–244.
16. *Ibid.*, p. 249.
17. *Ibid.*, pp. 257–261.
18. *Ibid.*, pp. 293–294.
19. *Ibid.*, pp. 307–311.
20. *Ibid.*, pp. 324–328.

VI. Incarceration

1. Truong Nhu Tang, p. 272.
2. *Ibid.*, p. 273.
3. Desbarats, "Repression in the Socialist Republic of Vietnam," in Moore, p. 195.
4. Le Huu Tri, p. 21.
5. Jamieson, p. 364.
6. Taylor, p. 241.
7. Tran Tri Vu, p. 17.
8. Freeman, p. 89, 211.
9. Le Huu Tri, p. 31.
10. Le Thi Duc, "The Vigil," in Santoli, p. 281.
11. Truong Nhu Tang, p. 274.
12. *Ibid.*, p. 275.
13. *Ibid.*, p. 278.
14. *Ibid.*, p. 279.
15. Son Ha, "After the Communist Takeover," in Hawthorne, p. 141.
16. Chanoff D., p. 193.
17. Tran Tri Vu, p. 301.
18. McKelvey, p. 86.
19. Tran Tri Vu, p. 23.
20. *Ibid.*, p. 34, 110; Huynh Jade, p. 106.
21. Huynh Jade, pp. 113–114.
22. *Ibid.*, pp. 143–144.
23. Tran Tri Vu, p. 203.
24. Chanoff, p. 193.
25. Tran Tri Vu, "The Discipline House," in Santoli, p. 277.
26. *Ibid.*, p. 309.
27. *The Soldier*, Asia Video 36, Westminster, CA.
28. Huynh Jade, p. 54.
29. Taylor, p. 241.
30. Metzner, p. 69.
31. Tran Tri Vu, p. 108.
32. Taylor, p. 241.
33. Tran Tri Vu, pp. 73–74.
34. Huynh Jade, p. 57.
35. Tran Tri Vu, p. 91.
36. Le Huu Tri, pp. 208–209.
37. Huynh Jade, p. 54; Tran Tri Vu, p. 269.
38. Le Huu Tri, p. 99.
39. *Ibid.*, p. 202.
40. *Ibid.*, pp. 184–185.
41. McKelvey, p. 89.
42. Le Huu Tri, p. 57; Huynh Jade, p. 87; Tran Tri Vu, p. 17, 310.
43. McKelvey, p. 70.
44. Hawthorne, p. 82, 145.

VII. Southern Gulags

1. Engelmann, p. 239.
2. Tran Tri Vu, p. 71.

3. Huynh Jade, p. 54.
4. Tran Tri Vu, "The Discipline House," in Santoli, p. 279.
5. Huynh Jade, p. 54.
6. Pham A., p. 16, 99.
7. Tran Tri Vu, pp. 38–42.
8. Huynh Jade, pp. 57–63.
9. *Ibid.*, p. 71.
10. *Ibid.*, p. 67.
11. Tran Tri Vu, p. 35.
12. Nguyen Ngoc Thuan, p. 107.
13. Tran Tri Vu, p. 23.
14. Ha Thuc Sinh, "Welcome to Trang Lon Reeducation Camp," in Huynh Sanh Thong, p. 95.
15. Nguyen Ngoc Thuan, p. 99.
16. Taylor, p. 243.
17. Huynh Jade, p. 54.
18. Taylor, p. 242.
19. Nguyen Ngoc Thuan, p. 98.
20. Tran Tri Vu, p. 12.
21. Taylor, p. 244.
22. Tran Tri Vu, pp. 199–200.
23. *Ibid.*, p. 22.
24. Le Huu Tri, p. 40.
25. Tran Tri Vu, p. 59.
26. *Ibid.*, pp. 21–22.
27. Le Huu Tri, p. 40.
28. Taylor, p. 245.
29. Tran Tri Vu, p. 23.
30. Le Huu Tri, p. 42.
31. *Ibid.*, pp. 83–85.
32. Tran Tri Vu, p. 101.
33. *Ibid.*, p. 32.
34. *Ibid.*, pp. 73–74.
35. *Ibid.*, p. 35.
36. Nguyen Ngoc Thuan, p. 125.
37. *Ibid.*, pp. 199–200.
38. Tran Tri Vu, p. 36.
39. *Ibid.*, p. 41.
40. *Ibid.*, p. 75.
41. *Ibid.*, p. 35.
42. *Ibid.*, pp. 120–121.
43. *Ibid.*, p. 262.
44. Huynh Jade, p. 105.
45. Tran Tri Vu, p. 263.
46. *Ibid.*, p. 274.
47. *Ibid.*, p. 34.
48. *Ibid.*, p. 110.
49. Huynh Jade, p. 66.
50. *Ibid.*, p. 106.
51. Tran Tri Vu, p. 50.
52. *Ibid.*, p. 122.
53. *Ibid.*, p. 87.
54. Nguyen Ngoc Thuan, "The Man Who Dreamed of Spring," in Huynh Sanh Thong, p. 114.
55. Vo Ky Dien, "Brother Ten," in Huynh Sanh Thong, p. 29.
56. Nguyen Ngoc Thuan, "The Man Who Dreamed of Spring," in Huynh Sanh Thong, p. 114.
57. Tran Xuan Ninh, "Why We Must Investigate Hanoi's Reeducation Concentration Policy," in Tran Xuan Dung, p. 534.
58. *Ibid.*, p. 535.
59. *Ibid.*
60. Tran Tri Vu, p. 227.
61. *Ibid.*, pp. 352–359.
62. *Ibid.*, p. 142.
63. *Ibid.*, pp. 167–170.
64. *Ibid.*, p. 252.
65. Taylor, p. 262.
66. Nguyen Ngoc Thuan, pp. 243–245.
67. Tran Tri Vu, pp. 270–271.
68. *Ibid.*, pp. 271–272.
69. *Ibid.*, p. 272.
70. Nguyen Ngoc Thuan, p. 263; Le Huu Tri, p. 162.
71. Nguyen Ngoc Thuan, p. 264.
72. Tran Tri Vu, p. 203.
73. Lu Thanh, pp. 49–52.
74. *Ibid.*, pp. 73–83.
75. *Ibid.*, pp. 84–85.
76. *Ibid.*, pp. 89–92.
77. *Ibid.*, pp. 96–111.
78. *Ibid.*, pp. 97–98, 105–106, 112.
79. Taylor, pp. 256–257.
80. *Ibid.*, pp. 258–260.
81. Story of "Dr. Do The Long." Private communication.

VIII. Northern Gulags

1. Vuong Thien, "Nhung manh vun cua cuoc doi," in Dac San Vo Khoa Thu Duc, pp. 90–95.
2. *Ibid.*, p. 91.
3. Freeman, p. 228.
4. Dac San, p. 92.

5. *Ibid.*, p. 93.
6. Nguyen Huu Hiep, "Postwar Memoirs," in Tran Xuan Dung, p. 424.
7. *Ibid.*, p. 440.
8. *Ibid.*, p. 442.
9. Nguyen Chi Thien, pp. 17–19.
10. Nguyen Huu Hiep in Tran Xuan Dung, p. 448.
11. *Ibid.*, p. 450.
12. Bao Ninh, p. 47.
13. *Ibid.*, p. 79.
14. *Ibid.*, p. 84.
15. Isaacs, p. 157.
16. Metzner, p. 11.
17. *Ibid.*, p. 18.
18. *Ibid.*, p. 19.
19. *Ibid.*, pp. 21–22.
20. Dommen, p. 947.
21. Metzner, p. 85.
22. *Ibid.*, p. 26.
23. *Ibid.*, p. 27, 84.
24. *Ibid.*, pp. 31–32.
25. *Ibid.*, p. 64.
26. *Ibid.*, p. 71.
27. *Ibid.*, p. 75.
28. Freeman, p. 237.
29. Metzner, pp. 76–77.
30. *Ibid.*, p. 78.
31. Freeman, p. 89, 231.
32. Metzner, p. 79.
33. *Ibid.*, pp. 90–91.
34. Freeman, p. 244.
35. *Ibid.*, p. 246.
36. *Ibid.*, pp. 251–252.
37. Interview with Col. Thi in October 1997.
38. Pham Anh Dung, "Souvenirs de Vu Duc Giang," in Tran Xuan Dung. p. 524.
39. Robinson, p. 196.
40. Freeman, p. 237.

IX. Starvation

1. Lu Thanh, pp. 94–95, 97.
2. Le Huu Tri, p. 31.
3. *Ibid.*, p. 119.
4. *Ibid.*, p. 104.
5. Lu Thanh, p. 92, 97.
6. Nguyen Ngoc Thuan, p. 98.
7. Son Ha, "After the Communist Takeover," in Hawthorne, p. 150.
8. Tran Tri Vu, p. 314.
9. Freeman, p. 238.
10. Le Huu Tri, pp. 57–61.
11. Tran Tri Vu, p. 107.
12. *Ibid.*, p. 282.
13. Nguyen Ngoc Thuan in Huynh Sanh Thong, p. 119.
14. Freeman, p. 89, 231.
15. Tran Tri Vu, p. 167.
16. Vo Hoang, "A New Place," in Huynh Sanh Thong, p. 113.
17. Bui Van Cao, "Living Under Communism," in Hawthorne, p. 167.
18. Freeman, p. 89, 217.
19. Ho Khanh, p. 137.
20. *Ibid.*, p. 139; Tran Tri Vu, p. 32.
21. Son Ha in Hawthorne, pp. 145–146.
22. Freeman, p. 89, 232.
23. Ho Khanh, p. 137.
24. Freeman, p. 249.
25. *Ibid.*, p. 248.
26. Ho Khanh, p. 140.
27. Huynh Jade, p. 71.
28. Ho Khanh, p. 139.
29. Huynh Jade, p. 67.
30. Freeman, pp. 89, 259–260.
31. Huynh Jade, p. 73.
32. Le Huu Tri, p. 168.
33. Tran Tri Vu, p. 80.
34. Freeman, p. 89, 265.
35. Taylor, p. 265.
36. McKelvey, p. 2, 43.
37. Freeman, p. 89, 260.
38. Tran Tri Vu, p. 167.
39. Tran Tri Vu, p. 209.
40. *Ibid.*, p. 203.
41. Nguyen Ngoc Thuan, pp. 262–263.
42. Tran Tri Vu, p. 219.
43. *Ibid.*, pp. 313–314.
44. *Ibid.*, p. 130.
45. Taylor, p. 266.
46. Nguyen Ngoc Thuan, p. 263.
47. *Ibid.*, p. 263; Le Huu Tri, p. 162.
48. Taylor, p. 266.
49. Freeman, p. 252.
50. Taylor, p. 292.
51. Le Huu Tri, p. 192.
52. Tran Tri Vu, p. 263.

53. *Ibid.*, p. 226.
54. *Ibid.*, p. 325.
55. *Ibid.*, p. 326.
56. Tuong Nang Tien, "Communism and Guigoz-canism," in Huynh Sanh Thong, p. 166.
57. *Ibid.*
58. Luu Thai Dzo, "The Guigoz Can," in Dac San, p. 69.
59. Tuong Nang Tien in Huynh Sanh Thong, p. 167.
60. *Ibid.*, p. 169.
61. *Ibid.*, p. 171.
62. *Ibid.*

X. Executions, Tortures, and Confinements

1. Mollica, 1998, pp. 543–553.
2. Huynh Jade, p. 79.
3. Lu Thanh, pp. 95–96, 97.
4. Freeman, p. 246.
5. Huynh Jade, p. 71; Le Huu Tri, p. 69.
6. Le Huu Tri, p. 137.
7. Huynh Jade, p. 67.
8. Lu Thanh, p. 97, 111.
9. McKelvey, pp. 2, 86–90.
10. Lu Thanh, p. 96, 97.
11. Huynh Jade, pp. 86–87.
12. Freeman, p. 213.
13. Huynh Jade, pp. 74–75.
14. Sagan, p. 30.
15. Tran Tri Vu, p. 296.
16. McKelvey, p. 90.
17. Lu Thanh, p. 97.
18. Nguyen Ngoc Thuan, p. 108.
19. Le Huu Tri, p. 52.
20. Tran Tri Vu, p. 91.
21. Al Santoli, p. 278.
22. Nguyen Ngoc Thuan, p. 140.
23. Le Huu Tri, p. 153.
24. Tran Tri Vu, p. 159.
25. Nguyen Ngoc Thuan, p. 108, 257.
26. Huynh Jade, p. 71.
27. Taylor, p. 249; Huynh Jade, p. 54.
28. Sagan, pp. 28–29.
29. Le Huu Tri, p. 153.
30. Tran Tri Vu, pp. 159–160.
31. Huynh Jade, p. 71.
32. Taylor, p. 249.
33. *Ibid.*, p. 255.
34. Sagan, pp. 29–30.
35. McKelvey, p. 85.
36. Huynh Jade, pp. 82–84.
37. *Ibid.*, pp. 109–111.
38. Pham X.A., pp. 14–15.
39. McKelvey, p. 208.
40. Taylor, p. 267; Le Huu Tri, p. 41.
41. Nguyen Ngoc Thuan, p. 116.
42. Freeman, p. 89, 216.
43. Lu Thanh, pp. 97, 98–100.
44. Le Huu Tri, p. 193.
45. *Ibid.*, p. 185.
46. Metzner, p. 71.
47. Taylor, p. 273.
48. Nguyen Van Canh, p. 215.
49. *Ibid.*, p. 126.
50. *Ibid.*, p. 128.
51. *Ibid.*
52. Desbarats in Moore, p. 194.
53. Hawthorne, p. 188.
54. Desbarats in Moore, p. 195.
55. *Ibid.*, p. 196.
56. *Ibid.*, p. 197.
57. Metzner, p. xiii.

XI. Thought Reform

1. Jamieson, p. 364.
2. Sagan G., "Prisoners of Conscience," in Santoli, p. 266.
3. Santoli, p. 273.
4. Tran Xuan Ninh in Tran Quoc Dung, p. 534.
5. Nguyen Ngoc Thuan, p. 123; Le Huu Tri, p. 37.
6. Tran Tri Vu, p. 69.
7. Son Ha in Hawthorne, p. 147.
8. Tran Tri Vu, p. 60.
9. Bui Van Cao, "Living Under Communism," in Hawthorne, p. 167.
10. Engelmann, p. 239.
11. Jamieson, p. 364.
12. Tran Tri Vu, p. 167.
13. Jamieson, p. 365.
14. Metzner, p. xiii.
15. Lu Thanh, p. 102.
16. *Ibid.*, p. 100.
17. Le Huu Tri, p. 89.

18. Tran Tri Vu, p. 112.
19. *Ibid.*, p. 217.
20. *Ibid.*, p. 113.
21. Lu Thanh, p. 97.
22. Tran Tri Vu, p. 112.
23. *Ibid.*, p. 114.
24. Young, S. "Village Development," in Santoli, p. 211.
25. Jamieson, p. 365.
26. Bui Tin, p. 66.
27. *Ibid.*, p. 90.
28. Jamieson, p. 366.
29. Nguyen Chi Thien, p. 117.

XII. Hard Labor and Poor Medical Care

1. Lu Thanh, p. 96, 97.
2. Le Tri, p. 01, 47.
3. *Ibid.*, p. 69.
4. McKelvey, pp. 154–156.
5. Lu Thanh, pp. 74–77, 97.
6. Le Tri, p. 87.
7. McKelvey, p. 89.
8. Sagan, p. 34.
9. Nguyen Chi Thien in Nguyen Canh, pp. 224–225.
10. Taylor, p. 258.
11. Nguyen Ngoc Thuan, pp. 102–104; Le Huu Tri, p. 54; Taylor, p. 258.
12. Pham X.A., p. 19.
13. *Ibid.*, p. 20.
14. Huynh Jade, p. 58; Le Huu Tri, p. 54.
15. Taylor, p. 259.
16. Nguyen Ngoc Thuan, p. 107.
17. Huynh Jade, p. 59.
18. Nguyen Ngoc Thuan, p. 107.
19. Nguyen Ngoc Thuan in Huynh Sanh Thong, pp. 188–189.
20. Freeman, p. 218.
21. *Ibid.*, p. 231.
22. *Ibid.*, p. 261.
23. Jade Huynh, p. 165.
24. Nguyen Ngan, pp. 199–200.

XIII. Defense Mechanisms

1. Le Huu Tri, p. 57; Huynh Jade, p. 87; Tran Tri Vu, p. 310.

2. Taylor, p. 260.
3. Freeman, p. 89, 241.
4. Tran Tri Vu, p. 311.
5. Freeman, p. 246.
6. Tran Tri Vu, p. 275.
7. Taylor, pp. 286–291.
8. McKelvey, p. 85.
9. McKelvey, p. 2, 42.
10. *Ibid.*, p. 63.
11. Freeman, p. 89, 220.
12. *Ibid.*, p. 264.
13. *Ibid.*, p. 220.
14. Nguyen Van Canh, pp. 142–143.
15. Tran Tri Vu, p. 304.
16. Baradacco, p. 73.
17. Tran Tri Vu, p. 271.
18. Tran Xuan Ninh in Xuan Tran Dung, p. 535.
19. Doan Van Toai, pp. 293–294.
20. Nguyen Ngan, p. 241.
21. Lu Thanh, p. 97.
22. Tran Vu, p. 326.
23. Freeman, pp. 252–253.

XIV. Well-Known Prisoners

1. Tran Tri Vu, "The Discipline House," in Santoli, p. 279.
2. Terzani in Taylor, p. 261.
3. Taylor, p. 261.
4. Metzner, p. 83.
5. *Ibid.*, p. 27.
6. *Ibid.*, p. 84.
7. Nguyen Cong Hoan in Taylor, p. 263.
8. Nguyen Canh, pp. 197–198.
9. Jamieson, p. 363.
10. Desbarats in Moore, p. 196.
11. Dommen, p. 957.
12. Nguyen Canh, p. 201.
13. Engelmann, p. 244.
14. Nguyen Canh, p. 201.
15. *Ibid.*, p. 215.
16. *Ibid.*, p. 216.
17. *Ibid.*
18. Bui Tin, p. 92.
19. Nguyen Canh, pp. 215–216.
20. Metzner, p. xiv.
21. Nguyen Canh, p. 216.
22. Templer, p. 273.

23. Brums W.R.
24. Desbarats in Thai Quang Trung, p. 50.
25. Jamieson, p. 364.
26. Isaacs, p. 186.
27. Metzner, p. xv.
28. *Ibid.*, p. 85.
29. McKelvey, p. 71, 90.

XV. Post-Reeducation Ordeal

1. Lu Thanh, p. 116.
2. *Ibid.*, pp. 112–113.
3. McKelvey, p. 5.
4. *Ibid.*
5. Lu Thanh, p. 119.
6. McKelvey, p. 45.
7. *Ibid.*, p. 6.
8. Lu Thanh, p. 123.
9. Le Tri, pp. 260–265.
10. Lu Thanh, pp. 125–128.
11. McKelvey, p. xii.
12. Cargill, p. 10.
13. Tran Tri Vu, p. 273.
14. McKelvey, pp. 46–49.
15. Ha Nguyen, "Our Lady of the Boat," in Cargill, p. 54.
16. Phung Le, "Flight from Classification 13," in Cargill, p. 107.
17. McKelvey, p. 54.
18. Desbarats in Thai Quang Trung, p. 48.
19. Interview with Xuan Hang Oct. 1997.
20. Son Ha in Hawthorne, p. 165.
21. Cargill, p. 181.
22. *Ibid.*, p. 182.
23. Kamm, p. 185.
24. Tran Tri Vu, p. 217.
25. Santoli, p. 274.
26. McKelvey, p. 6, 100.
27. *Ibid.*, p. 243.
28. Mollica, pp. 543–553.
29. Taylor, p. 292.
30. McKelvey, pp. 128–129.
31. *Ibid.*, p. xvii.
32. Tran Xuan Ninh in Tran Xuan Dung, p. 535.
33. Bao Ninh, p. 79.
34. *Ibid.*, p. 47.
35. Bao Ninh in Kamm, p. 185.

XVI. New Economic Zones

1. Tran Tri Vu, p. 228.
2. Desbarats in Moore, p. 197.
3. Hoang Ngoc Than Dung, "To Serve the Cause of Women's Liberation," in Huynh Sanh Thong. p. 74.
4. *Ibid.*, p. 73.
5. *Ibid.*, p. 68.
6. *Ibid.*, p. 77.
7. *Ibid.*, p. 74.
8. Desbarats in Moore, p. 199.
9. Cargill, p. 9.
10. Pham Lan, p. 181.
11. Huynh Jade, p. 68.
12. Pham Lan, p. 181.
13. Hung Truong, "Drowning the Boat," in Cargill, pp. 67–69.
14. Tran Tri Vu, p. 206.
15. Cargill, p. 71.
16. Tran Tri Vu, p. 206.
17. *Ibid.*, p. 250.
18. *Ibid.*
19. *Ibid.*, p. 203.
20. *Ibid.*, p. 244.
21. *Ibid.*, p. 286.
22. Desbarats in Moore, pp. 199–200.
23. Nguyen Ngoc Thuan, pp. 312–313.
24. Tran Tri Vu, p. 216.
25. Desbarats in Moore, p. 200.
26. Nguyen Canh, p. 221.
27. Jamieson, p. 365.
28. Jamieson, p. 366; Desbarats in Moore. p. 201.
29. Tran Thanh Son, "NEZ," in Santoli, p. 282.
30. Desbarats in Thai Quang Trung, p. 59.
31. Tran Tri Vu, p. 206.
32. Tran Thanh Son in Santoli, p. 282.
33. Desbarats in Thai Quang Trung, p. 60.

XVII. Disillusion

1. Doan Van Toai, p. 385.
2. Doan Van Toai, "Moral and Psy-

chological Lessons of Vietnam," in Moore, p. 32.
   3. Doan Van Toai, p. 311.
   4. *Ibid.*, p. 328.
   5. Nguyen Van Canh, p. 181.
   6. Dommen, p. 628.
   7. *Ibid.*, p. 957.
   8. Truong Nhu Tang, p. 260.
   9. *Ibid.*, p. 264.
   10. *Ibid.*, p. 282.
   11. Nguyen Cong Hoan, "Promises," in Santoli, p. 287.
   12. *Ibid.*, p. 288.
   13. Doan Van Toai, p. 339.
   14. *Ibid.*, p. 350.
   15. Dommen, p. 950.
   16. Summers, "Winners and Losers," in Santoli, pp. 283–284.
   17. Duong Thu Huong in Kamm, p. 145.
   18. *Ibid.*, pp. 148–149.
   19. Templer, p. 185.
   20. Bao Ninh, p. 15.
   21. *Ibid.*, p. 16.
   22. *Ibid.*, p. 20.
   23. *Ibid.*, p. 79.
   24. *Ibid.*, p. 47.
   25. Templer, p. 190.
   26. Bui Tin, p. 17.
   27. Templer, pp. 39–40.
   28. Bui Tin, p. 16.
   29. *Ibid.*, p. 167.
   30. *Ibid.*, p. 171.
   31. *Ibid.*, p. 174.
   32. Templer, p. 110.
   33. *Ibid.*, p. 113.
   34. *Ibid.*, p. 116.
   35. *Ibid.*, p. 118.
   36. Kamm, p. 190.
   37. *Ibid.*, p. 191.

XVIII. Of Cemeteries

   1. Isaacs, p. 158.
   2. Huynh Jade, pp. 48–49.
   3. Bui Tin, p. 95.
   4. *Asia Video 36: The Soldier.*
   5. Sheehan, p. 131.
   6. Tornquist, p. 111.
   7. Bui Diem, p. xiii.
   8. Sheehan, p. 130.
   9. *Ibid.*, p. 131.
   10. Lamb, p. 100.
   11. Kamm, p. 182.
   12. Heduy, pp. 23–33.
   13. Bui Tin, p. 95.
   14. Malarney S.K., "The Fatherland Remembers Your Sacrifice," in Hue Tam Ho Tai, p. 67.
   15. *Ibid.*, p. 60.
   16. Hue Tai, p. 191.
   17. Kamm, p. 83.

XIX. Epilogue

   1. Turner R.F., "Myths and Realities in the Vietnam Debate," in Moore, pp. 45–46.
   2. Summers, p. 188.
   3. *Ibid.*, p. 88.
   4. *Ibid.*, pp. 185–186.
   5. *Ibid.*, p. 90.
   6. Bui Tin, p. 94.
   7. Doan Van Toai, p. 324, 328.
   8. Wiesner, pp. 346–347.
   9. Bui Diem, p. 343.
   10. Desbarats in Thai Quang Trung, p. 47.
   11. Humana, p. 305.
   12. Sheehan, p. 14.
   13. Templer, p. 133.
   14. Frank 00.
   15. Lomperis, p. 173.
   16. Dommen, p. 1006.
   17. Courtois, p. xvii.
   18. Leeden 2002.

Bibliography

Asia Video 36: The Soldier. Thuy NGA Productions. Westminster, California: 2002.
Badaracco, J. L. *Leading Quietly: An Unorthodox Guide to Doing the Right Thing*. Boston: Harvard Business School Press, 2002.
Bao Ninh. *The Sorrow of War*. New York: Riverhead Books, 1993.
Brums, W.R. "Pope Names 37 Cardinals." *The Criterion*. 26 Jan. 2001: 1.
Bui Diem. *In the Jaws of History*. Bloomington: Indiana University Press, 1999. Reprint edition.
Bui Tin. *Following Ho Chi Minh: The Memoirs of a North Vietnamese Colonel*. Honolulu: University of Hawaii Press, 1995.
Bui Van Cao. "Living Under Communism." *Refugee: The Vietnamese Experience*, ed. L. Hawthorne. Oxford and New York: Oxford University Press, 1982.
Cargill, M.T. and J.Q. Huynh. *Voices of Vietnamese Boat People*. Jefferson, North Carolina: McFarland, 2000.
Chanda, Nayan. "Speeding Toward Reunification." *Far Eastern Economic Review*. 5 Dec. 1975.
Chanoff, D. and D.V. Toai. *Portrait of the Enemy*. New York: Random House, 1986.
Courtois S., et al. *The Black Book of Communism: Crime, Terror, Repression*. Cambridge, Massachusetts and London: Harvard University Press, 1999.
Dac San Vo Khoa Thu Duc Bulletin (Bulletin of the Thu Duc Military Academy), Houston, Texas: Summer 2000.
Dawson, A. *55 Days: The Fall of South Vietnam*. Upper Saddle River, New Jersey: Prentice Hall, 1977.
Desbarats, J. "Human Rights: Two Steps Forward, One Step Backward?" *Vietnam Today: Assessing the New Trends*, ed. Quang Trung Thai. New York: Crane Russak, 1990.
____. "Repression in the Socialist Republic of Vietnam." *The Vietnam Debate: A Fresh Look at the Old Arguments*, ed. J.N. Moore. Lanham, Maryland: University Press of America, 1990.
Doan Van Toai. "Moral and Psychological Lessons of Vietnam." *The Vietnam Debate: A Fresh Look at the Old Arguments*, ed. J.N. Moore. Lanham, Maryland: University Press of America, 1990.
____ and D. Chanoff. *The Vietnamese Gulag*. New York: Simon & Schuster, 1986.

Dommen, A.J. *The Indochinese Experience of the French and the Americans.* Bloomington: Indiana University Press, 2001.
Dooley, T.A. *Deliver Us from Evil.* New York: Farrar, Straus, Cudahy, 1956.
Duiker, W.J. *Ho Chi Minh: A Life.* New York: Hyperion, 2000.
Engelmann, L. *Tears Before the Rain: An Oral History of the Fall of South Vietnam.* Oxford and New York: Oxford University Press, 1990.
Frank, R. "In Paddies of Vietnam: Americans Once Again Land in a Quagmire." *Wall Street Journal* 21 Apr. 2000.
Freeman, J. *Hearts of Sorrow: Vietnamese-American Lives.* Palo Alto, California: Stanford University Press, 1989.
Giao Phan Quynh. "What Happened to My Village." *Refugee: The Vietnamese Experience,* ed. L. Hawthorne. Oxford and New York: Oxford University Press, 1982.
____. "Living with Communism." *Refugee: The Vietnamese Experience,* ed. L. Hawthorne. Oxford and New York: Oxford University Press, 1982.
Graetz, R. *Vietnam: Opening the Doors to the World.* Corinthian, 1988.
Hawthorne, L., ed. *Refugee: The Vietnamese Experience.* Oxford and New York: Oxford University Press, 1982.
Héduy, P. *Histoire de l' Indochine: La Perle de l'Empire.* Albin Michel, 1998.
Ho Khanh. "Hunger: Vietnam Forum." Yale Southeast Asia Studies, 1983 (2).
Hoang Ngoc Than Dung. "To Serve the Cause of Women's Liberation." *To Be Made Over: Tales of Socialist Reeducation in Vietnam,* ed. Sanh hong Huynh. Yale Southeast Asia Studies, 1988.
Hosmer, S.T. *Viet Cong Repression and Its Implication for the Future.* Lexington, Massachusetts: Heath, 1970.
____, and K. Kellen, and B. Jenkins. *The Fall of South Vietnam: Statements by Vietnamese Military and Civilian Leaders.* New York: Crane, Russack and Co., 1980.
Hue Tam Ho Tai. *The Country of Memory: Remaking the Past in Late Socialist Vietnam.* Berkeley: University of California Press, 2001.
Humana, C. *World's Human Rights Guide.* New York, NY: Pan Books, 1987.
Hung Truong. "Drowning the Boat." *Voices of Vietnamese Boat People,* ed. M.T. Cargill and J.Q. Huynh. Jefferson, North Carolina: McFarland, 2000.
Huynh Jade. *South Wind Changing.* St. Paul, Minnesota: Graywolf Press, 1994.
Huynh Sanh Thong, ed. *To Be Made Over: Tales of Socialist Reeducation in Vietnam.* The Lac Vieet series, No. 5: Yale Southeast Asia Studies, 1988.
Isaacs A.R. *Vietnam Shadows: The War, Its Ghosts, and Its Legacy.* Baltimore: Johns Hopkins University Press, 1997.
Jamieson, N.L. *Understanding Vietnam.* Berkeley: University of California Press, 1993.
Kamm, H. *Dragon Ascending: Vietnam and the Vietnamese.* New York: Arcade, 1996.
Kolko, G. *Anatomy of a War.* New York: The New Press, 1994.
Lamb, D. *Vietnam, Now: A Reporter Returns.* New York, NY: Public Affairs, 2002.
Lee J.E., and T. Haynsworth. *White Christmas in April: The Collapse of South Vietnam 1975.* New York: Peter Lang, 1999.
Leeden, M.A. "From Communism to Fascism." *Wall Street Journal* 22 Feb. 2002.
Le Huu Tri. *Prisoner of the Word.* Seattle: Black Heron, 2001.
Le Thanh Khoi. *Le Vietnam: Histoire et Civilisation.* Paris: Editions de Minuit, 1955.
Le Thi Duc. "The Vigil." *To Bear Any Burden,* ed. A. Santoli. Bloomington: Indiana University Press, 1999.
Li Tana. *Nguyen Cochinchina: Southern Vietnam in the Seventeenth and Eighteenth Centuries.* Ithaca, New York: Cornell, 1988.
Lomperis, T.J. *The War Everyone Lost—and Won.* Baton Rouge: Louisiana State University Press, 1984.

Luu Thai Dzo. "The Guigoz Can."
Lu Van Thanh. *The Inviting Call of Wandering Souls*. Jefferson, North Carolina: McFarland, 1997.
Malarney, S.K. "The Fatherland Remembers Your Sacrifice." *The Country of Memory: Remaking the Past in Late Socialist Vietnam*, ed. Tam Ho Tai Hue. Berkeley: University of California Press, 2001.
Mallin, J. *Terror in Vietnam*. Princeton: D. Van Nostrand, 1966.
Marr, D.G. *Vietnam 1945: The Quest for Power*. Berkeley: University of California Press, 1985.
McKelvey, R.S. *A Gift of Barbed Wire*. Pullman: University of Washington Press, 2002.
____. *The Dust of Life: America's Children Abandoned in Vietnam*. Pullman: University of Washington Press, 1999.
Metzner, E.P., et al. *Reeducation in Postwar Vietnam*. College Station: Texas A&M University Press, 2001.
Mollica, R., et al. "The Dose Effect Relationships between Torture and Psychiatric Symptoms in Vietnamese Ex-Political Detainees and a Comparison Group." *Nervous and Mental Disease*. 1988: 543–553.
Moore, J.N. *The Vietnam Debate: A Fresh Look at the Arguments*. Lanham, Maryland: University Press of America, 1990.
Mydans, S. "Old Wounds Slow US-Vietnam Reconciliation." *New York Times* 29 Apr. 2000.
Ngoc Dien. "Life as a Schoolteacher." *Refugee: The Vietnamese Experience*, ed. L. Hawthorne. Oxford and New York: Oxford University Press, 1982.
Nguyen Chi Thien. "Flowers from Hell." The Lac Viet series, No. 1: Yale Southeast Asia Studies, 1984.
Nguyen Ha. "Our Lady of the Boat." *Voices of the Vietnamese Boat People*, ed. M.T. Cargill and Jade Huynh. Jefferson, North Carolina: McFarland, 2000.
Nguyen Huu Hiep. "Postwar Memoirs." *Medical Corps of the Armed Forces RVN*. Melbourne, Australia: Corporate Printers, 2000.
Nguyen Kien. *The Unwanted*. London: Little Brown, 2001.
Nguyen, Ngoc Thuan. "The Man Who Dreamed of Spring." *To Be Made over: Tales of Socialist Reeducation in Vietnam*, ed. Sanh Thong Huynh. Yale Southeast Asia Studies, 1998.
____ and E.E. Richey. *The Will of Heaven*. New York: EP Dutton, 1982.
Nguyen, Ngoc Thong. "A Prisoner's Funeral in Huynh Sanh Thong." *An Anthology of Vietnamese Poems*. New Haven, Connecticut: Yale University Press, 2001.
Nguyen V. Canh. *Vietnam Under Communism, 1975–1982*. Stanford, California: Hoover Press, 1983.
Nguyen Tuong Lai. "New Socialist Man." *To Bear Any Burden*, ed. A. Santoli. Bloomington: Indiana University Press, 1999.
Nguyen Cong Hoan. "Promises." *To Bear Any Burden*, ed. A. Santoli. Bloomington: Indiana University Press, 1999.
Nhat Tien. "In the Footsteps of a Water Buffalo." *To Be Made Over: Tales of Socialist Reeducation in Vietnam*, ed. Sanh Thong Huynh. Yale Southeast Asia Studies, 1988.
Nhu, Van Lo. "Flea Market in Thai Nguyen." *Nguoi Viet Tu Do*. Japanese edition. Jan. 1978.
Pham Anh Dung. "Souvenirs de Vu Duc Giang." *Medical Corps of the Armed Forces RVN*, ed. Xuan Dung Tran. Melbourne, Australia: Corporate Printers, 2000.
Pham D.L. *Two Hamlets in Nam Bo: Memoirs of Life in Vietnam*. Jefferson, North Carolina: McFarland, 2000.
Pham X.A. *Catfish and Mandala*. New York: Picador, 1999.

Phung Le. "Flight from Classification 13." *Voices of the Vietnamese Boat People*, ed. M.T. Cargill and Jade Huynh. Jefferson, North Carolina: McFarland, 2000.
Quan Doi Nhan Dan (People's Army). June 27, 1977.
Robinson, W.C. *Terms of Refuge: The Indochinese Exodus and the International Response*. London: Zed Books, 1998.
Sagan, G. "Prisoners of Conscience." *To Bear Any Burden*, ed. A. Santoli. Bloomington: Indiana University Press, 1999.
____. "Vietnam's Postwar Hell." *Newsweek*, 3 May, 1983: 13.
____, and S. Denney. *Violations of Human Rights in the Socialist Republic of Vietnam: 1975–1983*. Berkeley, California: Aurora Foundation, 1983.
Santoli, A., ed. *To Bear Any Burden*. Bloomington: Indiana University Press, 1999.
Sheehan, N. *After the War Was Over*. New York: Random House, 1992.
Sinh Ha Thuc. "Welcome to Trang Lon Reeducation Camp." *To Be Made Over: Tales of Socialist Reeducation in Vietnam*, ed. Sann Thong Huynh. Yale Southeast Asia Studies, 1999.
Smith, H.D. "Setting the Record Straight." *White Christmas in April: The Collapse of South Vietnam 1975*, eds. J.E. Lee and T. Haynsworth. New York: Peter Lang, 1999.
Son Ha. "After the Communist Takeover." *Refugee. The Vietnamese Experience*, ed. L. Hawthorne. Oxford and New York: Oxford University Press, 1982.
Summers, H.G. *Historical Atlas of the Vietnam War*. Boston: Houghton Mifflin, 1995.
Summers, H.G. "Winners and Losers." *To Bear Any Burden*, ed. A. Santoli. Bloomington: Indiana University Press, 1999.
Taylor, T. *Where the Orange Blooms*. New York: McGraw Hill, 1989.
Templer, R. *Shadows and Wind: A View of Modern Vietnam*. New York: Penguin Books, 1999.
Thai Quang Trung, ed. *Vietnam Today: Assessing the New Trends*. New York: Crane Russak, 1990.
Thanh Dung. "To Serve the Cause of Women's Liberation." *To Be Made Over: Tales of Socialist Reeducation in Vietnam*, ed. Sanh Thong Huynh. Yale Southeast Asia Studies, 1988.
Thien Vuong. "Nhung manh vun cua cuoc doi." *Dac San Vo Khoa Thu Duc Bulletin*, Summer 2000.
Tornquist, D., et al. *Vietnam*. New York: Mallard Press, 1991.
Tran Thanh Son. "NEZ." *To Bear Any Burden*, ed. A. Santoli. Bloomington: Indiana University Press, 1999.
Tran, Tri Vu. "The Discipline House." *To Bear Any Burden*, ed. A. Santoli. Bloomington: Indiana University Press, 1999.
____. *Lost Years: My 1632 Days in Vietnamese Reeducation Camps*. Berkeley: University of California Press, 1988.
Tran Xuan Dung, ed. *Medical Corps of the Armed Forces RVN*. Melbourne, Australia: Corporate Printers, 2000.
Trar Xuan Ninh. "Why We Must Investigate Hanoi's Reeducation Concentration Policy." *Medical Corps of the Armed Forces RVN*, ed. Xuan Dung Tran. Melbourne, Australia: Corporate Printers, 2000.
Truong Nhu Tang. *A Vietcong Memoir*. New York: Vintage, 1986.
Tung Tri-Thien. Private communication.
Tuong Nang Tien. "Communism and Guigoz-canism." *To Be Made Over: Tales of Socialist Reeducation in Vietnam*. Yale Southeast Asia Studies, 1988.
Turner, R.F. "Myths and Realities in the Vietnam Debate." *The Vietnam Debate: A Fresh Look at the Old Arguments*, ed. J.N. Moore. Lanham, Maryland: University Press of America, 1990.

____. Vietnamese *Communism: Its Origins and Development*. Stanford, California: Hoover Institution Press, 1975.
"Vietnam Then and Now." *Wall Street Journal* 28 April 2000.
Vo, N.M. *The Duality of the Vietnamese Mind*. Dac San Hoi Y Si Vietnam tai Hoa Ky, August 2001.
Vuong Thien. "Nhung Manh Vun cua cuoc doi [Fragments of Life]." Bull Thu Duc Military Academy: 3–2000.
Webb, J. "History Proves Vietnam Victors Wrong." *Wall Street Journal* 28 April 2000.
Wiesner, L.A. *Victims and Survivors: Displaced Persons and Other War Victims in Vietnam 1954–1975*. Westport, Connecticut: Greenwood Press, 1988.
Young, S. "Village Development." *To Bear Any Burden*, ed. A. Santoli. Bloomington: Indiana University Press, 1999.

Index

A-30 camp 68, 84–5, 174
airplane position 49, 136
Amerasians 44–5
Amnesty International 59, 101, 168, 171, 202
amputation 62, 78, 156–7
An, Mai Van 170
antenna 47, 66, 120, 122, 124, 145, 160
Apartheid 162–4, 174–8, 214
August revolution 24
auto position 136

Ba, Gen. Ly Tong 17, 169
beatings 47, 64, 91, 133–5, 154, 160, 171
Bien Hoa: jail 48–9; national cemetery 209, 211–213
biography 68, 75–6
boat people 1, 182, 187, 204, 217
Bo bo 99, 103, 119, 129
Bo doi 51, 53, 56–7, 62, 64–5, 69, 74–5, 78–80, 83–4, 89–90, 116–8, 120–1, 123, 126–31, 133–8, 147–8, 157–160, 162–65, 184–5, 194
Bong, Col. Chung Van 171
bribes 18, 38, 46, 51, 79, 86, 139, 160, 170, 173–4, 181, 183, 188
Bu Gia Map camp 60, 77, 82–4, 87–8, 194
Buu Loi camp 82–4

cadre 84, 87–8, 121, 125, 128, 134–5, 140, 144–6, 152, 164, 185, 190, 205, 222
cage 206–7
Cai, Cap. Ben 125, 128, 138, 140, 155, 160, 173, 185
Cam Ranh: airport 13; bay 65
Cao Dai 42
cassava 39–40, 45, 72, 79, 86, 99, 117, 118–9, 123–4, 193
Cham 67
Chi Hoa jail 42, 170
Chi Lang camp 60, 68
Chieu hoi 169
Chinh, Col. Huynh Van 102–3, 168
Chinh, Truong 25, 27, 45
Coercion 190, 194
Communism 8–9, 13, 48, 71, 132, 147–9, 185–6, 195
Conex 59, 70, 72, 81, 120, 137–8, 164, 210
confinement 29, 49, 51, 59, 70, 75, 98, 115, 125, 133, 137, 171, 185, 199
convoy of tears 13–15
Corruption 38–9, 86, 148, 202, 221

D1 camp 153
Da Ban camp 68, 84–6, 153
Dai, Col. 86
Dang Ngoai 5
Dang Trong 5

Dao, Gen. Le Minh 16–7, 169
De Behaine, Bishop 212
depression 63–4, 97, 101, 104, 115, 146–8, 165, 183–4, 187
Desbarats 33–4
Diem, Pres. Ngo Dinh 8, 9, 12–3, 24, 31, 42, 170, 199–200, 208, 217
Dinh, Col. Ton That 100, 171
Dinh Thanh camp 140
discrimination 195
disinformation 167–8
Do, Nguyen Thon 170
Do, Thich Quang 200
Doan, Fr. Nguyen Cong 171
Dong, Pham Van 47, 81, 205
Duan, Le 204
Dung, Gen. Van Tien 11, 19
dysentery 63, 72, 74, 78, 103, 106, 121, 156

escape attempts 1–3, 8, 14–5, 18, 21, 32, 36, 48, 50, 54, 59, 61, 63, 65, 82–3, 85–7, 95, 102–3, 128, 136, 140, 148–9, 160–1, 172, 177, 181–2, 193, 201
executions 1, 3, 26, 29–30, 32–5, 133, 139–142, 210

food rations 57, 64, 72, 74, 104, 117–120, 129, 138, 145, 155, 193

Gia Long (king) 33, 213–4
Giao, Cao 205
Giap, Gen. Vo Nguyen 19, 27
Guigoz-canism 129–132
guillotine center 136, 138
Gulag 1, 3, 27, 58–63, 86, 143, 220

Ha Tay camp 98–100, 165–6
Hai, Gen. Tran Van 20
Ham Tan camp 6, 47–8, 170, (takeover) 161
Hanoi 1–2, 10, 12, 24, 27–8, 40, 48, 54–5, 61, 65, 67, 93, 99, 101, 110, 116, 142, 160, 166, 169–170, 176, 180, 186, 189, 191, 195, 198, 201–2, 204, 212, 214, 221
hard labor 3, 18, 60, 76–7, 83, 90, 96, 99, 101–3, 130, 147, 151–4, 220
Hiep, Dr. 95–8
Hiep Tan camp 74

Ho Chi Minh 3, 8, 23–4, 26, 149, 199, 206, 220; autobiography of 204; and revolution 220–222; trail 94, 216; wives of 204
Ho, Nguyen 205
Hoa, Lt Col. 147
Hoa Hao 8, 42, 208, 217
Hoan, Nguyen Cong 59, 127–8, 168, 201, 212
Hoang, Dr. Vu Ngoc 115
Hoang Lien Son camp 93
Hoc Mon camp 80–2, 140
Hoc, Col. Nguyen Van 100, 171
Hoi chanh 35, 50–1
Honda position 136
Hue (city) 6, 21, 24, 29–30, 109
human rights 1, 9, 34, 60, 71, 142, 149, 163, 171, 173, 181, 199, 205, 220–1
Hung, Gen. Le Van 18–9
hunger 14–5, 42, 51, 57, 63, 66, 72, 75, 82–3, 96, 103, 111, 118, 121–6, 143, 198, 220; *see also* starvation
Huong, Duong Thu 202–3
Huong, Tran Van 28–9

incarceration 1–2, 17, 46, 48, 53, 67, 75–6, 79, 83, 92–3, 104, 115–6, 125, 129, 136, 151, 164–6, 170, 172–3, 178, 183–4, 205, 210
Indochine 177
intimidation 10, 134
isolation cell 51

KaTum camp 60, 86–92, 137, 152
Khmer 5–7
Khmer Rouge 44, 61, 82, 87, 98, 157, 182
Kien Giang camp 68–73
Ky, Marsh. Nguyen Cao 12

land reform: northern 25–7; southern 40–2
Lang Son camp 105–7
Lao Kai camp 95–8
latrines 42, 47, 62–3, 71,194
Le Van Duyet (jail) 50–51
Linh, Nguyen Van 186
lizards 72, 123
Loc, Nguyen Van 170
Long, Do The 88–92
Long Khanh camp 60, 77–8, 80, 93, 117

INDEX

looting 45

Mac Dinh Chi (cemetery) 207–9
malaria 36, 61–2, 77, 82–3, 85, 152–3, 191, 197, 203
malnutrition 2, 17, 51, 64, 88, 95, 97, 103, 121, 125–6, 153, 197
Marx 96, 150, 202
medical care 1, 156–8, 205
Mekong River 7
mental illness 97
mines 40, 64, 73, 87, 90, 140, 151, 154–6
Minh, Gen. Big 19–20
Minh, Thich Thien 170
Minh, Tran The 170
Minh Luong camp 139, 155
mistreatment 63–7, 147–8, 164, 170, 186
monks 37, 42, 170, 199–201
Montagnards 14, 82, 89, 190, 196
mortality 2, 116
Muoi, Do 200

Nam, Gen. Nguyen Khoa 18–20
Nam Ha camp 101
Nam Tien 5, 9
Nazis 126, 143, 168
new economic zone 32, 36, 38, 43, 90, 141, 177, 185, 188–97
Nghe An camp 104–5
Nguyen Anh (prince) 6, 33, 213
Nguyen Hoang 5
Nguyen Hue 6, 33, 164, 214
Nha Ca 171
Nhu, Gen. Bui Van 169
Ninh, Bao 98, 187, 202–3
Ninh, Dr. Tran Xuan 80–1, 185–6
North Vietnamese 10, 12, 15, 17, 37, 109, 169, 186, 200–2, 216
northern camp 93–116

ODP 182
oppression 154, 164, 193–4

Paris Accords 10–11, 170, 215
Phong, Nguyen Xuan 170
Phu, Gen. Pham Van 13
Phu Quoc camp 119, 152, 155
Phuc, Col. Tran Van 101
priests 29–30, 42, 49, 86, 136, 165, 201, 212

Progressive 57, 65, 75, 87, 128, 146
PTSD 184, 186

Quang, Col. Phan Duy 171
Quang, Thich Huyen 42, 199
Quang, Thich Tri 42, 199
Quat, Dr. Phan Huy 170
Que, Dr. Nguyen Dan 171
Quynh, Fr. Hoang 170
Quynh Luu 27

rats 30, 72, 123, 129, 146
Red River Delta 5, 7
reeducation 1, 3, 18, 27, 33, 35–6, 41–2, 46–7, 49, 53–5, 59–60, 63, 81, 101, 117, 126, 128, 130, 142–3, 146, 148–9, 154, 157, 171, 173–87, 211
revenge 33, 55, 122, 133, 141, 149, 161, 207
rice 7–8, 18, 38–40, 47, 49, 57, 59, 70, 72, 74–5, 79, 85–6, 99, 106, 116–20, 129–30, 132, 183, 192–3

Sagan, Ginetta 1, 59
Saigon 1, 3, 6, 10–11, 14, 16–7, 21, 28–9, 31–4, 37, 43–5, 49, 53–4, 59–60, 73, 77, 79, 89, 99–100, 119, 127, 141–2, 149, 169–70, 185–6, 194–5, 199–201, 207, 211–2
sanctions 66, 91, 133–4, 175
sanitation 62, 77, 106
scabies 63, 77, 102, 115
self-criticism 68–71, 81, 85, 144, 151, 155, 164
Smith, Gen. Homer 17
snakes 72, 77, 123, 125, 130, 181
Son La camp 93–5
Song Mao camp 152
South Vietnamese 3, 6–7, 10–11, 13, 16, 19, 21, 24, 28, 30–2, 34, 39, 53, 59, 73, 93–4, 97, 99, 142, 144–5, 164, 170, 186, 201, 208, 211, 213, 217–8
Southern camp 68–92
starvation 1, 26, 51, 59, 72, 76, 88, 120–1, 129, 146, 168 *see also* hunger
suicide 18, 20, 26, 34, 38, 42, 64, 78, 105, 146, 165
Sumners, Col. 201–2
Suoi Mau camp 62, 81, 140, 160

T–50, T–51, T–52, T–53 camps 59, 62

Tang, Truong Nhu 47, 54, 200, 217
Tan Lap camp 97
Tet offensive 29–30
Thach, Nguyen Co 142, 169
Than, Lt Comm. 148, 164
Thien, Capt. Vuong 93
Thien, Nguyen Chi 96, 150, 154, 206
Thieu, Pres. Nguyen Van 11–3, 20, 31, 40, 42, 46, 99, 144, 168, 209
Tin, Bui 149, 204, 207, 213
Tien, Capt. 86, 135
Tiet Thuong sculpture 164, 208–10
Thao, Truong 171
Tho, Le Duck 31, 55, 142, 204
thought reform 29, 53–4, 59, 64, 143–6
Thu, Capt. Nguyen Thanh 164, 209–10
Thu Duc (camp) 47, 62, 99, (military academy) 18, 105
Thu, Tran Dinh 171
Thuan, Fr. Nguyen Van 170
Thuan, Nguyen Ngoc 156
Toai, Doan Van 49–51, 199, 217
Ton, Col. Nguyen Van 171
Torture 1, 27, 33, 35, 49–51, 59, 64–5, 70, 82–3, 86, 100–1, 133–6, 146, 154, 163, 170, 184–5, 200
Trang Lon camp 60, 73–7, 87, 140, 155

Tran Hung Dao (jail) 49–50
Trinh, Tran Khuong 170
Trung, Hoang Xuan 78
Tu, Nguyen 171
Tu, Tran Da 171
tuberculosis (TB) 96, 101, 153
Tung, Vo Van 81
Tuong, Cao Van 170
Tuu, Hoang Xuan 170
Tuyen, Tran Tam 170
Tuyen, Tran van 170

Vinh Phu camp 107–114
voting rights 176, 178
Vy, Gen. Le Nguyen 20

warden 51, 61, 64–7, 70, 73, 76, 81, 114–6, 122, 148, 155, 162, 174
wives 21, 26, 58–9, 67, 75, 111, 126, 176, 178–9, 185, 204; assault of 84

Xuan loc: camp 77–80, 171; town 16–7
Xuyen tam lien 100, 103

Yen Bai camp 102–4
Yew, Lee Kwan 218

www.ingramcontent.com/pod-product-compliance
Ingram Content Group UK Ltd.
Pitfield, Milton Keynes, MK11 3LW, UK
UKHW041938140426
5217IPUK00014B/539